Business Process Management

D0218042

This book introduces students to business process management, an approach that aims to align the organization's business processes with the demands of the marketplace. Processes serve as a coordination mechanism, and the aim of business process management is to improve the organization's effectiveness and efficiency in adapting to change and maintaining competitive advantage.

In *Business Process Management*, Kumar argues for the value of looking at businesses as a collection of processes that cut across departments, and for breaking down functional silos. The book provides an overview of the basic concepts in this field before moving on to more advanced topics such as process verification, flexible processes, process security and evaluation, resource assignment, and social networks. One chapter of the book is also devoted to process analytics. The book concludes with an examination of the future directions of the discipline.

Blending a strong grounding in current research with a focus on concepts and tools, *Business Process Management* is an accessible textbook full of practical examples and cases that will appeal to upper level students.

Akhil Kumar is Professor of Information Systems at Pennsylvania State University, USA. He has over 25 years of experience teaching a variety of information systems courses to undergraduate and graduate students. He was a co-program chair for the International Business Process Management conference in 2017.

Business Process Management

Akhil Kumar

Routledge
Taylor & Francis Group

NEW YORK AND LONDON

First published 2018
by Routledge
711 Third Avenue, New York, NY 10017

and by Routledge
2 Park Square, Milton Park, Abingdon, Oxon OX14 4RN

Routledge is an imprint of the Taylor & Francis Group, an informa business

Library of Congress Cataloging in Publication Data
Names: Kumar, Akhil, author.
Title: Business process management: by Akhil Kumar.
Description: First Edition. | New York: Routledge, 2018. |
Includes bibliographical references and index.
Identifiers: LCCN 2017036684 | ISBN 9781138181816 (hardback) |
ISBN 9781138181854 (pbk.) | ISBN 9781315646749 (ebook)
Subjects: LCSH: Industrial management. | Workflow–Management. |
Information technology–Management. | Organizational change.
Classification: LCC HD31.2.K86 2018 | DDC 658.5/3–dc23
LC record available at https://lccn.loc.gov/2017036684

ISBN: 978-1-138-18181-6 (hbk)
ISBN: 978-1-138-18185-4 (pbk)
ISBN: 978-1-315-64674-9 (ebk)

Typeset in Times New Roman
by Sunrise Setting Ltd, Brixham, UK

Visit the companion website: www.routledge.com/cw/kumar

To my parents who designed the process, my wife with whom I implement it, and our children who will rediscover it

If you can't describe what you are doing as a process, you don't know what you're doing.
W. Edwards Deming

At the heart of business reengineering is the notion of discontinuous thinking—identifying and abandoning outdated rules and fundamental assumptions that underlie current business operations... These rules are based on assumptions about technology, people, and organizational goals that no longer hold. Unless companies change these rules, any superficial reorganizations they perform will be no more effective than dusting the furniture at Pompeii.
Michael Hammer & James Champy, *Reengineering The Corporation*

Contents

Figures

Tables

Preface

In 1993, in Ithaca, NY, I picked up a copy of the book *Reengineering the Corporation*, by Michael Hammer and James Champy, that had just been published. I was an assistant professor at Cornell University at that time, working in the area of replication in databases. The book was transformational because it opened my eyes to an entirely new area of research. I soon realized that business process management (BPM) was an important and fertile field of research for a business school information systems professor like myself. Over the next several years, my research interests shifted towards BPM and workflow systems.

In the fall of 1999, when I was at the University of Colorado, Boulder, a fortuitous meeting with Wil van der Aalst, who was visiting Clarence (Skip) Ellis and giving a seminar, turned out to be a milestone. This chance meeting led to a collaboration (and a visit to Eindhoven the next summer) with Wil through which several papers came out in the next few years. His fountain of ideas and enthusiasm gave a booster shot to my research in this area. I am very grateful to Wil for the collaboration in the early years, and also for his support since then. Skip, for his part, did some pioneering research in workflow systems, and was a friend and mentor at Colorado. We kept in touch until his passing in 2014.

This book is an effort to capture and consolidate some of the work in the last 20 years in BPM and workflow systems. I have tried to organize and present it in a way that would be useful both to students (as a textbook in senior undergraduate and first-year masters programs in business, information science and industrial engineering) and also to practitioners in the real world who wish to learn more about this relatively new area of growing interest. What distinguishes this book from others is that it attempts a comprehensive treatment of BPM topics that is lacking in current books.

In particular, this book discusses multiple approaches to modeling business processes, taking into account various perspectives like control flow, data flow, resource, and time. Further it goes on to explain concepts related to performance evaluation, security and compliance, analysis of temporal workflows, social processes, and process mining. In the last chapter on future directions, I give readers a glimpse of some new topics of interest such as decision modeling notation, blockchain technology, and organizational routines.

There are numerous short cases and examples throughout the book, and it also introduces a variety of tools as they relate to the different topics. Finally, I have spread out a number of exercises in different chapters of the book. A reader or student can work on them at their own pace or as directed by an instructor. A disclaimer is that some of the exercises are also answered in the body of the text. So it is better if you try to answer them yourself first before proceeding. The chapters have summaries with a list of readings for going deeper into each topic. They will be particularly useful in a graduate program where the instructor may wish to have the students study the material at a deeper level. A few sections of the book where the material is of a more advanced or mathematical nature are marked with asterisks (***). They can be skipped without loss of continuity.

I wish to thank Paul Grefen, Rong (Emily) Liu, Irene Vanderfeesten, and Josep Carmona for reading parts of the manuscript and giving me suggestions for improvement. Emily also did her PhD with me, and was a research scientist at IBM Watson Research Labs for the last 10 years, during which time we have collaborated off and on. Many of the ideas in this book, especially in Chapters 6 and 10, were developed jointly with her. I also thank a large number of colleagues, students, and friends with whom I have collaborated over the years. Among them are: Amit Basu, Sujoy Basu, Remco Dijkman, Rik Eshuis, David Knuplesch, Kees van Hee, Manfred Reichert, Jerome Rolia, Zhe (Jay) Shan, Jacques Wainer, Lijie Wen, Jianmin Wang, Jianrui Wang, Wen Yao, Kang Zhao, and Leon Zhao. Rick Hull arranged for me a one-year visiting position in his department at Bell Labs, NJ, in 2000–2001, and I learnt a lot from him there. I also want to thank my colleagues at Penn State, and particularly my current department chair, Nick Petruzzi, and his predecessor, Gene Tyworth, as well as my associate dean, Russell Barton, who was a co-author too. Achal Goel, a bright master's student in the Industrial Engineering department at Penn State, gave me invaluable assistance in drawing final versions of several of the figures in this book.

One day about five to six years ago, an avuncular looking editor from Routledge, John Szilagyi, wandered into my office at Penn State. He wanted to chat and ask if I had thought about writing a book, and suggested I consider a book on ERP systems. I told him I had not, but would. I sent him a proposal for a book on ERP a couple of years later. By that time, he was retiring and passed on the proposal to his successor Sharon Golan. Sharon decided against that proposal, but encouraged me to propose a BPM book project. I did so, and after reviewing it she was supportive, and later sent me a contract that I signed in summer of 2015. It was the start of my sabbatical year at Penn State. I started writing in that year, but the bulk of the work happened during the last year. I am very appreciative of all the support from Sharon and her editorial assistants, Erin Arata and Samantha Phua. The project manager for the book, Sharon Nickels at Sunrise Setting Ltd., partners of Routledge, was also very helpful and cooperative.

I extend my deepest gratitude to my parents, Saroj and M. B. Lal, for all their love and support, and for fostering my passion for learning at an early stage by filling the house with books. I also thank my brother Ankur and sister Anju, and both their families. My journalist father has written many books and has wanted me to write one too. This is my humble attempt at it. Last but not least, my special thanks to Nilima, Anurag, and Anshul and Dayita, for everything.

Akhil Kumar
State College, PA
June 5, 2017

1 Evolution of Process Thinking

What Is a Process?

Processes are the lifeblood of an organization. Michael Hammer and James Champy argued in the early 1990s that by redesigning their business processes, organizations could achieve large improvements in productivity. These improvements translated into faster deliveries for customers, shorter order-to-cash cycle times for the business, and savings in the manpower needed to work on the processes. Many organizations did not and still do not have formal processes for how things are done. People are expected to "know" how things are done and follow the routine. However, unless a process description is written down explicitly, it is not possible to analyze it, find inefficiencies in it, or even make improvements to it. Many organizations have continued to carry out unnecessary tasks for decades without pausing to consider why they are doing them. They might send extra copies of a document to more people than need to look at it, or require more approvals than are necessary, etc. If you ask someone in an organization why they are doing it, they will tell you "this is how we have always done it." It happens because of organizational inertia, and often nobody may have even paused to reflect on why things are done in the way they are done!

1   A process is a way of performing activities to achieve an objective.
2   A process model is a formal representation of a series of related activities that are performed in a specific order to achieve a clear objective.
3   A business process is a collection of activities that takes one or more kinds of inputs and creates an output that is of value to the customer.
4   A business process is defined as a chain of activities whose final aim is the production of a specific output for a particular customer or market.

The focus of this book is on process thinking. This is a way of thinking logically about how various activities or groups of activities in an organization are carried out.

In their 1993 book, Hammer and Champy [3] urged organizations to think of their business in terms of their major processes, and to organize activities and people around processes rather than functions.

Figure 1.1 shows a function-centric view of a business, where each function reports to the top management. In such an organization, information flows between functions take place through the senior management. In contrast, Figure 1.2 shows a process-centric view of a business. Notice how the information flows directly across the functional areas. Which organization do you think is more efficient?

The functional organization leads to silos by creating somewhat artificial functional boundaries. On the other hand, the process-centric perspective helps to break down the functional boundaries to improve the information flow, and thus the flow of work, in an organization.

Business Processes in the Real-World

A real business has lots of processes. Some example processes are listed in Figure 1.3. If you have worked in a business or been a customer of a business you will be familiar with such processes. Most businesses have processes for selling their products to customers, for purchasing raw materials from vendors, and for manufacturing goods. In addition, they have a variety of processes related to hiring employees, approving expense claims when an employee goes on travel, approving requests for vacation, etc. As retail customers, we have all taken part in sales processes, returns processes, and repair processes. Each of these processes requires certain steps to be followed.

For instance, to return an item to an online merchant you must first have a return merchandise authorization from them. To obtain this authorization, you have to visit their website or call them on the phone and explain why you are returning the item. Some merchants will return the full amount of your purchase, while others will charge a restocking fee. The amount of refund is calculated based on their individual policies.

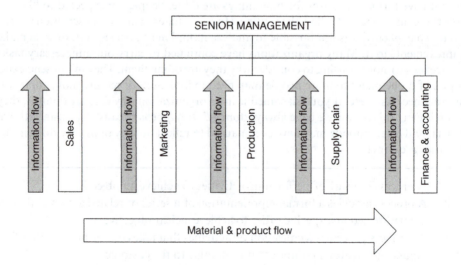

Figure 1.1 A function-centric view of a business

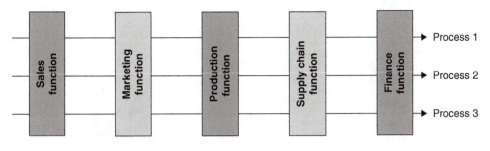

Figure 1.2 A process-centric view of a business

1	Travel expense report approval
2	Ordering a book at Amazon.com
3	Return a book at Amazon.com
4	Hiring a new employee
5	Transferring an employee
6	Auto insurance claim process
7	Mortgage loan application processing
8	30-year Mortgage processing

Figure 1.3 Some examples of business processes

Some merchants might accept returns only within four weeks from the date of the sale. Moreover, every return may require a manager's approval. If the sales clerk decides to make an exception and accept a return that is made more than four weeks after the sale, then a senior manager or a director's approval may be needed. Some key steps required in dealing with a return of a product are:

(agent) check that the returned product is complete and in good condition
(agent) check if a return merchandize authorization document is included
(agent) decide whether to accept returned item and ask manager for approval
(manager) approve or disapprove recommendation of agent
(agent) if return is not accepted: notify the customer and send the product back to them
(agent) if return is accepted: issue credit and send returned item to the manufacturer.

Ideally, a process description must capture not only the steps that must be performed, but also such details as the policy of the merchant. In addition, the process description should capture all the data pertaining to each activity. For instance, when an order is submitted it must have a customer name, address, phone number, item(s) ordered (and quantities), date, shipping method, payment method, etc.

A Sales Order Process

One process that occurs in almost every organization is a typical sales order process (see Figure 1.4). This is also called the order-to-cash process, and it is by far the most important process in most organizations. It starts with an order from a client and ends after

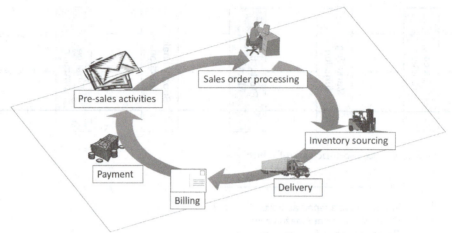

Figure 1.4 A sales order process cuts across functional areas

the payment is received for the fulfilled order. A client receives a quotation from a sales representative in your company as part of the pre-sales activities. Then the quotation is converted into a firm sales order in the ERP (Enterprise Resource Planning) system. This triggers the inventory sourcing task that in turn is followed by the delivery task. After the order is shipped, a bill is sent to the customer and finally the payment is received. In case the inventory has to be sourced in-house, the production process may have to be triggered to produce the order.

It is also important to note that the sales order process cuts across many functions or departments like Sales, Inventory/Production, Logistics, and Accounting.

This is a simple example of process thinking, where a certain way of doing things is formalized. The fruits of process thinking are realized in ERP systems. ERP systems help to automate business processes within an organization, as we discuss in the next section.

An ERP System

An ERP system, such as the old workhorse SAP R/3 from SAP Corporation, views a business as a collection of processes related to sales, purchasing, production, and accounting. This viewpoint offers many advantages. First, this leads to integration among different functional areas through better exchange of information. Second, inventory levels, sales orders, purchase orders, production orders and status of payments can be tracked in real-time. Third, the business can better manage its revenue cycle from invoice through cash receipt. Fourth, better production planning can help to shorten production lead times and delivery times across the supply chain of the company. Finally, marketing can make more accurate forecasts, which further reduce inventory levels and lead to higher profits for your company. Thus, an ERP system can improve communication, productivity, and efficiency of an organization in a variety of ways.

One can think of an ERP system as the nervous system of an organization. It is a vast information system that manages information about a company's products, customers,

Production	Sales	Marketing	Human relations	Accounting
Plants	Customers	Plans	Employees	Receipts
Machines	Prospects	Strategy	Departments	Payments
Products	Sales orders	Markets	Units	Receivables
Materials	Products	New products	Skills	Payables
Production orders	Prices		Contact	Asset values
Purchase orders				Liabilities

Figure 1.5 Physical and information resources of an organization

suppliers, employees, production facilities, financial balances, etc. It is used by every department in an organization and by most employees. The sales department can check prices of products and their inventory levels, enter sales orders from customers, make deliveries, issue invoices to customers and receive payments. The production department uses it to check inventory balances of products, create production orders, manage production schedules, and record the receipt of finished or in-progress orders. The marketing department can plan demand and make sales forecasts for the next sales period. The finance department uses it to manage accounts payables and receivables, enter payments made by customers and payments made to suppliers, and generate the balance sheet and profit and loss statements at the end of an accounting period. The human relations department tracks all employees in a company, their title, date of joining, department, and salary. Every new employee is added to the system as soon as they join the company.

In order to execute important processes in an organization, an ERP system needs to have access to resources and information about them. Figure 1.5 shows a list of resources used by various departments of a company. The information about these resources is stored in a database system.

An ERP system in effect manages all the resources of an organization or enterprise. Hence it is also called an enterprise (-wide) system. It knows how many manufacturing facilities belong to a company, and what machines are available at each facility and their capacities. It is almost like a "big brother" watching all the activities and transactions in a company. How is this possible? Well, the trick is that every transaction that takes places in a company gets recorded in the centralized database of the ERP system in real-time. By *real-time* we mean that every transaction, such as a sales order, delivery, purchase order, payment, etc. is recorded as soon as it occurs.

Role of Technology in Processes

Technology plays a major role in processes. A process can be redesigned as new hardware or software technology becomes available. Take the case of the supermarket. In the 1950s and 1960s, a cashier would calculate the bill for a customer by manually typing the prices and quantities of each item into a desk calculator and then tallying the total. This required manually looking up the price of each item in a book or register and separately measuring the weight of each product that is sold by weight, by placing it on a weighing machine. Moreover, the payment was usually received by cash or check. This meant that additional time was consumed in counting the tendered amount, calculating the change, and returning it to the customer from the cash drawer. Later, the advent of bar code technology made it possible to scan each item on the scanner so that its price could be looked up automatically. Subsequently, the weighing scale was also integrated with the cash register so that the weight of an item placed on the scale would be directly captured by the Point of Sale system. This saved the clerk the time spent entering two important pieces of information, the price of each item and its weight.

As you can see, with the advent of this technology the process for checking a customer out at a cash register was redesigned. Moreover, newer payment methods, notably with credit cards, were introduced in the 1950s. This was a faster form of payment than cash because no change had to be returned. In the earlier days of credit cards, a checkout clerk would record the credit card information by taking an impression of it on a manual machine. The information would be transmitted to the card issuing bank later in batch mode. This arrangement continued for many decades. In the 1990s, when computer networks became more prevalent, a clerk could swipe the card herself on a new device that was connected to the network of the card issuing bank and which would also enter the amount of the purchase. The credit card information, along with the purchase amount, would be transmitted to the computer system of the card issuing bank. The computer would verify the credit availability of the customer for the amount of the purchase being made, and then print out a receipt which then had to be signed by the customer. The account of the merchant would also be credited in real-time for the amount of the purchase. Nowadays, this technology has also changed. Vendors have introduced new machines that allow customers to swipe the card themselves without giving it to the clerk. Moreover, most vendors do not require signatures on sales under $50.

A further redesign has taken place in the last ten years, in that supermarkets have introduced self-checkout lanes where a customer can scan items herself. All of these transitions represent process changes. Processes are linked and inter-related. Payment technology has implications for inventory ordering. Every time an item is sold, the inventory is updated in real-time. New orders for replenishments are placed with the vendor of the product as soon as the inventory level drops below a certain reorder point.

Hammer and Champy have described in their book how they re-engineered the purchase process at Ford Company by replacing their paper-based system with a fully automated system where purchase orders were sent electronically using EDI (Electronic data Interchange) technology, and payments were also made electronically to the supplier upon receipt of goods. By eliminating several manual steps like matching and reconciliation of documents that were slow and tedious, they were able to reduce the headcount of the purchase department from 500 to125.

Features of Processes

As you may well imagine, processes come in a variety of shapes and sizes. We can characterize them along various dimensions (see Figure 1.6).

The first important feature of a process is its *size*. The size is the number of activities in it. In addition, there is the issue of complexity that relates to the structure of the process. A simple process may have a series of five activities in a straight sequence one after another, and so there is exactly one path in this process. However, in a complex process with the same number of activities there may be many possible paths from start to finish. We shall later see ways of characterizing the complexity of a process.

Another consideration in describing a process is its *duration*. A short duration process may typically run for a few minutes or hours. Most of the examples of the processes we

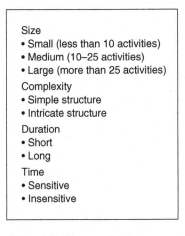

Size
• Small (less than 10 activities)
• Medium (10–25 activities)
• Large (more than 25 activities)
Complexity
• Simple structure
• Intricate structure
Duration
• Short
• Long
Time
• Sensitive
• Insensitive

Figure 1.6 Characterizing a process along various dimensions

have listed in Figure 1.3 fall into this category. However, consider the mortgage loan process on this list. This is a process that manages the issuance of a 30-year mortgage followed by the monthly payments to be received and processed for it. Pause for a minute to reflect on the issues involved in designing such a process. When does it start? When does it end? Further, note that the payments must be made at regular intervals, and so it has a temporal aspect too. Many processes are also time sensitive, i.e. they must finish by a certain deadline.

After the mortgage is issued there are steps like sending monthly bills for this mortgage, receiving payment and crediting the customer account, sending annual tax statements to show how much interest has been paid by the customer in the prior year, and finally closing the mortgage at the end of its life. In addition, there are other complicating factors in this process that must be considered, such as: sending overdue notices if the payment is late, transferring the mortgage to another lender, handling early pre-payment of the mortgage if the customer decides to sell her house, reissuing the mortgage if the customer decides to refinance her mortgage, etc. A process designer trying to design a process for this application must consider all of these issues. Hence, process design is a difficult and challenging exercise.

BPM Lifecycle and Reference Model

Process development is similar to any software application development. Just like any software, the development of a process follows a process lifecycle. These are stages in business process development. The typical business process management (BPM) lifecycle is shown in Figure 1.7.

In this figure, there are five main stages of process development. A process is first designed informally. Then the informal design is converted into a formal process model using a modeling tool or language. Sometimes these two steps are combined into one. During the execution phase, the process is run on an execution engine that can understand the process modeling language. The process should also be monitored to measure its performance. Monitoring can be done through dashboards and by measuring KPIs

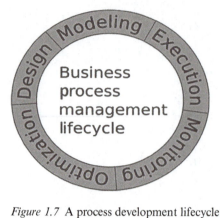

Figure 1.7 A process development lifecycle

(key performance indicators), as we shall see in a later chapter. Finally, the process is optimized by making any small changes to it to improve its performance.

It is important to note that the stages of this lifecycle are by no means sacred or engraved in stone. In a very comprehensive survey that is still quite current, Wil van der Aalst [1] has proposed three main stages in the BPM lifecycle: (re)design; implement/configure; and run and adjust. In another well-known text by Dumas et al. [2] the authors have proposed six stages in the BPM lifecycle: process identification; process discovery; process analysis; process redesign; process implementation; and process monitoring and controlling. It also bears mention that the term *business process* is often used synonymously with *workflow*. However, sometimes the scope of the term workflow is limited to the modeling and control flow aspects of a process. On the other hand, BPM is an umbrella term that encompasses many other issues of process management as well, such as security, compliance, resource allocation, etc., that we discuss in this book.

There are three types of roles that are involved in process development: *business roles, IT roles* and *operational roles*. Business analysts fall into the business role. Their job is to apply their understanding of business and process design concepts to design the process. These roles are often filled by students from information systems programs who have training in systems analysis and design, databases, process design, etc. They have both domain knowledge about the actual process and also an understanding of process modeling approaches. The people in IT roles are called *system architects* and *system administrators*. They understand the technology aspects of the execution environment in which the process will actually run. They are also familiar with software applications or workflow engines that execute the processes. In fact, they could even fix any runtime issues that arise when the processes are being executed. The operational role is filled by the process owner. The overall responsibility for the process and for the success of its implementation lies with the process owner. She would typically be an administrative person who understands the business aspects well and may not know much about the technology. The process owner would coordinate the activities of the other roles.

Finally, Figure 1.8 shows a workflow reference model or architecture that was developed by the Workflow Management Coalition (WfMC) [4] in the mid- to late-1990s in an effort to standardize workflow development in industry. Although it did not become a

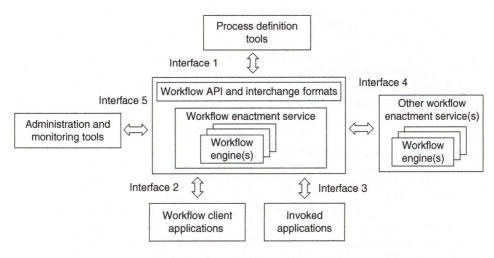

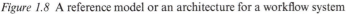

Figure 1.8 A reference model or an architecture for a workflow system

Source: Workflow management coalition, www.wfmc.org/index.php/standards.

widely accepted standard, it is a helpful reference to understand a workflow system from a broader perspective. The architecture identifies the major components and interfaces. The workflow engine or enactment service lies in the center of this architecture and has five major interfaces. The interfaces shown here were partly specified by WfMC but no precise semantics of the interface specifications were given. The process-definition tools allow the process to be specified. The client applications can access the workflow engine over a network. The administration tools are for managing and monitoring the workflow engine. Finally, there are interfaces meant for invoking other workflow services and applications.

A Roadmap for the Book

This chapter has introduced the subject of business process management. The reader is directed to the classic book by Hammer and Champy [3] for its excellent examples of real-world processes that can be improved by applying BPM techniques. The works of van der Aalst [1] and Dumas et al. [2] are more recent and provide in-depth studies of various aspects of BPM. Finally, further details on the reference model for the architecture of a workflow system proposed by the workflow management coalition may be found in WfMC [4]. This book takes a holistic view of business processes. A suggested roadmap for this book is shown in Figure 1.9. It is organized into three sections: foundations, intermediate, and advanced. After this introduction, we direct the reader towards foundational material in Chapters 2, 3, and 4. This deals with concepts of process modeling based on traditional approaches that focus more on the control flow aspect of a process (Chapter 2), and more holistic kinds of modeling methods that include modeling of resources and data (Chapter 3). Then, Chapter 4 covers data-centric business process modeling.

The intermediate level material appears in Chapters 5, 6, and 7. Chapter 5 builds on the basic foundational material and discusses flexible and declarative workflows. Chapter 6 turns to issues involved in process verification. Chapter 7 deals with various metrics

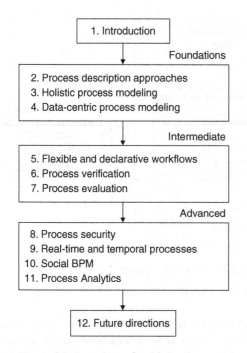

Figure 1.9 A roadmap for this book

for process evaluation. These metrics are crucial for a deeper understanding of process performance.

The next four chapters cover slightly advanced topics. It is not necessary that they are covered in the same sequence in a class. Chapter 8 discusses the issue of process security. Security is naturally important because processes deal with sensitive company or customer data, e.g. a loan application process deals with information that only authorized staff should be privy too. Policies are also required for the delegation of such data.

Chapter 9 is about temporal and real-time processes where time is of the essence. These processes interact with other processes and often have to observe real-time deadlines. We shall consider issues related to modeling, verifying, monitoring, and managing them. Chapter 10 pertains to an emerging area called social BPM. Activities in a process are performed by teams and the teams are fluid, i.e. they grow and dissolve somewhat organically. Many such processes can only be "loosely" defined. Finally, Chapter 11 goes into process analytics or process mining. Each executed process instance creates a log showing the various activities performed by it. Analyzing such logs can provide valuable insights into the nature of the process itself. This chapter looks at ways to analyze such process data and extract valuable information from them related to performance. Moreover, the log can also be used to extract a process model. The extracted process model can then be compared against a designed process model. Deviations between the two models can show the degree to which the actual process model is out of line with the designed process model.

Lastly, in Chapter 12, we shall briefly introduce some new directions that the BPM area is exploring such as decision modeling notation, blockchain technology and organizational routines. Exercises are scattered throughout the book at relevant places.

You should make an effort to answer them as you proceed. A few sections in this book are marked with (***) to indicate that they contain material of a more mathematical nature. For the most part, they can be skipped without loss of continuity.

References

1. W. van der Aalst. Business process management: a comprehensive survey. *ISRN Software Engineering*, Article ID 507894, pp. 1–37, 2013.
2. M. Dumas, M. La Rosa, J. Mendling and H. A. Reijers. *Fundamentals of Business Process Management*. Springer, February 2013.
3. M. Hammer and J. Champy. *Reengineering the Corporation*. Harper Business, New York, USA, 1993.
4. Workflow Management Coalition. www.wfmc.org/index.php/standards.

2 How to Model a Process

Introduction

The starting step in process development is process design and modeling. This is simply a way to describe the process formally. A formal process model describes a process unambiguously so that two or more people reading the model will interpret it in the same way. In this chapter we will look at various approaches to describe a process in a formal way. There are many techniques for describing processes. Rather than go into the detailed syntax of every modeling technique, we will cover a few selected methods for process modeling that are used commonly in practice. These are quite intuitive once you get the general principle of process modeling. Hence, our focus is on making you understand the basic principle based on the main features that are commonly used. While you are actually modeling a process, you can look up specific features for each approach on the web (some resources are given at the end). There are many formalisms that have been developed. We will discuss some of the important ones here, such as flowcharts, EPC diagrams, and BPMN. We also cover Petri nets, which provide a powerful modeling tool for researchers and scientists. But our focus is more on business languages and tools. Finally, we introduce you to process redesign and improvement techniques.

What Is Process Modeling?

A process description can be thought of as writing a program or a recipe; you are simply describing in a logical way the steps that should be performed. You want the description to be simple, clear, and unambiguous. Say you have bought a smartphone recently from an online retailer and you wish to return it because you don't like it. To describe the **returns process**, you could start by writing a description in English as follows:

- Log in to the merchant's website.
- Enter order information and retrieve the order.
- Select return option from a menu.
- Fill the return request form explaining the reason for return.
- Submit the form.
- Wait for an email from the vendor approving the return.
- If the vendor approves the return, then:

  o Click on the return label in the vendor email.
  o Print the return label.
  o Prepare package and post the return label on it.
  o Mail the package.
  o Check your credit card account to see if the credit for the return has been issued.

If the vendor does not approve the return then:

  o Call the customer service department of the vendor.
  o Resolve the matter on phone.

In this example it was straightforward, but it would be difficult to write all the steps in English if the process was too long.

During the process modeling or design phase, a process analyst will normally sit down with the manager or staff in the department(s) that is likely to participate in the process and understand the activities they perform in considerable detail. The analyst will also try to find out what information they need for each activity, and what is the output result of the activity, as well as the next step. Sometimes several meetings between the analyst and the staff of the end user department(s) are needed. After each meeting, the analyst should prepare notes describing her understanding of the process and share them with the staff of the user department. After a few meetings, the analyst will make a more formal rough-cut design of the process, and try to explain it to the staff to make sure that all the intricacies of the process have been captured accurately. Again, the formal design may also need multiple iterations before it is finalized. This is an important and non-trivial activity that can take from several weeks to a few months depending upon the complexity of the process. The first formal approach for describing a process that we shall discuss is flowcharts.

Flowcharts

Consider that a pizza delivery store has to deliver an order for a 16-inch cheese pizza with toppings of tomato, onion, and mushroom. It must prepare the pizza first. To make the pizza, it must have the ingredients readily available. If all the ingredients are in the store, then the cook can prepare the pizza and hand it to the delivery person, who will deliver the pizza to the customer and collect the payment. But, say the store is out of mushrooms! This is a special situation that our process must handle too. The helper will be sent to a nearby grocery store to fetch them before the pizza can be prepared. After the mushrooms arrive, another check is performed to ensure that all items are in the inventory. Perhaps another order has consumed an item that was needed, or the helper may have forgotten to procure it. If all ingredients are available, the pizza is prepared. When the pizza is ready it must be packed in a box and handed over to the delivery driver with an address and a bill so he can collect the payment. Figure 2.1 describes this process in a flowchart. There are six activity nodes corresponding to activities T1–T6.

Try to follow the logical flow in this figure. The rectangles represent an activity and the directed lines with arrows show the natural sequence in which they are performed. The diamond symbol with two outgoing branches means that one of these two branches will be taken depending upon whether the condition inside the diamond is true or false. The result of checking the condition is written on each outgoing path for it to be followed. The main symbols in a flowchart are summarized in Table 2.1.

The nice feature of flowcharts is their simplicity. By just using a few symbols (or "boxes and arrows" if you like), it is possible to express a variety of processes and even quite complicated logical flows. You can imagine the flowchart as a graph with nodes (e.g. event, activity, and decision nodes) that are connected together with directed links in a logical manner. Another powerful feature of the flowchart is the loop. Notice how in Figure 2.1, after fetching the toppings (T6) an inventory check (T2) is performed. This is an example of a loop between T2 and T6. A loop can be repeated multiple times. However, also notice that there is a decision point (or node) after T2. If the decision

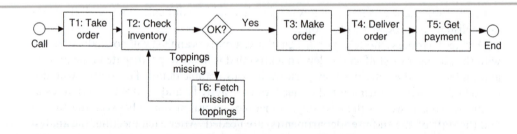

Figure 2.1 A pizza ordering workflow (Scenario 1)

Table 2.1 Standard flowcharting symbols

Symbol	Meaning
◯	An event indicating start or end of a process
▭	An activity node
⟶	Flow of logic
◇	Decision node

point were not there we would be stuck in the loop and could never get out of it. This would not make sense! But at the decision node there is one path towards T3 that exits the loop.

Exercise 1: Make a flowchart for the returns process for the smartphone described in the previous section. How will you check whether it is correct?

Flowcharts with Parallelism

We can think of flowcharts as simple boxes and arrows diagrams. However, they have one shortcoming. Let us revisit the pizza ordering example from Figure 2.1. In this scenario, if toppings are missing the helper has to fetch them before the cook can start preparing the pizza. However, there is another scenario in which the cook may just start preparing the pizza base with cheese on it while the helper is away fetching the toppings.

Exercise 2: Pause to think about why this scenario may be a better alternative. Also, think about how you would modify the flowchart in Figure 2.1 to describe this scenario.

After some thought you might realize that the flowchart cannot represent this scenario properly. The problem is that we are trying to perform two activities *simultaneously*, or *in parallel*. The flowchart can only model strictly sequential processes where only one activity can be in progress, or running, at a time. Hence, we need a new way to represent Scenario 2. We will extend the flowchart with one more modeling symbol to capture parallel activities and call it a *flowchart with parallelism*.

Let's take a look at the process in Figure 2.2. How is it different from the process in Figure 2.1? You will notice that we have added a new diamond with the "+" symbol inside it. This represents a *fork* or a *split* in the process flow and it means that at this point all branches that exit (i.e. have outgoing arrows) will be activated. Notice also the second diamond with a "+" symbol inside it in this figure. This diamond corresponds to a join node where the parallel branches coming in must meet and synchronize, i.e. the flow of logic cannot proceed until all the incoming branches have been completed. This is how we represent parallel activities in a process model. *The advantage of performing activities T6 and T7 in parallel is that the pizza will be prepared faster.* This means that the store will be able to provide better service to its customers.

This example also shows you how process improvement occurs. A pizza store (or any organization) might have started out with an initial process model that captures its work

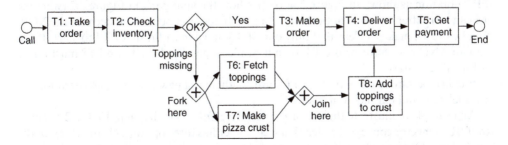

Figure 2.2 A pizza ordering workflow (Scenario 2)

practice. In the course of time, it will dawn upon the store manager that by modifying their practice they can improve their process and make it more efficient. Thus, they would gravitate towards it and also modify their formal process model accordingly. Process improvements happen over time, often as a result of watching or monitoring a process in action. We shall talk about techniques for process redesign and improvement later on in this chapter. But next, we will discuss process modeling techniques like EPC diagrams and BPMN. You can think of them as sophisticated flowcharts with parallelism and other features.

EPC Diagrams

Another approach for modeling business processes is based on Event-Process Chains (EPC). This is used widely by the company SAP in their ERP systems and hence it is useful to have a knowledge of this as well. The symbols used in EPC diagrams are summarized in Table 2.2 and will be discussed shortly.

This is a different set of symbols than we saw in the flowcharts. Using this notation we would model the process of Figure 2.1 by Figure 2.3. You will probably appreciate that the semantics or "meaning" of the two figures is exactly the same. However, notice that the notation is different for representing splits and joins. An *AND split* symbol (or node) is used to create two or more parallel paths and an *AND join* to synchronize (or join) them. By *synchronization*, we mean that any task that appears after an *AND join* node can start only after *all* the incoming branches at the *AND join* have completed.

Also, there are two types of ORs: exclusive and inclusive. An exclusive OR (XOR) is like the diamond symbol in a flowchart. Multiple (two or more) paths emanate from an *XOR split* but only and exactly one may be taken. Usually there is a corresponding *XOR join* node, where two or more paths meet. As soon as one of these paths is finished, the *XOR join* node is "activated," and the subsequent task or activity in the process may be performed. A loop can be created in an EPC diagram by using two XOR structures that create a cycle, as we shall illustrate shortly in the context of the cases.

A *function* in EPC notation is the name given to a task or an activity. An event records the state of the process. For instance, in Figure 2.3, the first event "call" represents the occurrence of an incoming call into the pizza store when the phone rings. Similarly, the end event signifies the end of the process, i.e. the state of the process instance becomes "end" or "ended."

Now we can also represent the second version of the pizza ordering example using the EPC notation as shown in Figure 2.4. Notice how the ambiguity in Figure 2.2 (whether T4 can start after only one or both of T3 and T8) does not occur here because the XOR join before T4 makes it clear that only one of T3 or T8 must finish for T4 to start. If we had an AND connector before T4, then it would imply that *both* T3 and T8 must finish before T4 can start.

Further, be sure to observe that in Figure 2.4 there is a new construct ($\wedge$) used for the parallel-split and parallel-join nodes.

An example to illustrate the use of the inclusive OR ($\vee$) is shown in Figure 2.5. Here, the OR connector conveys the idea that a customer has three options: (1) to pay by credit card alone; (2) to pay by gift card alone; (3) to pay partly by credit card and partly by gift card. Next, we shall look at some case examples of EPC diagrams.

Table 2.2 Standard symbols used in EPC diagrams

Symbol	Name	Description
	Event	Denotes the occurrence of an event
	Function	Denotes performance of an activity
XOR	Exclusive OR (XOR split)	A node in the process where the flow splits and *only one* of multiple branches is taken
XOR	Exclusive OR (XOR join)	A node in the process where multiple branches join
∧	AND split	A node in the process where the flow splits along multiple branches and they are *all* pursued in parallel
∧	AND join	A node in the process where the flow along multiple parallel branches joins (or synchronizes). The process cannot continue until activities along all branches are completed
V	Inclusive OR split	A node in the process where the flow splits and *at least one* of the multiple branches is taken
V	Inclusive OR join	A node in the process where the flow joins and all the branches that were taken at the corresponding split node are completed

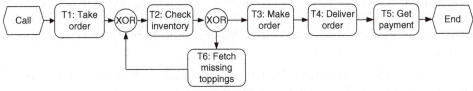

Figure 2.3 An EPC diagram to represent the pizza ordering process (Version 1)

Exercise 3: Show how you might express the idea of the inclusive OR in Figure 2.5 by using only XOR and AND connectors?

Case Example 1: Consider the process to order several items at an online website Orders-R-Us. A customer visits this site and performs various steps like logging in to

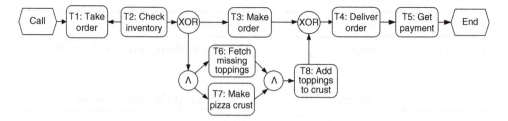

Figure 2.4 An EPC diagram to represent the pizza ordering process (Version 2)

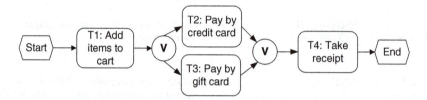

Figure 2.5 An example to illustrate the inclusive OR (∨) connector

the website, searching for an item, optionally adding it to a shopping cart, repeating the search-add steps multiple times, then proceeding to check out and completing the order by providing information such as shipping address, billing address, payment method, etc. This process is shown in Figure 2.6 as an EPC diagram. This diagram has been drawn using the Signavio software (www.signavio.com).

In this diagram, the various steps of the process are arranged in the correct order in which they occur. It also shows branching and parallel structures as needed. So, after searching for an item, a shopper may either decide to add it to the cart or just discard it. Similarly, some steps like authorizing the credit card and checking if the ordered items are in the inventory may be carried out in parallel with one another. In particular notice how loop structures are created by combining two XOR symbols. First, after searching for an item and adding it to the cart, the shopper may decide to either go to checkout or return to search for more items. This is shown in the model by two XOR split symbols arranged in a cycle. Also, don't overlook the second loop that appears after the display of the final order and gives the customer a chance to reject the order and start shopping further.

Exercise 4: In the example EPC diagram of Figure 2.4, what further improvements/ changes would you make so that it becomes more realistic?

Case Example 2: This case describes the process followed by an insurance company PEICO to handle an insurance claim. Figure 2.7 shows the EPC diagram of this process drawn using the Signavio software (www.signavio.com). After a claim is received, it is recorded. Then, in parallel, two checks are performed: (1) a check to ensure that the claim is covered by the policy of the customer; and (2) a check to verify that the premium payments are up to date. If either of these conditions is not true, then the claim

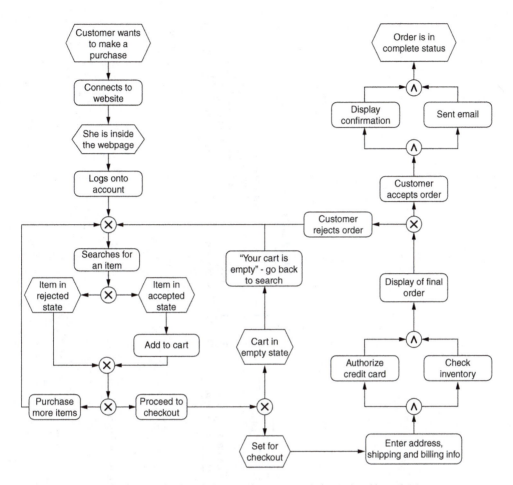

Figure 2.6 An EPC diagram for making a purchase at a website (using Signavio)

is rejected and closed. Otherwise, based on the size of the claim, an assessment is per-formed by an assessor for the company (for large claims only) to determine the amount of the damage that was sustained. Next, a settlement is proposed to the customer. If the customer accepts the settlement, then the payment is made and the claim is closed. How-ever, if the customer disputes the settlement, then a negotiation step is performed and a new settlement is offered. The propose settlement-negotiate loop may occur multiple times until the customer accepts the proposal. Every company will have its own policy for what a "large claim" means. In Figure 2.7, the condition to check for a large claim may alternatively be represented as:

if (amount_of_claim > 500) then perform assessment

Thus, only claim amounts in excess of $500 would qualify a claim as "large." From the company's point of view, the extra cost of assessing the claim may render unnecessary the need to assess smaller claims.

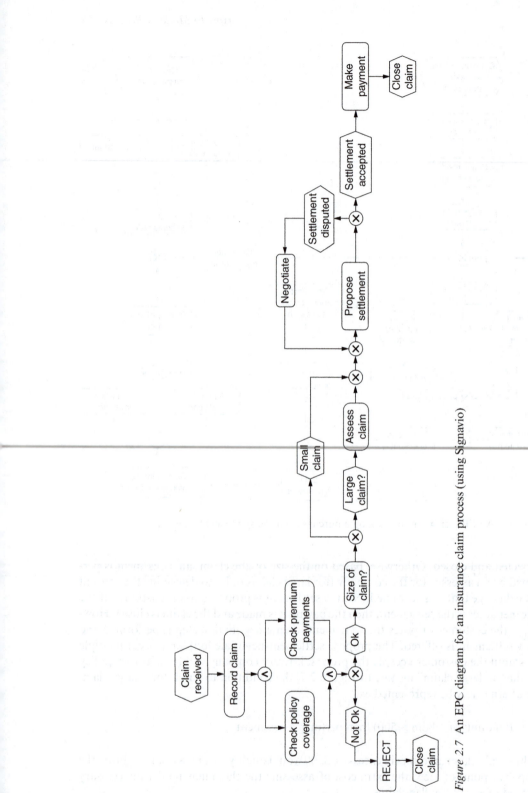

Figure 2.7 An EPC diagram for an insurance claim process (using Signavio)

BPMN

Another modeling notation that is becoming a de facto standard for process modeling is called BPMN or *Business Process Modeling Notation*. It uses a different set of symbols. The key symbols are shown in Table 2.3

The start, end and intermediate symbols are straightforward. At an exclusive gateway, only one outgoing branch is taken based on the value of a data item. At a parallel gateway all the outgoing branches are taken. An inclusive gateway allows one or more outgoing branches to be taken. An event-based gateway is similar to an exclusive gateway, except that the decision on which branch to take is made based on the occurrence of an event. Finally, the complex gateway allows testing of multiple conditions to decide which combination of outgoing branches should be taken.

Notice that many of the symbols in the BPMN notation have corresponding symbols in EPC notation. Thus, the first version of the pizza delivery process is shown in BPMN in Figure 2.8. It is very similar to Figure 2.4 for EPC diagrams with the different symbols for start, end, and exclusive OR nodes. It is important to realize that the two process models are identical in terms of the underlying process that they are describing. However, the description languages are different. It is like expressing the same idea in German or Italian.

In a similar vein, Figure 2.9 shows the second version of the pizza delivery process in the BPMN notation. Again, on comparison you will see that this process is identical

Table 2.3 Some key symbols of BPMN

Symbol	Name	Description
	Start event	This is a signal (or event) to start the process
	End or Terminate event	This is an event that indicates the end of the process
	Intermediate event	This event occurs between the start and end of a process
	Exclusive Gateway (or data-based gateway)	This is a node where the control flow diverges into multiple branches. Exactly one branch is selected based on the value of a data item obtained from a previous task
	Parallel Gateway	This is a node where the control flow selects all of the multiple outgoing branches
	Inclusive Gateway	This allows one or more outgoing branches to be taken
	Event based gateway	This is similar to an exclusive data gateway. But the decision is made based on the occurrence of an event
	Complex Gateway	At this node the control flow selects one or more outgoing branches based on testing one or more conditions

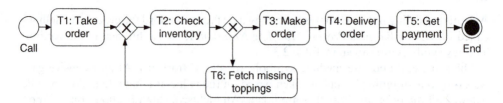

Figure 2.8 A BPMN diagram for the pizza delivery process (Version 1)

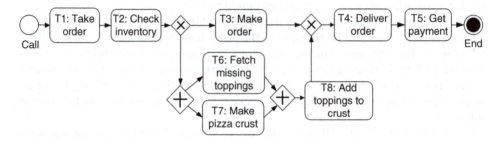

Figure 2.9 A BPMN diagram for the pizza delivery process (Version 2)

to the EPC process description for this process. The only difference is in the symbols. In this figure, as you can see, there is a new symbol for depicting parallel activities.

Exercise 5: Redraw Figure 2.4 that describes the web ordering process as a BPMN diagram.

Exercise 6: Make a BPMN diagram of the insurance claim process of Figure 2.7.

Extended BPMN Notation

The full BPMN notation offers a more extensive set of symbols for modeling. The additional symbols are shown in Table 2.4.

These additional symbols make it possible to model more advanced processes. We illustrate the use of these additional symbols with examples. Figure 2.10 shows a modified version of the pizza ordering example to illustrate the use of the *timer, signal,* and *compensation* symbols. In this example, the timer is set for 15 minutes as soon as the sub-process inside the box starts. If the subprocess does not complete within 15 minutes, then a *hold signal* is generated and task T9 causes the pizza preparation to be suspended. Then a call is made to the customer to ask if a delay is acceptable. If the customer consents, then the pizza preparation process receives a signal to resume. However, if the customer refuses to accept the delay then the pizza process is "rolled back," i.e. the incomplete work on the pizza is undone, and the payment is refunded to the customer. A *subprocess* like the one inside the box in Figure 2.10 is simply a process in itself that is a part of a larger process.

A BPMN model also has a feature to allow *process escalation*. To illustrate escalation in the context of Figure 2.11, say again that the pizza order is running late. An escalation can involve asking another partner store to deliver the pizza. If the subprocess for

Table 2.4 Additional symbols used in BPMN modeling

Symbol	Meaning
(envelope icon)	Send a message
(clock icon)	Set a timer
(triangle icon)	Send a signal
(up arrow icon)	Escalate the process
(X icon)	Cancel process
(rewind icon)	Compensate a step or steps of a process
(lightning/N icon)	An error will cause the process to interrupt
(right arrow icon)	Link to a sub-process that is a part of a larger process

making the pizza in-store described in the rectangular box in Figure 2.11 takes more than 10 minutes, a timer event is generated. As a result, the sub-process is put on hold. A check is performed to see if the delivery will be late. If so, an order is sent to the partner store to prepare a pizza (T10), and a payment is made to them (T11). Although not explicitly stated here, this process assumes that the pizza prepared at the partner store will be delivered to our store. Then our store will deliver it to the customer (T4).

BPMN 2.0 also allows you to specify a task type. The tasks we have used so far are called abstract tasks. Table 2.5 summarizes the seven main task types with brief descriptions. Note that all modeling tools do not support the task types.

In the rest of the book, we shall use BPMN primarily as the modeling notation to represent process models. So you will get to see many more examples. Next we'll briefly introduce Petri nets.

Petri Nets (PN)

Petri nets are not really meant for use by business people. Since our focus in this book is on business applications, we prefer to use BPMN as the modeling language for the most part. However, we give a brief introduction here.

A Petri net (PN) is a common tool for graphically and mathematically modeling the states of concurrent, parallel, asynchronous, and distributed controls systems, e.g. a process model. A PN is a directed bipartite graph, i.e. one where there are links between two non-intersecting sets of nodes. The two types of nodes are called *places* and *transitions*. Places and transitions are depicted as circles and rectangles, respectively. The directed

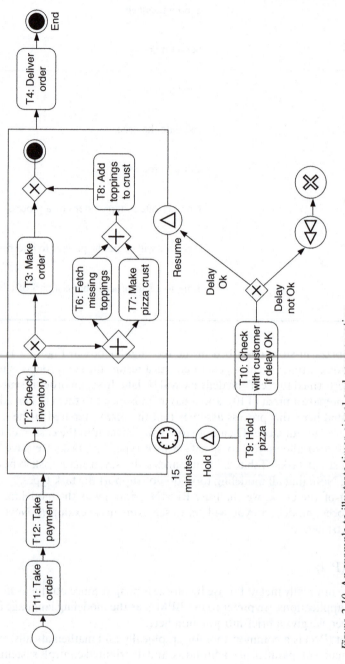

Figure 2.10 An example to illustrate timer, signal and compensation

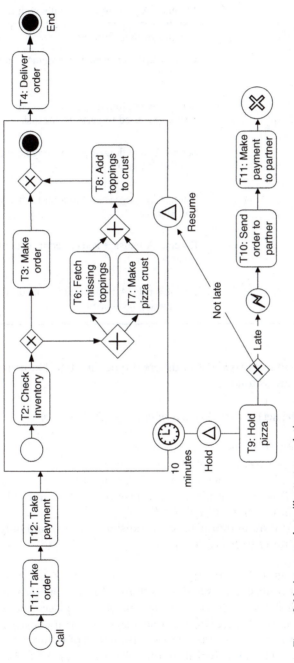

Figure 2.11 An example to illustrate escalation

Table 2.5 Different task types in BPMN 2.0

Task type symbol	Name and description
Manual	Manual: A task done manually without any system or application; for example, picking goods from inventory
User	User: A task performed by a human on the system
Service	Service: An automated application or web service is used to perform the task
Script	Script: A workflow or process engine executes a script, e.g. in Javascript
Send	Send: A message is sent to another party or process
Receive	Receive: A message is received from another party
Business Rule	Business rule: A business rule is invoked in making a decision

arcs are used to connect two nodes of different types in a PN. The definition and related concepts of PNs are as follows:

Definition 1: **(Petri net)** *A Petri Net is a tuple* $N_1 = (P, T, F)$ *where*

- P is a finite set of places
- T is a finite set of transitions such that $P \cap T = \phi$
- $F \subseteq (P \times T) \cup (T \times P)$ is a set of arcs (flow relation)
- A place $p \in P$ is an input place of a transition $t \in T$ if and only if there exists a directed arc from p to t, i.e., $(p, t) \in F$
- A place $p \in P$ is an output place of a transition $t \in T$ if and only if there exists a directed arc from t to p, i.e., $(t, p) \in F$

As shown in Figure 2.12, $P = \{p_1, p_2, \ldots, p_{13}\}$, $T = \{t_1, t_2, \ldots, t_{13}\}$, and set F indicates all arcs that connect places and transitions. The marking (*or state*) M_1 of a PN is represented by black tokens distributed over one or more places (see p_1 in Figure 2.12). A transition t is *enabled* if there is at least one token in each input place p, $(p, t) \in F$. If an enabled transition t *fires*, it removes one token from each of its input places p_1, $(p_1, t) \in F$ and generates one token in each of its output places p_2, $(t, p_2) \in F$. In general, it is possible to have more than one token in a place but here we will limit our discussion to Petri nets with no more than one token in a place. Also, note that places and transitions always alternate with each other in a Petri net.

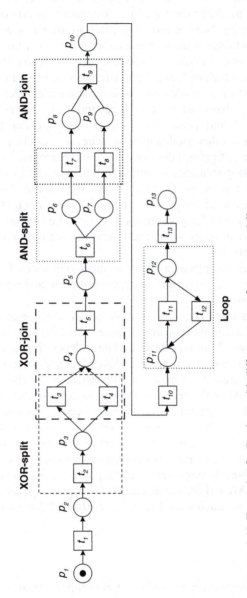

Figure 2.12 Example of a Petri net with different types of process modeling structures

Based on the causal relationships among its elements, four basic structure types of a PN can be classified as sequence (SEQ), parallel (AND), exclusive-choice (XOR), and iteration (Loop). The XOR and AND are shown in terms of their split and join representations in Figure 2.12. The representation of the Loop pattern is also shown here. A sequence is simply represented by the directed arcs, e.g. task t_2 follows t_1 in a sequence.

In Figure 2.12, we show an abstract example of a Petri net. At the start the token (black dot) is in place p_1. After the transition (or task) t_1 occurs or fires, it causes the token to move to place p_2. Next, it moves to place p_3 after t_2 fires. When the token is in place p_3, one of two things could happen: either t_3 fires or t_4 fires. However, t_3 and t_4 cannot fire together. This is like a choice or XOR construct. A condition may be attached to place p_3 to determine which of t_3 or t_4 fires. Alternatively, other factors may determine the decision and in that case we say that "the environment decides." Subsequently, the token moves to place p_5. Now, after t_6 fires, it generates two tokens that occupy p_6 and p_7 *simultaneously*. Next t_7 and t_8 can fire in parallel or in any order. This is like a parallel construct we have seen in other modeling approaches above. The parallel paths from t_7 and t_8 synchronize after t_9 fires and deposits a token in place p_{10}.

Finally, note how a loop structure is created by placing t_{11} and t_{12} in a cycle. In particular, when the token is in place p_{13}, it can either cause t_{12} to fire, thus making a loop, or t_{13} to fire, leading to the end of the process. The decision on which of the two transitions will fire can be made by attaching a condition to p_{12}. The various boxes shown in the figure are only meant to illustrate where the different structures that we have introduced earlier appear in the Petri net.

A Petri net in which any place can have at most one token for all possible firing sequences is said to be a *safe Petri net*. A large number of real-world processes can be modeled by such Petri nets.

Figure 2.13 shows a more concrete example of an expense claim process. After a claim is prepared and submitted by an employee the company may perform one of two approvals, Approval 1 or Approval 2. Then, depending upon the outcome of the approval (accept, or reject), the process moves forward to "Notify employee" and "Update records" (in parallel), or makes a loop whereby the claim is returned to the employee for revision. After the revision, the employee resubmits the claim. After the approval is complete, the payment is made. This places a token in place $p5$. The transition after $p5$ marked "X" denotes an empty or *silent transition*. This transition does not correspond to a real step; however, it is included to ensure the correct construction of the Petri net. The effect of this transition is to simply create two places, $p6$ and $p7$. Now tasks, "Notify employee" and "Update records" can proceed in parallel with one another. After there are tokens in both places $p8$ and $p9$, the transition "Close claim" can fire, producing a token in place $p10$ and thus completing the process instance.

BPMN vs. Petri Nets

Now that we have reviewed these methods, a brief comparison between them is in order. Clearly both methods are using basic control flow modeling patterns as building blocks to create process designs. In the case of BPMN, the patterns are created directly by symbols that can easily be recognized. However, for Petri nets they are created by using places and transitions as we showed above. These are more primitive constructs and hence are more difficult for an end user to understand.

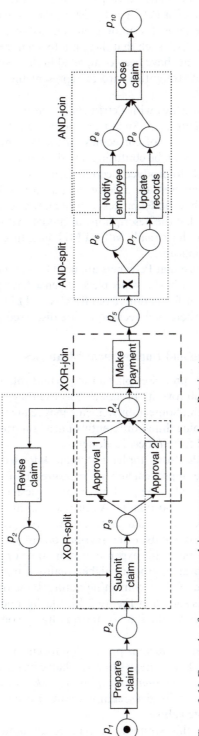

Figure 2.13 Example of an expense claim process represented as a Petri net

Another difference is that Petri nets are said to be "state aware" because it is possible to record the exact state of a Petri net by listing the number of tokens in each place. Thus, if we represent the state of a running process instance represented by the Petri net process model of Figure 2.13, such that there is a token in place *p5*, it means that all the tasks until "Make payment" have been completed in the instance. In the case of BPMN process models, it is not straightforward to represent the state of a running instance created from that model.

Yet another issue that arises with Petri nets is that of silent transitions like the one marked with "X" in Figure 2.13. Such transitions are artificial in that the modeler is forced to use them for the sake of correctness of the Petri net, but they do not have any real meaning. Hence, they can be confusing. On the other hand, sometimes silent places may be used intentionally to produce a certain behavior.

Finally, in terms of representation power and accuracy, Petri nets have a more precise semantics because they model processes using lower-level primitives like places and transitions. This means that the descriptions of models with Petri nets are more precise and less ambiguous than those made with BPMN diagrams. In most realistic situations, this difference is not significant.

It is important to realize that Petri nets are used by academicians, while BPMN (and EPC) are more suitable for business people and hence have greater practical value. It is also possible to make transformations from BPMN and EPC to Petri nets. We shall give references to literature where such techniques are discussed at the end of this chapter.

Basic Process Redesign and Improvement Strategies

As we saw in Chapter 1, processes play an important role in a business. A business is constantly striving to improve its processes because they have a direct impact on the efficiency of its operations. Some improvements may relate to advancements in IT, while others result from just doing things differently or in a "smarter" way based on experience. Improvement is realized from process redesign.

Process redesign results from applying domain knowledge about a process to find improvements in it. The improvements are measured by four metrics: *cost, time, flexibility*, and *quality*. Naturally, the goal of process redesign is to reduce cost and time while increasing flexibility and quality. As they say, in life there is no such thing as a free lunch, or at least they are hard to come by! Accordingly, these objectives tend to be conflicting in nature, i.e. one must often sacrifice one objective to attain another. Thus, greater flexibility may come at the expense of more time or cost. For faster service, you have to pay more. Moreover, to produce higher quality you incur a higher cost and it may take more time. Because of their conflicting nature, these objectives are said to form a "Devil's Quadrangle," as shown in Figure 2.14. Ideally, one would like to redesign the process in a way that reduces the span of the quadrangle on the X-axis and increases it along the Y-axis.

In the academic literature, various process improvement strategies to redesign a process are discussed. Some key strategies that we shall cover first here are *task elimination, task replacement, task combination, task splitting, task restructuring*, and *task postponement*. For each strategy, we'll give examples and also discuss its likely effect on the performance metrics noted above.

Task Elimination. In this strategy we remove an optional task, e.g. task T2 in Figure 2.15. An example of this strategy is eliminating a car wash task at a car rental

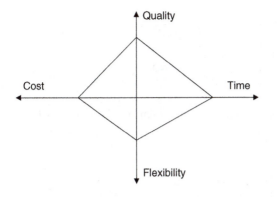

Figure 2.14 The Devil's Quadrangle

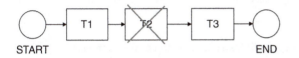

Figure 2.15 Task elimination, e.g. skip the car wash task

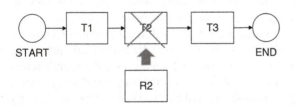

Figure 2.16 Task replacement, e.g. replace a regular car wash with express car wash

company before renting out a car. This will save time and cost, but it could hurt quality because a dirty car may be rented and the customer may not be satisfied. Note that customer satisfaction is a key component of quality after all.

Exercise 7: How will the quadrangle of Figure 2.14 shift if a car rental company omits the car wash task altogether before renting out the car?

Task replacement. In this strategy, we can replace an existing task with an alternative task (see Figure 2.16). For instance, a car wash (T2) may be replaced by an express car wash (R2). This task will take less time than a full car wash and it will also be less expensive, so there is a saving in both cost and time. However, it may hurt quality slightly since the express car wash may not make the car as clean as a full car wash.

Task combination. In this strategy two existing tasks may be combined into a single task as shown in Figure 2.17. An example of combination may occur in an insurance claim process. Say two separate agents are performing the tasks of receiving the customer claim (T1) and checking if the claim is covered by the customer's policy (T2).

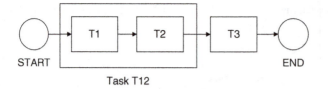

Task T12

Figure 2.17 Task combination, e.g. combine the receive claim and check claim tasks

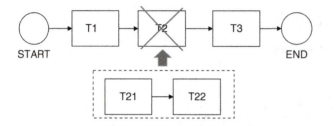

Figure 2.18 Task splitting strategy, split loan approval and notification task

These two tasks could be merged into a single task (T12) that is assigned to one agent. In doing so, the cost and time may likely decrease, since there is less set up time involved because the same agent executes both tasks. The quality would remain the same if the new task is properly designed. Perhaps, such a process was designed many years ago and information technology was not very advanced then. With the aid of new technology, it is now possible to merge these tasks easily. For example, the system can automatically check if the premium payments are on time and flash an alert on the agent's screen to warn her that the premiums have not been paid by the customer. Similarly, advances in technologies such as text mining and databases make it possible to type the description of the damage and have the system look up if it will be covered by the policy.

Task splitting. This is the opposite strategy of task combination, as shown in Figure 2.18. In this strategy, one task is split into two different tasks.

An example of task splitting would arise when the task of loan approval and customer notification (T2) being done by one person is split into two tasks: loan approval (T21) and customer notification (T22). The rationale for this split is that the two tasks are different in nature. The approval task requires a manager, while the notifications can be handled by a representative. The time of the manager is more precious and can be better utilized exclusively for approvals. In this way the cost of executing the process may drop and the time will remain about the same. In fact, the quality might improve slightly also on account of specialization.

Exercise 8: How will the quadrangle of Figure 2.14 change upon making the above redesign to a process?

Task restructuring. This strategy changes the structure of a process by combining two adjacent sequential tasks into a parallel structure as shown in Figure 2.19. Of course, this is possible only when the two tasks do not have a dependency between them. While processing a customer order, checking the credit status of the customer and checking

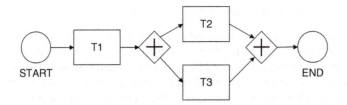

Figure 2.19 Task restructuring strategy – T2 and T3 are moved into a parallel structure

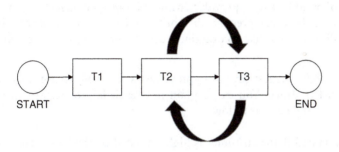

Figure 2.20 Task postponement – T2 is postponed until after T3 (e.g. perform credit approval after shipping)

available inventory of the items ordered can be done in parallel. The downside of this strategy is that sometimes the outcome of only one of the tasks is required to terminate the process, thus making the second task unnecessary. This is called *knock- out*, i.e. the output of the task may knock the process instance out by termination. For the example at hand, if the credit check failed then the process instance may terminate, eliminating the need for checking the inventory level altogether. However, if the knock-out probability is small, then restructuring would be worth considering.

The biggest advantage of parallel activities accrues from the time savings realized from multi-tasking. The cost would remain about the same and the quality is higher because the process will run faster, leading to a better response time for the customer. This strategy can only work when the output of one activity is not needed as in input for the second one. In general, even more than two tasks may be performed in parallel.

Task postponement. In this strategy a task may be postponed to a later point in the process, as shown in Figure 2.20. While processing a customer order, the credit approval step may be deferred until after the goods are shipped if the approval task is running slowly. In the context of Figure 2.20, we may consider that task T1 takes the customer order, T2 is the credit approval task, and T3 is the shipment task. Here, in some cases, we may do shipment before approval on the assumption that most credit checks are successful. In some cases, where the credit approval fails, the business may contact the customer later to recover the payment or even write it off as a cost of customer service. By doing postponement the timeliness can improve, leading to higher customer satisfaction and overall quality. The cost may rise on account of some losses incurred. It is also possible to make a rule that for orders below a certain level, the business will apply this strategy so as to reduce their risk.

Next, we describe an example to illustrate how performance improvement may be carried out in the context of a mortgage loan approval process.

Case Example 3. Figure 2.21 shows the loan approval process for Loans-R-Us bank. In this process, an application is received (T1), then a credit report for the applicant and an appraisal report for the property are obtained (T2) from an external service provider. Depending upon the contents of the reports, some applicants are automatically rejected and in these cases the instance follows the lower path at the XOR node. Along this path, a manager approves the rejection (T4), an assistant prepares the rejection notice (T5) and then the applicant is notified (T10). If the reports are "OK," then the instance follows the upper path at the XOR node. Along this path a financial officer makes a recommendation (T3) and this is followed by two approvals (T6 and T7 – by a manager and a VP) in the next two steps. An assistant then prepares the notification (T8) and it is sent to the applicant (T10). Loans-R-Us would like to examine ways to improve this process and make it more efficient.

As a consultant, you might suggest several improvements for them to consider by applying the strategies listed above. You can explain how each improvement can be applied and discuss its pros and cons as follows.

- Task T2 can be eliminated if the customer is highly trusted by the bank. There is a risk of higher rate of delinquencies that should be captured as a cost element for removing this task in a process instance. Moreover, this strategy can be applied only when the workload is high and the deadline is imminent. In this way, this strategy also increases flexibility.
- Task T2 may be replaced by another task R2 that takes less time at a higher cost. Thus, there is a clear trade-off between time and cost. Of course, often the cost may be passed on to the customer by the bank in the form of a fee for faster processing of their application.
- Tasks T6 and T7 are both approval tasks, so one may be skipped. Again, there is a trade-off involved in that the risk of making a bad loan goes up if only one approval is performed. This risk should be factored in as a cost and weighed against the benefit of faster processing and lower cost, since it would free up the time of one senior bank officer for other more important tasks. This strategy also increases flexibility.
- Tasks T6 and T7 may alternatively be performed in parallel. Often organizations require that approvals take place in sequence in order of seniority. Thus, in Figure 2.21, the manager is required to approve the loan first before it goes to the VP. If it is done in this manner, then the VP would have access to any comments or suggestions noted by the manager and this may lead to a better final decision. However, in conducting these approvals in parallel there is a clear saving in time. Since the loan would be approved only if both the officers approve it, the increase in risk is very small. This increased risk may be modeled in the cost of restructuring the task.
- The two approval tasks T6 and T7 may be combined into a single new task T67. This may correspond to a situation where the manager and VP jointly approve the loan. In doing so the duration of the combined activity would be less than the total duration of the two activities in sequence. There is clearly a saving in time in this arrangement.

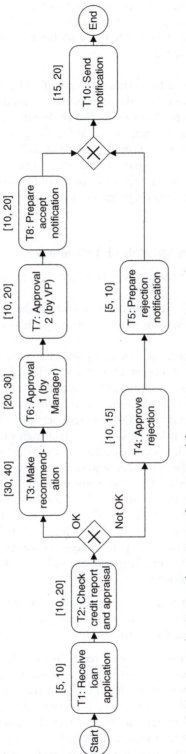

Figure 2.21 An example mortgage loan approval process model

- The loan may initially be approved and the customer notified based on the manager's approval, and the VP's approval may be carried out later as a verification step. If necessary, the VP may provide feedback to the manager or take other action as suitable for future reference.

All these strategies involve trade-offs in terms of time, cost, quality and flexibility. An organization that is trying to make improvements can quantify these metrics along a common scale and then try to evaluate the trade-offs before making a decision on how to modify its process. A common scale for the four metrics can be derived by converting each dimension into monetary terms. Cost is usually stated in monetary terms directly. Time can be converted into monetary terms by using an imputed hourly rate for each category of resource. Quality and flexibility are somewhat harder to convert into monetary terms, and some judgment may have to be applied by the functional managers.

More Redesign Strategies and Role of Technology

In addition to the above strategies, there are some more strategies that we shall mention briefly.

Resequencing. Modifying the sequencing of tasks in the process, to unleash more efficiencies from the process based on various criteria. This is also a variant of the task postponement idea.

Knock-out. As noted earlier if two tasks are in sequence and they do not have a strict dependency between them then they can be arranged in increasing order of effort required for the task and decreasing order of termination probability. Thus, we are able to discover instances that have to be terminated by investing less effort.

Analysis of performance metrics. Process designers at Infosys in India found that a process with three sequential tasks, A – B – C had high variability in the duration of task B. This was measured by calculating the standard deviation of the processing time of each task. They also noticed that there were many instances where task B had a very short processing time. Based on this, they came up with the idea of splitting task B into an exception path and a normal path, such that short duration instances would take the exception path and all others would take the normal one. Of course, this assumes that it is possible to predict the approximate duration of task B. This idea has been applied in supermarkets by the creation of express checkout counters (i.e. an exception path) for customers with ten or fewer items. This is an example of task restructuring based on the performance metrics of a process.

Exercise 9: What are other metrics or considerations that might influence the decision to create exception paths? In the supermarket example above, when would it make sense to create more than one exception path?

Technology plays a big role in process redesign as well. Think about how technology has impacted the checkout process in your neighborhood supermarket. Figure 2.22 shows how this process has evolved. Figure 2.22(a) shows the traditional process that most stores have followed for a long time. In recent years, however, many stores have introduced self-checkout lanes that allow customers to scan their items themselves (see Figure 2.22(b)). According to a Dutch colleague, in Europe often an additional sampling step is done to check if a customer scanned every item and did not miss anything

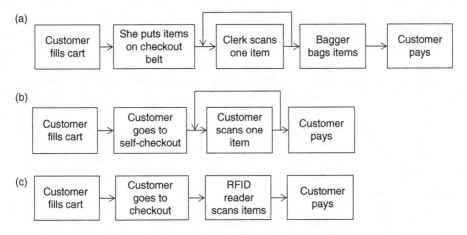

Figure 2.22 Evolution of the checkout process at the supermarket: (a) cashier checkout process (the loop is shown informally without gateways); (b) self-checkout process
(the loop is shown informally); (c) a fully automated checkout process

inadvertently or otherwise. This random check is done by a dedicated clerk if the
customer is flagged by the system, perhaps based on the customer's history.

With rapid advances in technology, the day is not far away when you will be able
to simply walk out with your cart through a checkout gate and an RFID scanner will
automatically receive signals from all the items in your cart (see Figure 2.22(c)). It will
then be able to calculate your bill and show you a total on payment display. You simply
swipe your card, put your items in a bag, and leave. The payment could also be made by
a mobile device. Thus, technology will continue to have a large influence on the design
of processes.

Chapter Summary

EPC is used widely in SAP [5]. It is also a part of ARIS [1], an approach to enterprise
modeling that offers methods for analyzing processes taking a holistic view of process
design, management, workflow, and application processing. Some references to EPC
are [1, 5].

The BPMN Quick Guide [6] and Lucid Charts [11] are convenient references for
BPMN 2.0 that covers all the visual elements, the basic rules, best practices and more.
Another useful reference [2] gives many interesting examples to illustrate the use of
various BPMN elements. Van der Aalst et al. [17] have enumerated a large number of
generic patterns that can be applied to design workflows in a plug-and-play manner.
Many of these patterns have been implemented in the Yawl academic product [19]. Signavio (www.signavio.com) is a very user-friendly web based tool for making EPC and
BPMN diagrams. These diagrams can also be made in Microsoft Visio using predefined
templates. But they cannot be saved in Visio in XML format which you can do in Signavio. Lohmann et al. [9] describe approaches to transform EPC and BPMN models
into Petri nets. In this way, an end user can design a model in a business language and a
tool or a workflow engine can transform it to a Petri net for internal representation and

analysis in a system. A Petri net based approach for describing and analyzing workflow management systems is presented in van der Aalst and van Hee [18].

The book by Hammer and Champy [4] that was published in the 1990s is a classic work on business process management and it gives numerous interesting cases and examples of successful process redesign efforts in industry. The approach they advocated was called business process re-engineering. While it worked in some companies that tried it, many others found it to be too radical and instead preferred more incremental approaches to process redesign. The Devil's Quadrangle was proposed by Brand and van der Kolk [3] to show that different goals might lead to completely different redesign options. Mansar and Reijers made the first effort to examine process redesign in a systematic way. In [12, 13] they discuss many different best practices and heuristics for redesign. Jansen-Vullers et al. [7] have studied performance measures like cost, time, quality and flexibility for evaluating a new design.

An evolutionary approach for generating redesign alternatives by applying best practices to an existing process is proposed by Netjes et al. in [14, 15]. This work resulted from the PhD thesis of Mariska Netjes on creation and evaluation of process alternatives at the University of Eindhoven. Van der Aalst [16] has done an analysis of knock-out strategy to determine under what conditions it works well. There has also been work on process improvement patterns in Lohrmann and Reichert [10]. A recent work by Kumar and Indradat discusses a formal approach for optimizing process model redesign by applying various improvement strategies [8]. In this work, an optimization model is developed to minimize the cost of applying a redesign strategy subject to a set of constraints that capture the effect of the redesign.

Some well-known BPM products and platforms are: Activiti (www.activiti.org/), Bizagi (www.bizagi.com/), Camunda (https://camunda.org/), and jbpm (www.jbpm.org/).

References

1. Aris Community. Basic Rules of EPC Modeling. http://www.ariscommunity.com/users/rbaureis/2010-03-22-basic-rules-epc-modelling.
2. BPMN Modeling Reference. https://camunda.org/bpmn/reference/.
3. N. Brand and H. V. der Kolk. *Workflow Analysis and Design*. Kluwer, Deventer (in Dutch), 1995.
4. M. Hammer and J. Champy. *Reengineering the Corporation: A Manifesto for Business Revolution*. Harper Business Editions, New York, 1993.
5. T. A. Curran and A. Ladd. SAP R/3 Business Blueprint (2nd Ed.): *Understanding Enterprise Supply Chain Management*. Prentice Hall PTR, Upper Saddle River, NJ, USA, 1999.
6. D. Gagné and S. Ringuette. *BPMN Quick Guide* (2nd Ed.). www.bpmnquickguide.com/view-bpmn-quick-guide/.
7. M. H. Jansen-Vullers, P. A. M. Kleingeld and N. Mariska. Quantifying the performance of workflows. *IS Management*, Vol. 25, No. 4, pp. 332–343, 2008.
8. A. Kumar and P. Indradat. Optimizing process model redesign. *ICSOC*, pp. 39–54, 2016.
9. N. Lohmann, E. Verbeek and R. M. Dijkman. Petri net transformations for business processes—a survey. *Transactions on Petri Nets and Other Models of Concurrency*, Vol. 2, pp. 46–63, 2009.
10. M. Lohrmann and M. Reichert. Effective application of process improvement patterns to business processes. *Software & Systems Modeling*, Vol. 15, No. 353, pp. 1–23, 2014.
11. Lucid Charts. www.lucidchart.com/pages/bpmn/activities/tasks.
12. S. L. Mansar and H. A. Reijers. Best practices in business process redesign: validation of a redesign framework. *Computers in Industry*, Vol. 56, No. 5, pp. 457–471, 2005.

13. L. Mansar and H. A. Reijers. Best practices in business process redesign: use and impact. *Business Process Management Journal*, Vol. 13, No. 2, pp. 193–213, 2007.
14. M. Netjes, S. L. Mansar, H. A. Reijers and W. M. P. van der Aalst. Performing business process redesign with best practices: an evolutionary approach. *ICEIS* (Selected Papers) 2007, pp. 199–211, 2007.
15. M. Netjes, S. L. Mansar, H. A. Reijers and W. M. P. van der Aalst. An evolutionary approach for business process redesign – towards an intelligent system. *ICEIS*, Vol. 3, pp. 47–54, 2007.
16. W. M. P. van der Aalst. Reengineering knock-out processes. *Decision Support Systems*, Vol. 30, No. 4, pp. 451–468, 2000.
17. W. M. P. van der Aalst, A. H. M. Ter Hofstede, B. Kiepuszewski and A. P. Barros. Workflow patterns. *Distributed and Parallel Databases*, Vol. 14, No. 1, pp. 5–51, 2003.
18. W. M. P. van der Aalst and K. Van Hee. *Workflow Management Models, Methods and Systems*. Cambridge, MA, MIT Press, USA, 2004.
19. Yawl, University of Queensland. http://yaug.org/node/21.

3 Data and Resource Modeling

Introduction

In the previous chapter, we only considered the control flow of a process, i.e. the order in which tasks had to be performed in a process and the coordination among them. By now, we hopefully understand that ordering and sequencing the tasks correctly is important for a proper description of a process. We cannot, for instance, make a pizza unless all the ingredients for it are there, or deliver it before it has been prepared. However, it is equally important to realize that there are many other aspects of a process that bear description before it can actually be executed.

The perspective we described in the previous chapter is called the *control flow perspective* because it emphasizes the control flow of a process. But let's not forget that, after all, the eventual goal of process modeling is to be able to execute the process. To do so, we must add two other perspectives – the *data perspective* to specify the input and output data of each task in a process; and the *resource perspective* to specify who is qualified to perform what task (e.g. an individual or a resource).

When you think about it, you will realize that we must also know the role or person that is actually going to perform a task; after all, a surgery cannot be performed by a lab technician, rather it needs a surgeon, or it may even need a team of participants. The **resource perspective** is concerned with the assignment of tasks to suitably qualified resources. In the pizza example from the last chapter, the order is received by an *agent*, the pizza is actually prepared by the *cook*, and the delivery is made by the *delivery person*. These are three different roles. In a medical process, there are roles like *receptionist, nurse, physician, technician, surgeon*, etc.

Moreover, the surgeon will require a lot of information about the patient to be able to plan for and perform the surgery. This would perhaps include the patient's full electronic medical record (EMR) that contains basic information like the patient's name, age, gender, etc. along with more detailed information about results of blood tests, imaging tests, etc. Such information is called data of a process. In general, each task in a process consumes information from previous tasks and generates fresh information for use by later tasks. This data may be in the form of messages sent from one task to another, or it can be data that are generated and stored in a database. Thus, after a purchase order is created, it is stored in a database. Then the information in the purchase order is used to perform additional tasks to fulfil the purchase order. Fulfilment in turn includes other steps such as order preparation, shipping, billing, etc. The **data perspective** refers to the data needs of various tasks of a process.

A *holistic process model* must consider the resource and data perspectives in addition to the control flow perspective to produce a complete process model. Moreover, it is also possible to take a broader notion of a resource that extends beyond just human resources. For instance, to perform a surgery a surgeon will need an operating room. Further, the operating room must have a set of machines or equipment that will be required to monitor the condition of the patient as the surgery proceeds. Thus, the room and the equipment are additional resources that are needed to perform the surgery. Ideally a workflow management system should be able to manage the assignment of all such resources. In this chapter, we shall start with the resource perspective, and then move on to the data perspective, to be followed by a healthcare case example. The rest of the chapter will focus on concepts and actual practice of resource allocation.

Adding Resource Information with Swimlanes

We have just seen that a task cannot be assigned to a worker or an agent if the model does not have resource information. A resource model should show the information about who actually performs a task. One way in which this is done is by means of a *swimlane diagram*. This diagram is divided into horizontal lanes and each lane corresponds to one resource, as shown in Figure 3.1. This is a blank swimlane diagram consisting of pools and lanes. There are two pools for customers and the ABC insurance company. The pool for the company is divided into multiple lanes that correspond to separate departments or units where work is performed. In general, a pool represents a separate entity or an organization, such as a customer or a company, while the lanes correspond to departments, divisions, groups, etc. of the company.

Now let us fill this swimlane diagram with an actual process that belongs here. An insurance claim process is shown in Figure 3.2.

This figure shows a typical insurance claim process with two pools, one for the customer and another for the insurance company. The pool for the insurance company is split into multiple lanes that correspond to different units such as receiving, reviewing, assessing, approval, and payment. These lanes may also correspond to various roles within the company, such as finance manager, accounts vice-president, etc. In this process, the claim is submitted by the customer and received by the receiving department

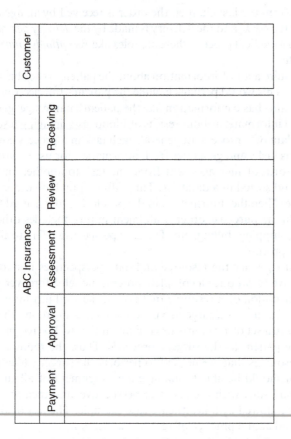

Figure 3.1 A blank swimlane diagram showing pools and lanes

of the company. In turn, it is sent to the reviewing department for review to ensure that all the information has been provided and the customer does indeed have policy coverage for the claim being made. Next, if it is complete and valid, then it is handed to an assessor, who is a specialist in determining the amount of damage and the appropriate compensation for it. The assessor prepares and submits a report that is sent to the approvals unit, where a manager approves the claim. Finally, the payment is made by the payment unit.

The purpose of the swimlanes is self-explanatory from this diagram. They are basically a way to enable someone looking at the model to easily see at a glance who performs what task. Another aspect of this model that must be noted is the dotted line link (in contrast to the solid line links within each pool) across the customer pool and the insurance company pool. This link denotes the passing of a message from the customer pool to the insurance company pool. The important point here is to realize that the customer and ABC Insurance are two separate entities and their internal processes are independent of one another. In general, company 1 would not like company 2 to see its internal processes, and vice versa. Yet, they should be able to communicate with each other. This is achieved through message passing. Hence, in general, we assume that they are not interoperable, and the only way for the two processes to interact is through the exchange

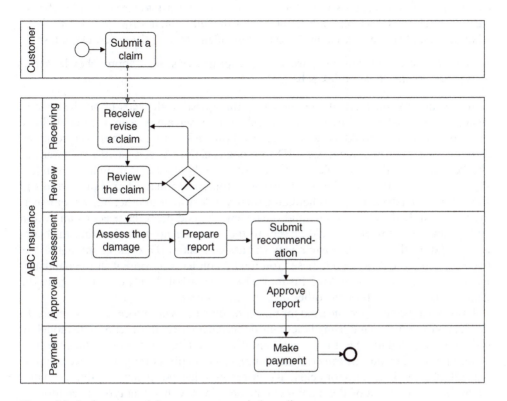

Figure 3.2 An insurance claim process on a swimlane diagram

of messages. On the other hand, even though there are several units or departments within a company, it is still a single entity and it is reasonable that one process cuts across several departments of the company. Hence, the solid lines across lane boundaries indicating the flow of control within a process are valid. Finally, note that in this context a message is a generic term for the passing of information across two parties. The message could be sent as an email, by a phone call, by filling a form on the web, etc.

Modeling of Data

A process model should also capture the data perspective, i.e. it should describe the data required and produced by each task in the process. In general, most activities will need to deal with data that relate to a specific case in order for work to be done. Try to make a list of the data that an activity in the above example of an insurance claim will need.

Well, if we consider the receive claim activity, it will strike you upon a little reflection that to process a claim we need some essential information from the customer, like *customer name, policy number, date of claim, details of claim*, etc. Moreover, this information will be required at every step of this process. From the point of view of modeling the data needs of this process, we can do one of two things: (1) we could capture the information at the start of the process at the receive claim task and then keep on passing it along to successive tasks; or, (2) we could capture this information at the receive claim task, assign a claim ID to it and then store it in the database of the company as a new claim. Then we can only pass along the claim ID from one task to the next and each task can use the claim ID to look up the database for the full claim information. Think about what task should assign the claim ID: the receive claim task or the review claim task.

Exercise 1: How would you compare the data capture and storage approaches described above? Which one do you think is better?

To be sure, to some extent the answer to this question depends upon the process designer. A normal procedure is to assign a claim ID when a new claim is entered. Some may argue that one should assign the claim ID only after the claim has been reviewed as there is no point in assigning an ID to a bogus claim. As soon as the reviewer has checked that the claim is complete and valid, she would press a button on her screen (see Figure 3.3). Upon this step, the system would automatically mark the claim as valid and store it in the database. On the other hand, there would also be another button for reject-ing the claim. If the claim is not valid the reviewer would press the reject claim button and a standard form letter would be sent to the customer notifying her that the claim is not valid. In this case, the system may still assign a claim ID to the claim, mark it as rejected, and store it in the database. You might wonder, why store it in the database? For future reference, so that ABC Insurance has a record of the claim. Think about the data inputs and outputs of the other tasks in this process.

Thus, having established the need for modeling data flows in a process, let us delve into the details of how data modeling is actually done. An important aspect of data modeling is data objects. A data object is a collection of related data items about some aspect of an application. For our insurance claim example, a data object is an insurance claim. It is a collection of data items (or fields) like customer name, policy number, date of claim, claim details, etc. Each of these items can be described with a data type. Therefore, we may describe the structure of this data object in semi-formal syntax as:

```
DataObject Claim{
Customer name String[50];
Policy number String[40];
Claim Date Date;
Claim details String[250];
}
```

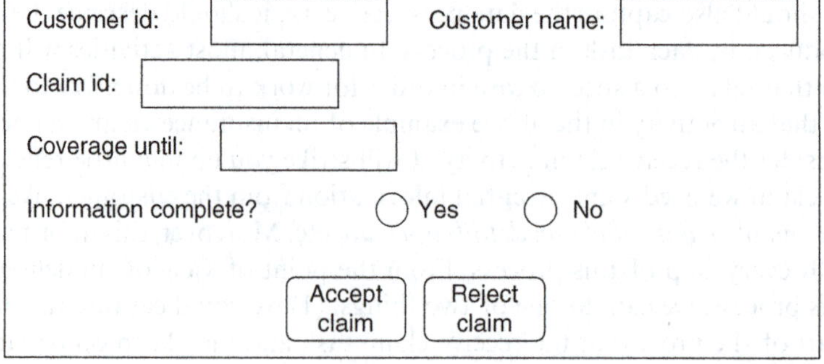

Figure 3.3 Screenshot of a review claim screen

Exercise 2: Now that you have seen the description for a data object, think of other data objects that are relevant for this example and write down their definitions in a similar format.

Representing Data in BPMN Diagrams

In BPMN, we use the notion of an association link to represent the input and output data of an activity. An association link is shown by a dotted line connecting an activity to an object. In Figure 3.4, we express the idea that the output of the "Research the topic" activity is a document of data object called "Research Notes," and the same data object is the input of the "Write text" activity that follows the "Research the topic" activity. It is important to clearly distinguish the control flow, i.e. the order in which the activities are performed (represented by solid lines) from the data flow, i.e. the input and output data needs of an activity (represented by dotted lines). Also note that the two different diagrams in Figure 3.4 represent the same idea. In the second diagram, the association link is made between the link and the data object to convey that the Research Notes data object is generated by one activity and is used by the next one.

With this background, it will be easier to understand Figure 3.5, which shows the full BPMN process model introduced earlier in this chapter, annotated with the data object information. The symbol for a data object is a rectangle with a fold at the top right corner. Notice how the three data objects are shown in this figure along with the tasks they relate to. The data objects are connected to the task that accesses them using a (dotted line) association link. This link should not be confused with a control flow link. The association link may have an arrow on it to indicate the direction in which the data is transferred. If an activity writes to the data object, then the link is directed outwards from the task to the object, while if it reads from it, then the direction of the arrow is reversed. An undirected link means that the activity both reads from and writes to the object. Most BPMN modeling tools such as Signavio, Visio, etc. allow you to make such models with the data object information.

For some modeling needs, it may suffice to simply describe the input and output data objects of each activity in a process model and stop there. However, for other process models, more details may be desirable to make the model complete. In particular, we may wish to know what kinds of information must be captured while recording a claim. Thus, it is necessary to provide specific inputs and outputs of an activity, e.g., as already noted above, the specific inputs of the Receive/Revise a claim activity are: customer

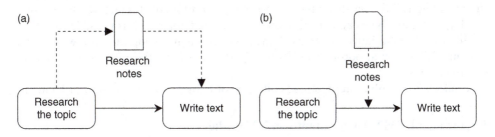

Figure 3.4 Representing a data association between two tasks: (a) one way to represent a data association; (b) an alternative way to represent a data association

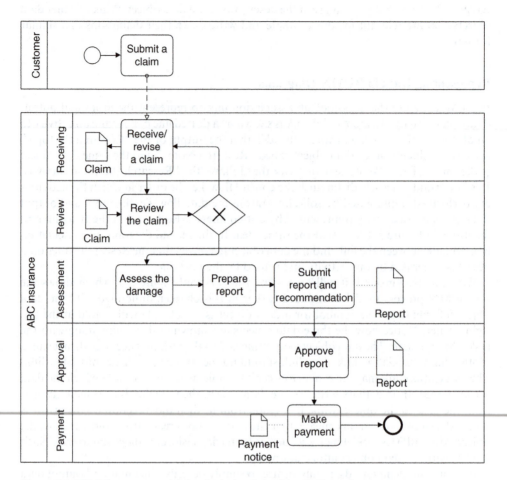

Figure 3.5 BPMN process model that includes data object information

name, policy number, claim date, and claim details. Several BPMN modeling tools allow a modeler to supply such information.

In Signavio (www.signavio.com) this is done through the attributes pane on the right of the designer screen. This attributes pane can be made visible by clicking the double arrows on the top right corner of your screen. A screenshot of the attributes pane is shown in Figure 3.6. The attributes are shown at the bottom of this picture. By selecting the data input attributes and clicking on the "…" that appears, it is possible to create, modify, or delete the data input fields of an activity through the pop-up window as shown in Figure 3.7. A similar pop-up window may be used to specify the outputs of an activity (see Figure 3.8).

A **collection** data object represents a collection of information, e.g. a list of order items.

Exporting a BPMN Diagram into an XML File

A BPMN model in the form of such drawings is useful for a visual understanding of the process. Thus, it is a valuable tool for one person to describe a process formally

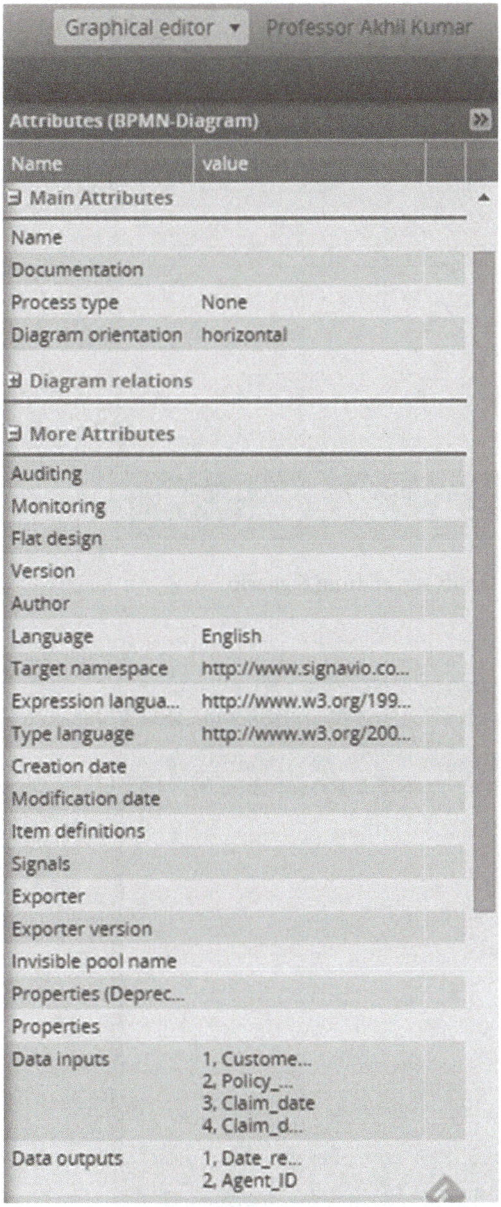

Name	value
Main Attributes	
Name	
Documentation	
Process type	None
Diagram orientation	horizontal
Diagram relations	
More Attributes	
Auditing	
Monitoring	
Flat design	
Version	
Author	
Language	English
Target namespace	http://www.signavio.co...
Expression langua...	http://www.w3.org/199...
Type language	http://www.w3.org/200...
Creation date	
Modification date	
Item definitions	
Signals	
Exporter	
Exporter version	
Invisible pool name	
Properties (Deprec...	
Properties	
Data inputs	1, Custome... 2, Policy_... 3, Claim_date 4, Claim_d...
Data outputs	1, Date_re... 2, Agent_ID

Graphical editor ▾ Professor Akhil Kumar

Attributes (BPMN-Diagram)

Figure 3.6 A screenshot of the attributes pane on the right margin of the Signavio modeler screen

so that another person can understand it and check it. However, it cannot be directly understood by a computer. To enable this, we must convert the drawing into a "machine readable format." The BPMN 2.0 specification defines a way for storing any BPMN process model as an XML file. The specification defines an XML schema (or a set of formatting rules) for storing this drawing in a file in XML format. The XML file can in

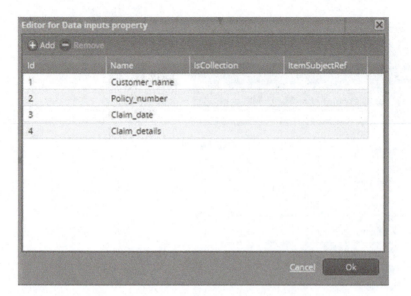

Figure 3.7 A screenshot of the data inputs screen from Signavio

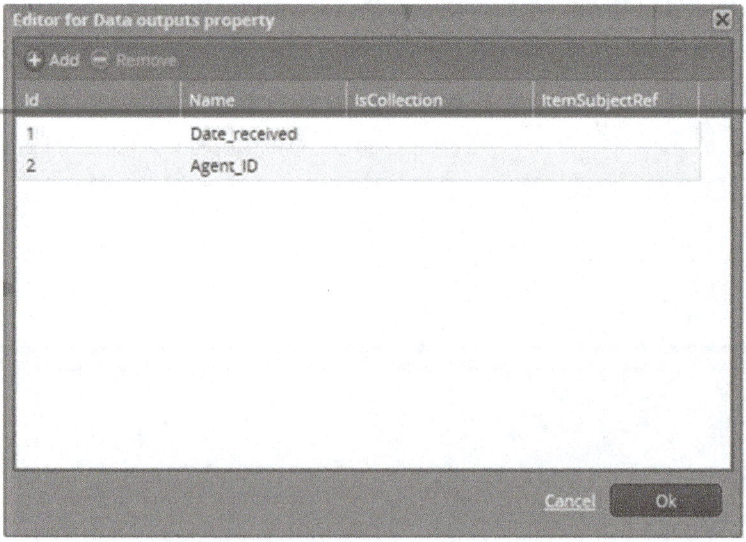

Figure 3.8 A screenshot of the data outputs screen from Signavio

turn be parsed by a workflow engine and executed. Many modeling tools, but not all, will allow you to save a model in XML format. This is a standard format that is recognized by most workflow execution engines. Each modeling construct of BPMN maps into an element name. The BPMN specification gives corresponding XML element names for the various drawing elements used on the canvas for creating a diagram. Examples of these element names are: <process>, <task>, <parallelgateway>, <exclusivegateway>, <pool>, <lane>, etc. The data inputs and outputs are specified with <iospecification>, <dataInput>, and <dataOutput> elements. Thus, the XML specification of the "Receive/Revise a claim" activity would be described as shown in Figure 3.9.

As an end user, fortunately, you need not concern yourself with the details of each and every element in this figure. However, it is worth noting that the <dataInput> and <dataOutput> XML elements are used to specify the names of the data object and the specific data fields in it referenced by the activity as part of the <iospecification> element. There is also additional information pertaining to <inputSet> and <outputSet> elements. The important point to remember is that a BPMN modeling tool should allow you to export a BPMN diagram into an XML file so that a workflow engine can execute it and other modeling tools can also interpret it. In this way, interoperability is considerably enhanced.

In general, the *dataInput* and *dataOutput* elements may be defined for a process, task, or event. For a process or task, they are part of the *ioSpecification* that defines one or more inputSets and outputSets. Each inputSet and outputSet references zero or more dataInputs and dataOutputs. The operational semantics of ioSpecification and inputSet say that a process or task cannot start until the inputSet data are available. In that sense, ioSpecification defines the data requirements of the process or task, which is also called its *interface* or *signature*.

```xml
<task completionQuantity="1" id="sid-47CE12C3-2405-4C86-A573-F879CF016CB2" name="Receive/Revise a claim">
    <incoming>sid-F56B5036-1C11-4E85-87F7-D58DCE11B16B</incoming>
    <outgoing>sid-B3F4BEFA-021C-40CF-92EA-3757B528E7C4</outgoing>
    <ioSpecification id="sid-373bbe6c-ba35-493a-91b6-3652a163c2d1">
    <dataInput id="1" isCollection="false" name="Customer_name"/>
    <dataInput id="2" isCollection="false" name="Policy_number"/>
    <dataInput id="3" isCollection="false" name="Claim_date"/>
    <dataInput id="4" isCollection="false" name="Claim_details"/>
    <dataInput id="sid-69A2A0F4-C936-4687-B767-39C69862F5DF" isCollection="false" name="Claim">
      <extensionElements>
        <signavio:signavioMetaData metaKey="bgcolor" metaValue="#ffffff"/>
      </extensionElements>
    </dataInput>
    <dataOutput id="1" isCollection="false" name="Date_received"/>
    <dataOutput id="2" isCollection="false" name="Agent_ID"/>
    <dataOutput id="sid-686EA308-7750-4A99-A4D0-F5501FED7AEF" isCollection="false" name="Claim">
      <extensionElements>
        <signavio:signavioMetaData metaKey="bgcolor" metaValue="#ffffff"/>
      </extensionElements>
    </dataOutput>
    <inputSet id="sid-9584aa82-4870-4e6e-a761-043efc5cd5e8">
      <dataInputRefs>sid-69A2A0F4-C936-4687-B767-39C69862F5DF</dataInputRefs>
    </inputSet>
    <outputSet id="sid-751174ef-0686-4e83-9f42-34dbfadb354f">
      <dataOutputRefs>sid-686EA308-7750-4A99-A4D0-F5501FED7AEF</dataOutputRefs>
    </outputSet>
    </ioSpecification>
    ...
</task>
```

Figure 3.9 A BPMN 2.0 XML snippet of the "Receive/Revise a claim" activity

A Case Example from Healthcare

Case Example 1: Eternal-Health is a small practice with five physicians, eight nurses, and about ten additional staff that include an office manager, reception staff, billing staff, etc. They serve as a primary care practice (PCP office) for about 50 families, which translates into roughly 200 individual patients. This practice serves as the first port of call for patients whenever they have any symptoms or issues, or even if they need a wellness exam. The practice has an automated clinical decision support system (CDSS) that allows patients to make appointments and it also keeps track of the patients' records and status. The PCP office interacts with a pharmacy where all prescriptions for medicines, drugs, etc. are sent, and with a lab where all the lab orders are sent. The managers at Eternal-Health are trying to streamline their processes, and as a first step they wish to make process flow maps to have a better understanding of their workflows and interactions with their partners.

Figure 3.10 represents a simplified BPMN clinical workflow for Eternal-Health created in the web-based Signavio-Oryx editor. BPMN 2.0 can support various types of tasks and workflow patterns. It is executable and supported by existing workflow engines. In this diagram, pools (represented by rectangular blocks) correspond to workflow participants, including patient, CDSS, PCP office, pharmacy, and lab. A message flow (shown by dotted lines) is used to coordinate communication between two participants. Lanes are used to organize and categorize activities within a pool, say between a doctor and a nurse. The control flow among activities within a pool is shown by solid lines. This pathway shows that a patient having any symptom visits the PCP office and is examined by the care providers. The doctor writes a prescription (Rx) and sends it to the pharmacy. The pharmacy prepares and dispenses the medicine, and the lab is responsible for various tests. Activities or tasks are shown in round rectangles, while events are in circles. Complex gateways (shown in diamonds with an asterisk) allow one or more outgoing branches based on the results of conditions. Parallel gateways (shown in a diamond symbol with a "+" symbol, e.g. see the top lane in Figure 3.10) create parallel paths without checking any conditions. This is a formal description of the coordination among activities in this process.

"Prepare Rx" is a reusable sub-process whose execution semantics are strictly and explicitly defined, while "Do tests" in the last lane in Figure 3.10 is an ad hoc sub-process that is realized from other isolated activities. It is "loosely defined" at design time because its instantiation is dynamically determined by the outcome of previous activities. For example, if a doctor upon examination suspects that a patient may have suffered a heart attack, then "EKG" and "ECG" would be executed in the subsequent pathway. In contrast, a "Blood test" might be needed if a patient is suspected of having hypertension. Thus, using a strictly predefined sub-process to design an uncertain and dynamic activity is not practical since it lacks flexibility and adaptability. Information from the actual context must be applied to provide execution semantics for the "loosely defined" regions of such clinical processes at runtime. Accordingly, a doctor may order only a blood test for one patient, an ECG and EKG for another patient, and yet another different combination of tests for a third patient.

It should also be noted that in this figure there are five pools and six lanes. As stated above, each pool corresponds to a different "organization" or entity. Hence, communication across lanes takes place by message passing (e.g. by email). A message can also be sent by logging into a website and filling a form. So, a doctor's office may send you an

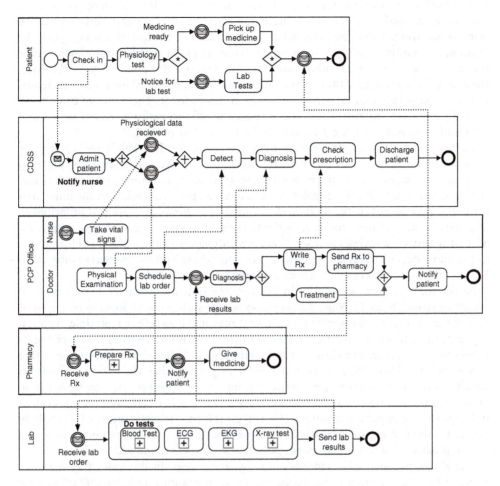

Figure 3.10 An example of a healthcare process for the treatment of an outpatient

email to remind you of an appointment you have with them in the near future. To con-firm the appointment, you may be asked to click on a link in the email. On clicking you may be directed to a website in your browser. On the website you can check the box for "confirm appointment" and then press the submit button. In this way, you can easily reply to a message you have received.

We omitted the data perspective from this figure to avoid cluttering it with too much detail. When a generic process model like the one in Figure 3.10 is actually executed for a specific patient, it is called a process instance. Thus, the process instance for patient "Sue" with Id "P1001" is different from that for patient "Jack" with Id "P1003," and so on.

Resource Allocation in a Workflow System

In this section, we discuss issues of resource allocation. There are two ways of allocating tasks to resources, by *offer* and by *assignment*, also called *pull* and *push* respectively.

In an offer-based allocation scheme, a resource is given an "offer" or an opportunity to work on a task and she can decide to accept or reject an offer within a certain time. An offer would also indicate the expected completion date of the task if it is accepted. An example of an offer-based allocation would be the manner in which the academic review process for a scholarly article submitted to a journal for possible publication works. After the article is received, an editor of the journal would normally invite a set of reviewers to review the article and prepare an evaluation report for it. The reviewer can decide, typically in a week, whether to accept or reject the offer to perform the evaluation and then notify the editor. Figure 3.11 describes a part of this process.

In this example, an editor contacts three reviewers, R1–R3. The inner sub-process shows that the editor waits for the three replies in a loop, and upon receiving each reply acknowledges it. If all three reviewers reply in less than seven days, then the inner sub-process is exited. If all the replies are not received in seven days, then the timer goes off and forces an exit of the loop, and the pending requests are canceled immediately after exit. Now, if all three reviewers agree to review the paper then there is a subprocess S2 that receives the reviews and sends acknowledgments to the reviewers. However, if one or more decline to review then the editor contacts substitute reviewers (subprocess S2), sets the timer to seven days again, and enters the inner subprocess.

Notice that the agent or worker, in this case the potential reviewer, has a choice to accept or refuse the task. While making an offer the system could do so in two ways: it may make an offer to one agent at a time or it may make an offer to multiple agents at the same time. If one agent accepts the offer then it is withdrawn from the other agents to whom it was made. The choice of the method would often depend upon the nature of the task involved. For a routine task with a tight deadline, the option of multiple simultaneous offers is more appropriate, but for non-routine tasks it may be better to make one offer at a time. Simultaneous offers are reasonable when, say, multiple evaluation reports of a paper are required. This is typical for the review process of a scholarly article as shown in Figure 3.11, where multiple reports are normally required. In such a case, it is reasonable to invite multiple potential reviewers simultaneously.

The alternative allocation mechanism is by *assignment*. In this case, a system may assign a task to a certain agent based on her qualifications and availability without checking with her if she would like to do it. An insurance claim assessor may receive an assignment for checking the damage to a car, while a photocopier repair technician may receive a daily assignment of repair tasks at various locations around a city. Of course, after the assignment is made, the agent may still decline it but that would require a separate (sub)process for declining and in that case the system would reassign the task to another agent.

Another aspect of resource allocation relates to *single v. multiple resources*. Some tasks are performed by individuals, whereas others require a group of people to work as a team. An example of a team task would be a surgery operation where a surgeon, an anesthetist, a nurse, and a medical technician may be required. In such a case, a system has to assign the surgery task to a group of people based on their respective schedules. As you can well imagine, an offer-based approach may not work well here. Another example of a team assignment would be to schedule a meeting for a group of people to discuss hiring a new senior executive for the company, or a team of people to evaluate the specifications of a new software product.

Yet another dimension of task allocation relates to *fixed v. flexible time tasks*. Some tasks, like approving an expense claim or a loan application, can be done in the approver's

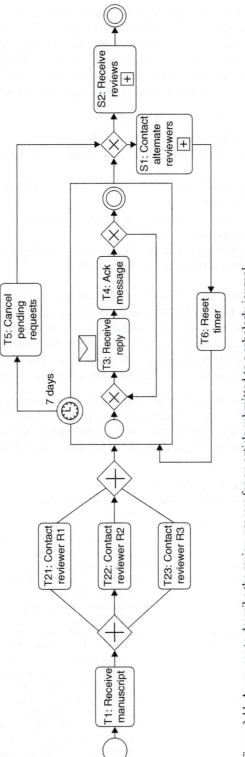

Figure 3.11 A process to describe the review process for an article submitted to a scholarly journal

own time from a mobile device, provided they are completed before the deadline. Other tasks, such as inspecting a vehicle to assess the damage to it, may require a prior appointment. In addition, team tasks would usually require a meeting time to be set up, when all concerned can discuss an issue in real-time even if it is through a virtual meeting. Table 3.1 summarizes various characteristics of task allocation.

Some other factors deserve consideration as well when dealing with team issues. Among them are:

Is everybody attending the meeting at the same location?
Will everybody be physically present, or will some participants join by audio/video conferencing?
For a virtual, geographically dispersed meeting what are the time zones in which the participants are located.
What kind of internet connections do they have? High speed, mobile, etc.?
What kind of meeting room is required?
What kind of computer hardware and software is required for the meeting?
Will there be a need for overhead projection equipment?

In making such assignments it is also important to consider how well the members of a team will be able to work together with each other. Unfortunately, most workflow systems do not provide much support for such considerations. Even support for assignment of teams to a task is rather limited. To make a proper assignment that considers various human and non-human resources, it is important to have a model that considers all these categories as class types and captures the relationships among them.

Exercise 3: Say, a team of five software engineers is distributed geographically across San Jose, California; Bangalore, India; and Singapore. They need to have a virtual meeting in a conference room equipped with high-quality video conferencing equipment and a high-end workstation on which computer-aided design and manufacturing software is

Table 3.1 Task allocation characteristics

Characteristic	Example
Offer v. assign	A task is offered to one or more agents, or it is assigned to a specific agent
Single v. multiple resource	One individual or several
Fixed v. flexible time	The task is done at an appointed time, or there is no specific time for it
Generic v. unique	Any surgeon from a group, or a specific surgeon ("Dr. Smith")
Transferrable v. non-transferrable	The same agent must be involved throughout a task, or an agent can handoff the task to another agent.
Multitask v. single task	An anesthetist may attend to two surgeries at the same time, or he must be present in one surgery for the entire duration of the surgery.
Atomic v. non-atomic	A senior nurse role may be replaced by two junior nurses, or it is not allowed.
Binding v. non-binding	The same nurse (say, Bob or Kim) must participate in all tasks (preparation, surgery, etc.) through a process instance when a nurse role is needed, or not.

installed. The time difference between San Jose and Singapore is 15 or 16 hours depending upon the time of the year. Between Bangalore and San Jose, it is either 12.5 or 13.5 hours. Singapore and India stay on the same time throughout the year, but San Jose shifts to daylight saving time between March and November. How would you schedule a team meeting that does not force anyone to work at awkward times across these countries?

To perform resource allocation effectively it is necessary to have an understanding of the resources in an organization. Resources are described by means of a resource model that captures information about each resource and also how they are related to each other.

Building a Resource Model – an Ontology of a Hospital

To allocate resources well, we first need to make a resource model that describes the resources and their relationships with each other. After all, the system can allocate only those resources it knows about. A resource model should be able to answer questions like: How busy is an employee? Is she on vacation? What role or position does an employee occupy? What role is required to perform a task? Is a technician qualified to operate a certain device? It is important to realize that the term resource is a broader concept than simply human resources. It encompasses non-human resources as well, like devices and equipment, locations, etc. Thus, an arterial defibrillator is a mobile resource in the context of a hospital. A resource model should be able to help determine the status of a specific arterial defibrillator, say, with ID AD8923, is it operational or not? Is it currently in use? What is its location?

An ontology is a convenient way of describing a resource model. Figure 3.12 shows an ontology in a hospital with Persons, Activities, Locations and Devices. The main idea being represented here is that in a hospital people perform activities at locations using devices and equipment. The ovals represent classes and subclasses, the solid lines with arrows point towards objects that are properties of another class object. For instance, an activity object points to a location object that denotes the location in which the activity is performed. Similarly, an activity object also points to a device object that is needed to perform it. Finally, the dashed lines point towards properties of data attributes of objects that belong to the class.

Using this ontology, we can determine that a **person**, say, Dr. Fick, is a heart surgeon who is participating in a triple bypass operation (Activity) with Activity ID A5643 in operating room 209 using a device with ID AD8923. We can also add temporal information such as what time the operation is expected to end. In addition, future activities that are scheduled can also be tracked using this schema.

Exercise 4: In the context of the above example related to the ontology of Figure 3.12, how can we find out what other staff members are assisting Dr. Fick with the operation he is performing?

A Model for Resource Allocation

Having discussed resource modeling issues and an ontology-based approach for resource modeling, we are in a position to discuss a resource allocation model. Figure 3.13 shows a model for resource allocation that covers some of the issues we have discussed thus

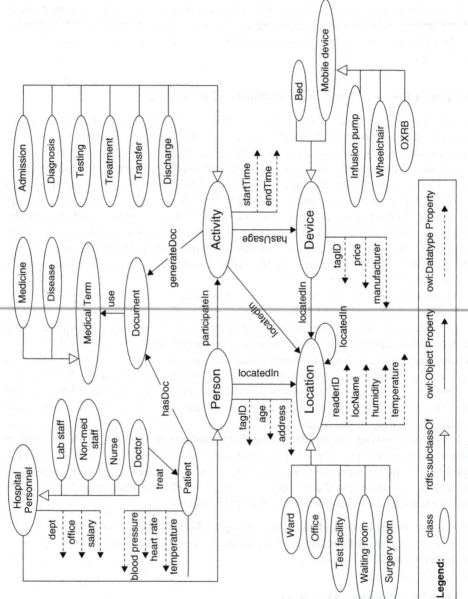

Figure 3.12 An ontology showing resource, location, and equipment

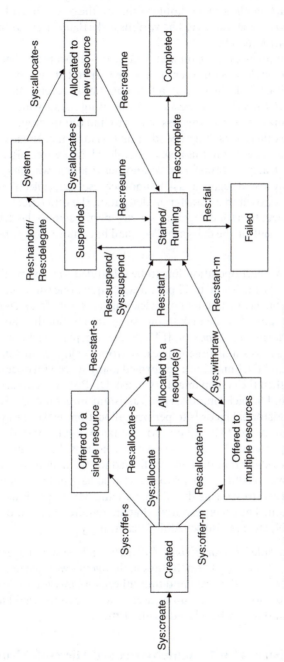

Figure 3.13 A work allocation framework (adapted from Russell [14])

far. It considers both offer-based and *assignment-based allocation*, and also shows what occurs after a task is allocated to a resource. In both cases the offer or assignment is made to users who satisfy certain conditions based on their role or position, qualifications, etc. In *offer-based allocation*, a resource would have to explicitly accept an offer before a task is assigned to it. Further, the system should withdraw the offer from other resources after it has been accepted by one resource. The various tasks that a user has to perform appear in her task list or work item list.

A resource(s) commences work on a task after it is allocated to her. If she is unable to complete it in a single session, then it may be suspended and resumed later. It may also occur that the task fails. In general, a task could be in several states such as *Started, Running, Suspended, Completed, Failed*, etc. Associating a state with a task helps various people in the organization query the task status to find out its progress or status. This is important because other tasks that depend upon this task may already have been scheduled, but they cannot begin until this task is completed. Moreover, after one resource has suspended a task, it may be transferred to another resource who may resume it. Similarly, a resource may also delegate a task to another resource, called the delegate, to do it on her behalf. As opposed to a transfer, in delegation the difference is that the resource carrying out the delegation (or delegator) is giving permission to the delegate to perform a specific task on behalf of the delegator. We shall have more to say about delegation in Chapter 8.

Case Example 2: A heart operation has to be scheduled for next week in a hospital in Operating Room 207 from 9 a.m. to 12 p.m. It will require one surgeon, one assistant surgeon, two nurses, one technician, and one cleaning assistant. To assemble this team, the workflow system might offer the task to one surgeon, Dr. Smith, who is most qualified and is not booked during that time slot. If Dr. Smith accepts, then the system might invite Dr. Jones to serve as assistant surgeon because from the log records it is evident that in the past Dr. Jones and Dr. Smith have performed many successful operations together. If Dr. Smith refuses, then the system might try to ask Dr. Robinson to serve as surgeon and ask another person, Dr. Jackson, to serve as assistant surgeon if Dr. Robinson accepts. Here we are using historical records to perform allocation. Next, the system might offer the operation to four nurses (Ms. Adams, Mr. Banks, Ms. Pike, and Mr. Sparks) who are available for the operation. As soon as two nurses accept the assignment, it is updated on their worklists to show that they are confirmed for the operation, and it is also withdrawn from the worklists of the other two nurses who have not responded so far. Finally, Mr. Garcia is assigned to serve as the technician and Mr. Lopez is assigned to serve as the cleaning assistant. The other resources that are required in the room such as arterial defibrillator AD259, etc. are also scheduled accordingly.

Another method called *Hierarchy-based allocation* allows a manager who sees that an agent in her department is busy to do the task in the agent's worklist herself. The manager has a higher privilege than the agent and thus inherits permission to do the task. In *User defined group*-based allocation a group of users may be defined who have the capability to perform a task and it may be offered to all of them.

Resource Allocation in TIBCO ActiveMatrix and Microsoft Sharepoint

TIBCO is a US company that provides integration, analytics and events processing software for companies to use on premises or as part of cloud computing environments.

The software manages information, decisions, processes, and applications. TIBCO acquired a company called Staffware that was a pioneer in business process management software in 2003. Staffware had developed many of the resource allocation techniques that were adopted into TIBCO software. ActiveMatrix is TIBCO's technology-neutral platform for composite business process management (BPM) and service-oriented architecture (SOA) applications. It includes products for service creation and integration, distributed services and data grids, packaged applications, BPM and governance. ActiveMatrix offers sophisticated resource allocation mechanisms.

A user or participant occupies a *position* in a unit of the organization. For each position you can specify properties like the location of the position and how long it should exist for, and you can also define capabilities and resources for a position. A group is a job type within the organization that allows resources to be grouped by their job characteristics. You can specify privileges and system actions associated with a position. As an example of privileges the *accounts organization* unit may be able to sign off expenses up to $500, but the *accounts manager* may be authorized to sign off expenses up to $1000.

There are several strategies for offering work to users:

Offer To All. This option is selected to specify that you want all users that match the participant definition to have the opportunity to accept or decline the work item. For example, if there is a claims handler organizational entity (such as a group), the work item is offered to all users in that group. Once a user opens the work item, it is allocated to her and removed from the work lists of other users in that group.

Offer to One. This option is selected to specify that you want only one user that matches the participant definition to have the opportunity to accept or decline the work item. If the user declines the work item, it is offered to another user that matches the participant definition.

Allocate to One. This option automatically allocates the work item to a user that matches the participant definition.

Allocate to Offer-set Member. This option allocates the work item to a specific user who is a member of the offer set defined by the user task's participant definition. A *performer* field must also be specified with this option, which the process must populate with the GUID (Globally Unique Identifier) of the specific member of the offer-set to whom the work item should be allocated.

There is also a *re-offer strategy* that allows a user task to be configured to re-offer the work item to any valid user when a user closes or cancels the work item.

Figure 3.14 shows how work views are presented in a folder/file type of display, where My Work and Supervised Work appear as folders, and work views you create under those categories appear as files. You can expand and collapse the *folders* by clicking the −/+ icon to the left of My Work and Supervised Work. When you click a work view, say, Request, a list of the work items in that view is displayed as shown in the figure. The Supervised Work views allow you to see the work of other individual resources or organizational entities that you are supervising.

SharePoint is a workflow tool from Microsoft that is used for simple office workflows. Its resource allocation features are less sophisticated than those of ActiveMatrix. A project task list displays a collection of tasks that are part of a project. A task is a discrete work item that a single person can be assigned to. A project is typically a series of activities that has a beginning, middle, and end, and which produces a product or service, such as producing a product demonstration for a trade show, creating a product proposal for stakeholders, or even putting together a corporate morale event.

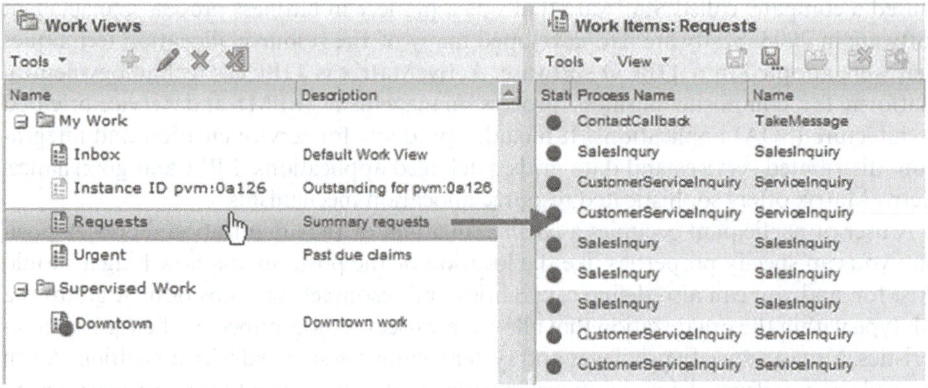

Figure 3.14 Work views in TIBCO ActiveMatrix and work items in the Requests view

Source: https://docs.tibco.com/pub/amx-bpm/3.1.0/doc/html/bpmhelp/GUID-879F8415-84FA-450D-80CE-1265DF9BFF6B.html.

After you create a SharePoint project task list, you can add tasks, assign resources to tasks, update the progress on tasks, and view the task information on bars that are displayed along a timeline.

Sharepoint can be accessed through a web-based interface, so there is no need for special software. It is simple to set up and use. Email notifications are sent when tasks are assigned. A user has an ability to create subtasks and to add tasks to the timeline. It has pre-built views for My Tasks, Late Tasks, Upcoming Tasks, Gantt Chart, etc.

Chapter Summary

In this chapter we tried to understand the importance of data and resource considerations as they apply to constructing business process models. We saw how data objects are associated with process models, and resource models are designed. Resource allocation mechanisms were also described and discussed in the context of actual products.

BPMN 2.0 [1] is the current de facto standard for modeling business processes with data. Protégé [11] is a tool for building ontologies like the one we described in this chapter. A variety of various workflow data patterns are discussed in [13].

Some early work on modeling of organizational resources was done by Zur Muehlen [20]. He has developed a generic meta model that shows relationships between resource classes like *person, position, position type, organizational unit, qualification, competence*, etc. Such a model can be helpful in understanding the resource capabilities of an organization so that appropriate resources can be selected. Unfortunately, a standard for resource modeling of a universal nature has still not emerged.

Resource allocation is an important issue in BPM. Some early work on resource allocation (e.g. [6]) was based on the ideas of pull and push mechanisms. Kumar et al. note that proper resource allocation is crucial in providing efficient usage of resources in business process execution. They discussed ways to balance quality and performance of a running process by considering metrics like suitability, urgency, conformance, and availability. Russell et al. [14] introduced workflow resource patterns as an extension of workflow patterns [16]. They have identified 43 workflow resource patterns (of both the push and pull type), which describe different ways of resource allocation. Many of these ideas have been implemented in the YAWL tool from the Queensland University of Technology. This is a successful tool from a university that is still being maintained and has been implemented in some businesses also, but it has not yet become a commercial product. Some of the experiences of YAWL are described in [15], in which Russell and Hofstede refer to several other related papers as well.

Pesic et al. [10] have also investigated the resource allocation mechanisms in the context of workflow products. Huang et al. have looked at a technique for resource allocation based on reinforcement learning [4]. Resource allocation should also consider factors like risk [3] and compatibility [7] in making assignments. Various other approaches are discussed in [2, 5, 8, 12, 17–19]. Finally, techniques for discovering staff assignment rules are described in [9].

References

1. BPMN Specification. www.bpmn.org/.
2. C. Cabanillas et al. *Priority-based Human Resource Allocation in Business Processes*. International Conference on Service-Oriented Computing. Springer, Berlin, Heidelberg, 2013.
3. R. Conforti et al. A recommendation system for predicting risks across multiple business process instances. *Decision Support Systems*, Vol. 69, pp. 1–19, 2015.
4. Z. Huang, W. M. P. van der Aalst, X. Lu and H. Duan. Reinforcement learning based resource allocation in business process management. *Data & Knowledge Engineering*, Vol. 70, No. 1, pp. 127–145, 2011.
5. Z. Huang, X. Lu and H. Duan. Mining association rules to support resource allocation in business process management. *Expert Systems with Applications*, Vol. 38, No. 8, pp. 9483–9490, 2011.
6. A. Kumar, W. M. P. van der Aalst and H. M. W. Verbeek. Dynamic work distribution in workflow management systems: How to balance quality and performance. *Journal of Management Information Systems*, Vol. 18, No. 3, pp. 157–193, 2002.
7. A. Kumar, R. Dijkman and M. Song. Optimal Resource Assignment in Workflows for Maximizing Cooperation. In: Daniel, F., Wang, J., Weber, B. (eds) *Business Process Management*. Springer, Berlin, Heidelberg, pp. 235–250, 2013.
8. Y. Liu, J. Wang, Y. Yang and J. Sun. A semi-automatic approach for workflow staff assignment. *Computers in Industry*, Vol. 59, No. 5, pp. 465–476, 2008.
9. L. T. Ly, S. Rinderle, P. Dadam and M. Reichert. Mining staff assignment rules from event-based data. *Lecture Notes in Computer Science*, Vol. 3812, pp. 177–190, 2006.
10. M. Pesic and W. M. P. van der Aalst. Modeling work distribution mechanisms using Colored Petri Nets. *International Journal on Software Tools for Technology Transfer*, Vol. 9, No. 3/4, pp. 327–352, 2007.
11. Protégé. http://protege.stanford.edu/.
12. H. Reijers et al. Workflow Management Systems+Swarm Intelligence=Dynamic Task Assignment for Emergency Management Applications. In: G. Alonso, P. Dadam and M. Rosemann (eds) BPM 2007. *LNCS*, Vol. 4714, pp. 125–140. Springer, Heidelberg, 2007.
13. N. Russell, A. H. M. ter Hofstede, D. Edmond and W. M. P. van der Aalst. Workflow Data Patterns: Identification, Representation and Tool Support. In: L. Delcambre, C. Kop, H. C. Mayr, J. Mylopoulos and O. Pastor (eds). *Proceedings of the 24th International Conference on Conceptual Modeling (ER'05)*, Springer-Verlag, Berlin, Heidelberg, pp. 353–368, 2005.

14. N. Russell, W. M. P. van der Aalst, A. H. M. ter Hofstede and D. Edmond. Workflow Resource Patterns: Identification, Representation and Tool Support. *Proceedings of the 17th International Conference on Advanced Information Systems Engineering (CAiSE '05)*, pp. 216–232, 2005.
15. N. Russell and A. H. M. ter Hofstede. Surmounting BPM challenges: the YAWL story. *Computer Science-Research and Development*, Vol. 23, No. 2, pp. 67–79, 2009.
16. W. M. P. van der Aalst, A. H. M. Ter Hofstede, B. Kiepuszewski and A. P. Barros. Workflow patterns. *Distributed and Parallel Database*, Vol. 14, No. 1, pp. 5–51, 2003.
17. J. Xu, C. Liu and X. Zhao. Resource Planning for Massive Number of Process Instances. In: *On the Move to Meaningful Internet Systems: OTM 2009* Germany, Vol. 5870. Springer-Verlag, Berlin, pp. 219–236, 2009.
18. X. Zhao, C. Liu, Y. Yang and W. Sadiq. Aligning collaborative business processes: An organization-oriented perspective. *IEEE Transactions on Systems, Man, and Cybernetics-Part A: Systems and Humans*, Vol. 39, No. 6, pp. 1152–1164, 2009.
19. W. Zhao, H. Liu, W. Dai and J. Ma. An entropy-based clustering ensemble method to support resource allocation in business process management. *Knowledge and Information Systems*, Vol. 48, No. 2, p. 305, 2016.
20. M. Zur Muehlen. Organizational management in workflow applications: issues and perspectives. *Information Technology and Management*, Vol. 5, No. 3–4, pp. 271–291, 2004.

4   Data-Centric Business Process Modeling

Introduction

In the previous chapter, we discussed the importance of data and resource modeling in a business process. In this chapter, we introduce new approaches that are data-centric in nature, i.e. they focus on data objects and artifacts as a primary basis for process modeling. Further, there is no well-defined control flow that can be visualized. Instead data elements or artifacts play a central role. As the process progresses, initial data inputs are used to produce new data by tasks that require those inputs. Eventually, a final data item or object is produced. Artifacts are also objects that contain data from entities or documents and they are associated with a lifecycle with stages. In each stage only some tasks can be performed subject to certain conditions being satisfied. As process execution proceeds, an artifact makes transitions through key stages of this lifecycle. In this way, the sequencing of activities of a process is enabled. In this chapter, we shall discuss two main data-centric methods based on PDM models and artifacts. After introducing the value of data-centric methods, we first describe the product data model (PDM) method, followed by a short digression into the value of dual control flow and data flow perspectives. Later, we discuss the artifact-centric approach at length.

Introduction to Data-Centric Methods

Let us introduce the data-centric approaches with a detailed example that compares a control flow-based workflow with the corresponding data flow-based approach. Figure 4.1 shows an order process using control flow design. In this process, an order is received, and then the customer's credit rating is checked. Based on the result of the credit check, either the order is cancelled or the steps of warehouse pickup, shipping, invoicing, and close order are performed. To simplify the case, we ignore the exception handling issues, such as what happens if the payment is declined, the item is out of stock, etc.

The control flow design puts emphasis on the execution sequence of the tasks. It does not explicitly explain why one task should be performed before another. For example, it is not clear why the Warehouse Pickup task is done before Ship (in Figure 4.1), or the Invoice task is done after Shipping. In general, control flow diagrams assume that the process designer has the business knowledge to lay out the task sequence. Often old practices become deeply ingrained into the fabric of an organization and nobody knows why it is done that way. If you ask somebody, the best answer you may get is "because we have always done it like that," or "we were trained to do it like that!"

The layout of the task sequence is related to *task dependencies*. Tasks have various kinds of dependencies between them. Zlotkin [13] summarizes three basic types of dependencies: Fit, Flow, and Sharing, as shown in Figure 4.2. Using this notion, we can observe that the tasks Warehouse Pickup and Ship have a *flow dependency* between them, i.e. the output of task Warehouse Pickup is one of the required inputs of (or flows into) task Ship. A *sharing dependency* arises when several tasks compete for the same resource or data object at the same time. In Figure 4.1, if we wanted to redesign the process and perform the Ship and Invoice tasks in parallel, then they may share some common data like "Package list" and "Shipping advice." *Fit dependencies* arise when multiple activities collectively produce a single resource. If three approval signatures are required on an application form to receive a bank loan, then each approval is an activity that must be performed (perhaps in parallel) to produce the final approved document.

If we take the dependency analysis approach one step further, and focus on data dependencies, then we can develop a data flow chart as shown in Table 4.1 for the order process of Figure 4.1. The data flow analysis provides the input data for a task to be executed, and its output data. Then we can draw a new diagram using data flow analysis as in Figure 4.3. In this figure, the focus is on the input and output data of each task.

It is evident that a task cannot be performed until its input data is available. As you can see in Figure 4.3, the task Invoice does not have to be performed after task Ship because there is no data dependency between them. However, a seller may have a policy or be

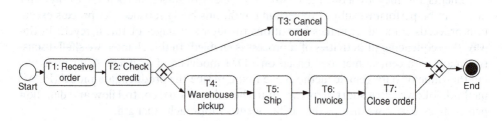

Figure 4.1 Order processing workflow modeled with the control and document flow approaches

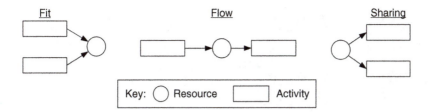

Figure 4.2 Three basic types of dependencies among activities (adapted from Zlotkin)

Table 4.1 Information or data flow analysis for tasks in an order process

Task	Input information	Output information

Receive order	Order information
	Payment information
	  (i.e. name, customer ID,
	  credit card)
	Order items (SKUs, unit
	  price, quantity, etc.)
	Shipping information
	  (i.e. UPS ground)
		The order information in the input
		  document is split into three documents:
		  • Payment information
		  • Order items
		  • Shipping advice

Check credit	Payment information	Approved or rejected
Warehouse pickup	Order items	Pick up list
Invoice	Payment Package list Shipping advice	Invoice
Ship	Pick up list Shipping advice	Proof of shipment (shipping report)

required by law to invoice the customer only after the shipment has been sent. Thus, we have two types of constraints which determine the sequence of tasks: data dependency constraints and business policy constraints. We call a data dependency a *hard constraint* and business policy a *soft constraint* because the former is a strict one arising from a data flow requirement, while the latter arises from organizational policy and may vary from one organization to another. The soft dependency is shown in Figure 4.3 by means of the dashed line from the Ship task to the Invoice task.

The example process also raises two important questions about information flow. The first question is: Why did the task Receive Order split the original order data into three documents (payment, order items, and shipping advice) instead of handling it as one document? There are two advantages of doing so. First, it is more efficient. If we simply send the whole order to task Warehouse Pickup, then the whole order is "locked" (i.e. inaccessible to another task) when the task is executing, which prevents other users from making changes to any part of the order. However, such a lock is unnecessary because the changes made to the "Shipping advice" have nothing to do with "Warehouse pickup." Second, it is more secure. The payment information is sensitive and should be only released to the relevant staff, i.e. the Finance staff. The second question is: Can the two

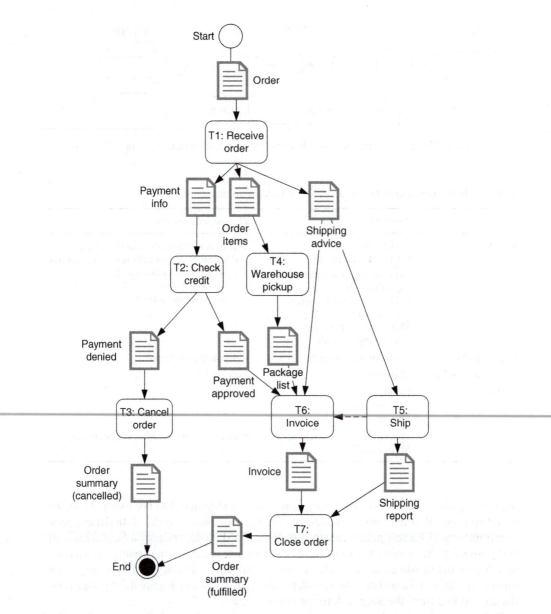

Figure 4.3 Data flow analysis for an order process (documents embedded in control flow)

tasks, Invoice and Ship, be performed concurrently? Since both tasks require Shipping Advice and Package List information, we may instead ask, can Shipping Advice and Package List information be accessed at the same time? The answer in this case is yes, because both tasks only need *read access* to the data in the documents, they will not modify them. Hence, the two tasks will not interfere with each other.

The above data (and document) flow analysis has two advantages. First, it provides a partial ordering for the tasks. Second, it imposes restrictions on the way in which the process can be reconfigured because of soft constraints. Next, we'll look at an approach that creates workflows simply by looking at the data input and output needs of different tasks, and does not require an explicit control flow to be created.

Product Data Model – Building Information Products

This approach is inspired by the Bill of Materials (BOM) used in manufacturing. Figure 4.4 shows a bicycle with nearly 50 parts. The BOM for a bicycle (see Figure 4.4) will include a handle bar, a seat assembly, two wheel assemblies, two brakes, a pedal, etc. A seat assembly consists of a seat post, a seat and two bolts to attach the seat to the post. Thus, the BOM is a tree structure that consists of the final product, in this case the bicycle at the root level, and it contains the components at the lowest or the leaf level. A bill of materials is an essential starting point in the manufacture of any product. By following the BOM, a manufacturer can build a product. In the case of a bicycle, for instance, separate sub-assemblies are made first for the frame, transmission, control, and wheel. Then these sub-assemblies are further assembled into the final bicycle, as shown in Figure 4.5.

Exercise 1: Make the three-level BOM for a car, showing its main sub-assemblies and their high-level components.

In workflows, instead of dealing with materials like parts and components, we are usually dealing with data items. So, the data items (or documents) are the equivalent of the parts and sub-assemblies, and the final product as well. Thus, the approach to making a process data model is to start with the initial data that is provided by a customer or user and then use it to create or derive new data in a systematic manner. The conversion of input data into output data is performed by tasks.

The idea behind the product data model (PDM) approach is to view business processes as ways to create an information product. An example of an information product is a loan approval document. To produce this document, other information products are required; for instance, for a loan approval some of the following information documents are necessary: *loan application, application check, applicant credit report, property appraisal report, title search report, manager approval, VP approval.* These are all documents or parts of documents and they have to be produced in a certain sequence. For instance, a credit report for an applicant cannot be obtained unless an application document is available and, moreover, it has been reviewed to check that it is complete. In this way, various dependencies are created between data items. We first give a definition of a PDM and then make a PDM for this example.

Definition 1: A PDM is a tuple (D, O, H, C, root) where:

D: is a set of data elements
O: is a set of operations on elements of D
$H \subset (D \times O \times [C]) \cup (O \times D)$ is a connected and acyclic graph connecting data elements and operations
C: is a set of conditions that may apply an (D, O) edge and must be satisfied along the edge.
root: is a node that corresponds to the final data item whose value is derived.

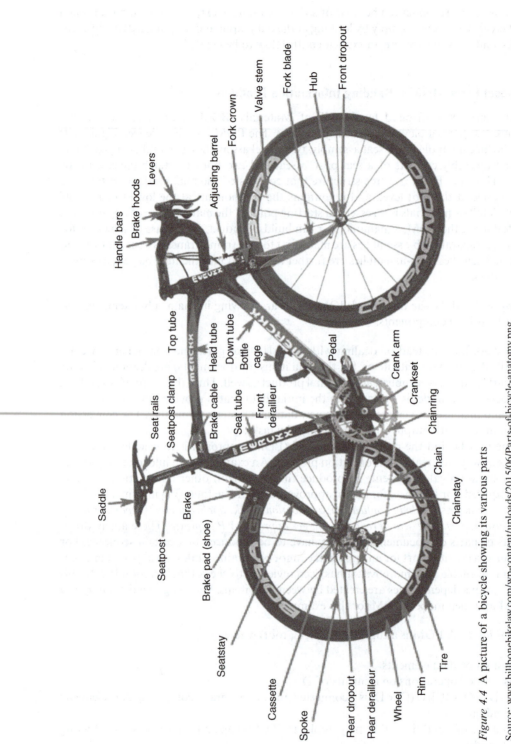

Figure 4.4 A picture of a bicycle showing its various parts

Source: www.billbonebikelaw.com/wp-content/uploads/2015/06/Parts-of-bicycle-anatomy.png.

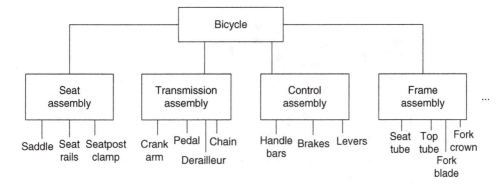

Figure 4.5 A partial bill of materials (BOM) for a bicycle

The condition is optional as indicated by the square brackets in the (D × O × [C]) tuple, and usually pertains to the data item whose value has just been determined. If a condition does not apply to an edge, then the condition element can be omitted. The typical structure of the condition is: {data-item} {operator: =, <, >, ≤, ≥} {data-value}. We will illustrate conditions with examples. A PDM also has a root node.

Case Example 1: Say, Loans-R-Us bank wishes to apply the PDM approach to develop their loan approval application. The application follows a standard procedure, such that a customer fills in and submits an application form. After the application is reviewed, the bank obtains a credit report for the customer, an appraisal for the property for which the loan is being obtained and a title search report for the property. After the reports are ready, they are reviewed separately by a manager and a vice president (VP). If both approve the application, then the loan is granted.

Figure 4.6 shows a PDM model for the mortgage loan example. In this PDM, a loan application (d1) is checked for completeness and an "application ok" field or data item d2 is created to note that it is ready for further processing. If any problem is found, then a resubmit notification (d11) is sent to the client. If it is ok then the applicant credit report (d3), property appraisal report (d4), and title search report (d5) are obtained. These reports are combined into a dossier (d6), which is then reviewed by a manager and a VP. The manager's recommendation is noted in document d7 and the VP's in document d8. If both approve the application then an approval notice (d9) is prepared, else a rejection notice (d10) is prepared. If any one of them disapproves, it is rejected. In both cases a document (d9) is prepared to notify the client. A notification (d11) is sent to the client in both cases. We can represent this PDM more formally as:

D = {d1, d2, d3, . . . , d11}
O = {Loan application, application review, prepare credit report, property appraisal, title search, manager approval, VP approval, make decision, notify approval, notify rejection, request resubmission}
H = {(loan application, d1), (d1, application review), (application review, d2), (d2, credit report), (d2, property appraisal, d2 = Ok), (d2, title search, d2 = Ok), (d2, request resubmission, d2 ≠ Ok), ({d3, d4, d5}, check reports), . . . , (notify rejection, d11)}.

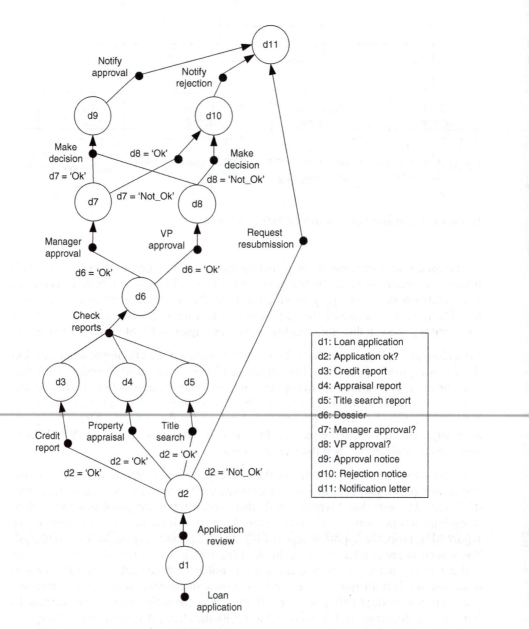

Figure 4.6 A mortgage loan PDM model

Exercise 2: Verify for yourself that with this information about D, O, and H it is possible to reconstruct the PDM in Figure 4.6.

In the set H, above, we have an entry for every link in the graph, either a data-operation link or an operation-data link. An alternative way of representing set H is as set H′ by noting each operation along with its the input and output sets as a 3-tuple. For instance,

H′ = {(loan application, {}, {d1}), (application review, {d1}, {d2}), (credit report, {d2}, {d3}), ..., (check reports, {d3, d4, d5}, d6), ..., (notify approval, {d9}, {d11})}

Duality of Control Flow and Data Flow Perspectives

Next, let us briefly discuss the relationship between the control flow and data flow perspectives in the context of the next example.

Case Example 2: For another example, let us consider how online orders for items are handled on the website of Orders-Unlimited. The control flow for this process is shown in Figure 4.7. It is a standard process where after the order is received, the credit information is checked. If the credit check does not pass, then the order is cancelled and closed. However, if the credit check passes, then the invoice is sent in parallel with "Pick goods" and "Ship goods" tasks. Finally, the order is closed. The data flows of elements d1–d11 described in this figure are shown along the edges between tasks.

The PDM for this order is shown in Figure 4.8. In this figure we have also shown the data flows that take place along various edges. By examining the data flows in this figure and applying knowledge about each activity, it is possible to develop the PDM diagram shown in Figure 4.8. This diagram shows the various data flows that take place while performing the various activities and also the dependencies between them. Two other observations are relevant here. First, once we have a PDM, it is in general possible to create multiple different control flow models with it. So, for the PDM of Figure 4.8, it turns out that Figure 4.7 is not a unique mapping. We could, for instance, create a control flow in which T4–T6 are in a sequence and this would be a correct control flow because the data dependencies are not violated. Second, a PDM by itself can be used to create an execution model of the process. If we have a list of tasks that are to be performed and their input requirements, then as soon as the input data is available we should be able to run the task. This style of execution can be implemented by a collection of production rules.

Figure 4.9 shows two abstract task- and data-centric representations of the same process. In Figure 4.9(a) the focus is on the tasks T1, T2, ..., that appear in the boxes, and the data flows occur along the edges. The interpretation here is that each task has inputs that lead to the production of outputs, and these outputs flow into the next task, and so on. This is the traditional and most common way to describe a process. On the other hand, Figure 4.9(b) is a data-centric representation where the data is shown in the boxes as D1, D2, ..., and the tasks appear along the edges. This representation can be interpreted in terms of data transformation. Thus, some initial data D1 is transformed into intermediate data D2, which is further transformed until the final data is produced. The transformation is performed by a series of tasks.

We may also think of Figure 4.9(b) as a dual of Figure 4.9(a) in the sense that they are representing the same information, but in different ways.

In a similar vein, Figures 4.7 and 4.8 represent the same information but from different perspectives. Observe how the data-centric view makes it easier to focus on the flow of data. By understanding data dependencies, we may realize that certain important data items that are needed for producing new data are missing. Similarly, by focusing on the flow of tasks, we may discover missing tasks that may be associated with the policy of an organization. Thus, by studying both the views together it is possible to design higher-quality holistic processes.

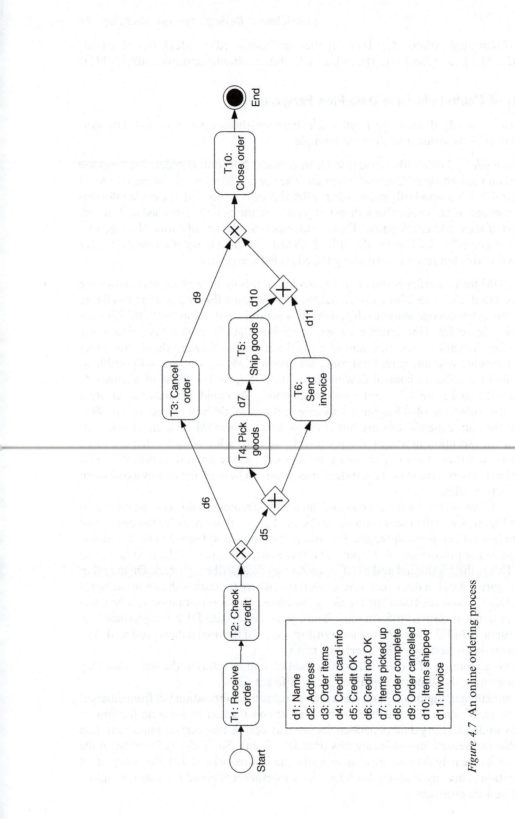

Figure 4.7 An online ordering process

d1: Name
d2: Address
d3: Order items
d4: Credit card info
d5: Credit OK
d6: Credit not OK
d7: Items picked up
d8: Order complete
d9: Order cancelled
d10: Items shipped
d11: Invoice

Start

T1: Receive order

T2: Check credit

d5

d6

T3: Cancel order

T4: Pick goods

T5: Ship goods

T6: Send invoice

d7

d9

d10

d11

T10: Close order

End

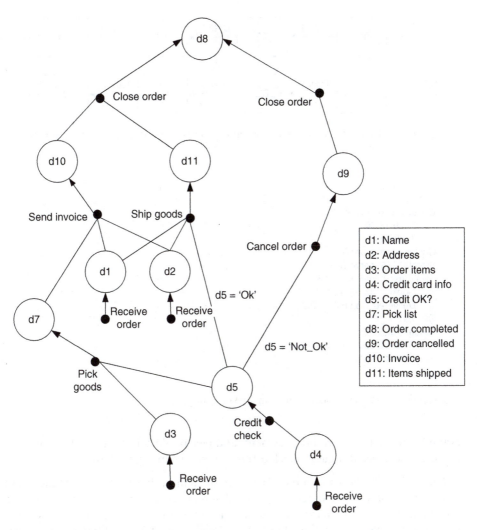

Figure 4.8 A PDM for the online order process

Artifacts

A business artifact includes business relevant data about a business entity. These are objects that play a central or significant role in the execution of a process. It is also a natural way of thinking about a business. Hence, the term *artifact-centric*. As stated in a seminal article by A. Nigam and N. S. Caswell of IBM Corporation [6], *artifacts are concrete, identifiable, self-describing chunks of information* that can be used by a business person to run a business. They emerged as a way of operational specification of an application and later found their way into business process modeling.

Example 3: Consider a typical restaurant, say Food-R-Us. An important process in this restaurant is the guest entry-to-departure process. It starts when a guest enters the restaurant and ends after she departs. The key artifacts, based on the definition above, in this

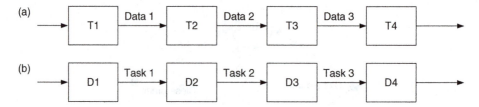

Figure 4.9 Two different views of the same process: (a) task-centric view; (b) data-centric view

```
Guest-check{
ID 123
Context(date 3/31/2017
        Time 18.30
        Table 6)
Customer (number 3)
Store(ID (55) server(2))
Item (desc hamB price 2.57
        Cooked "18.53 3/31/2017"
        Delivered "18.56 3/31/2017"
Tax 0.33
Tender (total 2.90
        Cash 20.000 coupon 1.00
        Change 18.10)
}
```

Figure 4.10 A guest-check artifact in a restaurant process

example are: menu, order, bill, payment, and receipt. Another way to think about this process is in terms of a guest-check artifact, as shown in Figure 4.10.

This artifact is shown as a data structure of name-value pairs. The artifact has the context information like date, time, and table number, along with the number of customers or guests in the party. It also has the ID of the restaurant and the server ID. In addition, it has information about the ordered items and quantities, and the times at which they are cooked and served. Finally, it has the billing information, including the tax, discounts, etc. Essentially, the guest- check artifact serves as a primary document for the entire application that involves managing materials, people and cash, and preparing reports, etc.

It is important to note that the reason the guest check is selected as the main artifact is because it is an *essential organizing structure* for this application that captures the information, function, and flow of the application. Another important idea in the context of artifact-centric models is that of a *lifecycle* of a process. In the case of Food-R-Us restaurant, the guest moves through various states, like: *entered, seated, order placed, order served, payment made,* and *departed.* These states describe the status of the guest in the restaurant process. As activities occur, the guest check moves from one state to another as shown in Figure 4.11. The collection of valid states and the permitted transitions between them is called the lifecycle. By keeping track of states of an artifact, one can monitor the status of a process.

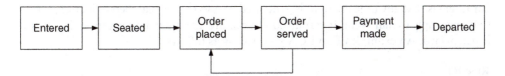

Figure 4.11 A lifecycle of the restaurant guest and the transitions among her states

The set of states that are selected for an application can be determined in consultation between a client and a process analyst. One way to think about states is that they are a series of (sub)goals or milestones a business would like to closely monitor during the process execution. Activities cause state transitions that usually lead to an update of some attributes in the artifact.

In this example at hand, one could well add a *waiting* state after the guest enters the restaurant. Another state called *menu offered* could also be added. Similarly, the payment made state could be replaced by three states, bill presented, payment offered, and receipt issued. The decision on now many states to have in the lifecycle is to some extent subjective and also depends upon the degree of detail that the client (in this case the restaurant managers) would like to capture about the process. Finally, notice that in Figure 4.11, a return edge from "Order served" to "Order placed" is present. This corresponds to a scenario where the guest might place another order, say for dessert, after the first order for the main meal. The details of this order would be added to the guest check artifact as well. After this order is placed, it would be served. This loop could occur multiple times.

Now, if this return edge was not present it would mean that only one order can be placed in one process instance that corresponds to a single guest-check artifact. If the customer wanted dessert, they should have ordered it in the first instance and if they failed to do so, then a new process instance with a new guest-check artifact would need to be created. Of course, they would not have to leave the restaurant and re-enter again. The first two steps in the lifecycle would simply be skipped. This shows that the design of the business process application must be closely connected with the actual business practice.

In the medical claims processing business, claims are received from doctors and hospitals and have to be processed. They pass through stages like *received, entered, checked, assessed, approved*, and *paid*. Here, the artifact is a *medical event authorization* document. Similarly, in a human resources application the main artifact is the *employee record*, while in an express shipping application it is an airway bill.

Exercise 3: What are the valid states in the lifecycle of an employee record artifact?

Exercise 4: What are the valid states in the lifecycle of an airway bill artifact?

Applying Artifacts in Process Modeling

Now let us turn to see how this idea of artifacts applies to business processes. This is an *event-driven approach*. The basic idea is that an event would be generated any time the state of an artifact changes. Thus, when an insurance claim is received, it would cause a received event to be generated. The artifact-centric approach works in conjunction with the ECA (event-condition-action) paradigm of computing. The essence of the ECA paradigm is that any time an event is generated, a rule-base is searched to identify a rule that may apply to that event. If certain conditions are met, then the corresponding action is performed. An example of an ECA style rule is as follows:

Rule R1
Event: A claim is received from the customer
Condition: The information on the claim is complete
Action: Enter the claim into the system
By: An authorized representative of the insurance company.

After the event occurs, the condition is checked. If it is true, then the action is performed. After the claim has been entered, *the state of the claim artifact is moved to "entered."* At this point, another ECA rule may become applicable. This is a declarative approach in that ECA rules "declare" what is to be done without specifying an actual order in which they are executed. Many different orderings are thus possible, depending upon what conditions are satisfied at a given stage of execution.

This is also called a *data-centric methodology* because the artifact in Figure 4.10 is a collection of data or information about a process. As data values change, they trigger events that in turn cause rules to fire. The high-level approach is summarized in Figure 4.12 in four main steps. In the first step, we determine the artifacts and the lifecycle of each artifact in terms of the key stages it passes through. The lifecycle also shows the permissible transitions that can occur among the various stages of the artifact by means of directed arrows. Thus, an order may go from state "received" to "verified," but not vice versa.

In Step 2, an artifact schema that maps out the relationships among artifacts is created. This is essentially an Entity-Relationship (ER) or a Unified Modeling Language (UML) diagram that shows the main relationships between the artifacts, and enables a better understanding of the operation of the business. In this step we also consider how an artifact moves from one stage to another. This happens by means of services or tasks.

Data-Centric Design Methodology

Step 1: *Business Artifacts Discovery*

(a) Identify critical artifacts for the business process
(b) Discover key stages of artifacts' lifecycles from the scenario-based requirements

Step 2: *Design of Business Operations Model (BOM)*

(a) Logical design of artifact schemas
(b) Specify services for artifacts needed for moving artifacts through the lifecycles
(c) Develop ECA rules that enable artifacts' progress in their lifecycles

Step 3: *Design of Conceptual Flow Diagram*

Step 4: *Workflow Realization*

Figure 4.12 Design methodology at a glance

Since we live in a service-oriented world, it is convenient to think of each task in a generic way as a service. Hence, each service must be defined. To do so, we need to specify its inputs, outputs, preconditions, and effects (or IOPE in short). As an example of a service, consider a credit report service that must be consulted while reviewing an applicant for a mortgage loan. This service is described as follows:

Inputs: Customer_name, social security number, Bank _ID
Outputs: Customer_name, credit rating, credit score, analyst name
Precondition: Application has been verified
(Conditional) Effects: Credit report has been received.

In a similar way, we can determine the IOPE values for an appraisal service or a title search service.

Exercise 5: Describe the IOPE for a property appraisal service in the context of a mortgage loan.

After a service is specified, we develop ECA rules to enable transitions to occur between stages of the artifacts connected with it. When there are multiple artifacts of interest, then we should also consider the relationships between intersecting artifact lifecycles.

Above, in steps 1 and 2, we focused on a *business operations model*, i.e. a detailed logical specification of the business artifacts, their lifecycles and logical relationships to describe the business-level operations of various parts of a business. Steps 3 and 4 focus on realization. In particular, a conceptual flow diagram (see Figure 4.13) is created. This is a graphical specification that represents procedurally how a business operations model can be implemented. However, it omits low-level implementation details.

In the conceptual flow diagram of Figure 4.13, an event E1 occurs that consists of an application being received from a customer. This application could be on a paper or an online form. This causes a check application service (or a task) to be invoked. In turn, the checked application is stored in an application container in a database with updates to appropriate fields. A field on the application will also be marked to indicate that the application has been checked and give the name of the individual who checked it. If there are errors in the application, they will be noted and the applicant will be asked to

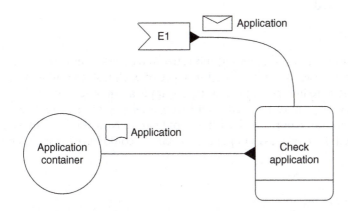

Figure 4.13 A conceptual flow diagram for an ECA rule

resubmit the application. This figure corresponds to a similar rule to the one described above, as follows:

Rule R1′
Event: An application is received from the customer
Condition: The application is complete
Action: Enter the application into the system
By: An authorized representative of the company.

In the last step, step 4, these flow diagrams are converted into actual implementations. An implementation needs a database engine that implements the artifacts and their logical ER model. We also need support for handling events and invoking services, e.g. using Web Services Description Language (WSDL). The implementation details are omitted from our discussion here.

An Example to Illustrate a Loan Application Process using an Artifact-Centric Approach

Example 4: Let us revisit the mortgage loan process for Loans-R-Us in Chapter 2, and see if we can describe it within the artifact-centric framework. Loans-R-Us gives loans to customers to buy residential properties. The application must be complete and accompanied by a non-refundable $500 application fee. Each application has to go through a credit check, a property appraisal, and a title search for the property. If the requested amount is less than $500K then a manager must approve the loan. For higher amounts, a VP approval is necessary, unless the manager has more than 5 years' experience.

First, we need to identify the critical artifacts in this process. The artifacts (and their states) are:

Artifact 1: Loan application
   States: received, checked, ready for approval, approved, denied
Artifact 2: Credit report (CR)
   States: undefined, received
Artifact 3: Property appraisal report (AR)
   States: undefined, received
Artifact 4: Title search report (TSR)
   States: undefined, received
Artifact 5: Property
   States: defined, undefined.

Again, the choice of these states is somewhat subjective and depends upon the desired degree of detail. In some sense, we want the performance of each task to lead to a new state. Thus, if we request a credit report in the mortgage application process then after it is received a new state credit_report_received would arise. Similarly, after we receive the appraisal report, an appraisal_report_received state would arise. Now think about what happens if we performed these two tasks in parallel. Then, we could have three possible state combinations:

credit_report_received
appraisal_report_received
credit and appraisal_report_received.

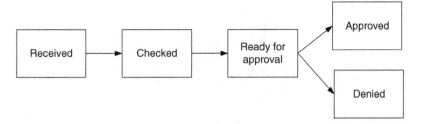

Figure 4.14 The lifecycle of the mortgage application artifact showing its key stages

An initial lifecycle for this process is shown in Figure 4.14. If we include the above states also in our example, the lifecycle will look as shown in Figure 4.15.

Exercise 6: Check if the modified lifecycle diagram in Figure 4.15 is correct.

And, by the way, in our example we have three such tasks in parallel, since we also need a title search report. In general, if you have n such tasks in parallel, you would have $2^{(n-1)}$ state combinations. It is not hard to see that this can quickly lead to a combinatorial explosion of states. This explosion only gets worse when you consider that for each of the three parallel requests there will be three parallel replies that may arrive in any order. So, is requesting a report a task by itself? We can answer this question in terms of task granularity. One way to think about an atomic task is by applying the criterion that a task must add significant business value to the artifact. By this criterion, requesting a report and receiving a report are probably not two different tasks. Instead we can just combine them into a single task, "request and receive a report" or "obtain a report."

A lifecycle diagram can also have implications for monitoring. If we keep the states at a finer level of granularity, then we will be able to respond to queries about the status of a running instance more accurately and precisely. Thus, by using the more detailed lifecycle it is possible to say that the credit report and the property appraisal reports have been received but the title search report has not been received.

The ER diagram in Figure 4.16 shows the various artifacts as boxes and the relationships among them by edges. Say a loan application is made for the purchase of a property. A credit report is obtained for the customer who submits the application. In addition, an appraisal report gives the appraised value of the property. Finally, a title search is a means of ascertaining that the person who is selling the property really has the right to sell it, and that the buyer is getting all the rights to the property (title) that he or she is paying for.

In addition to the artifacts, the ER diagram in Figure 4.16 also shows various attributes of each artifact. An application has an *ID, a customer name and address, social security number (SSN)*, etc. There are other attributes too that are not shown in the figure, such as *employment history, salary*, etc. that will be required for processing the application. The attributes of the credit report artifact are *credit score* and *credit rating*. The attributes of the property artifact are *address, year built, square footage*, and *price*. Finally, the appraisal report artifact will have attributes like *appraiser, checklist, notes*, etc. These are only partial lists of attributes.

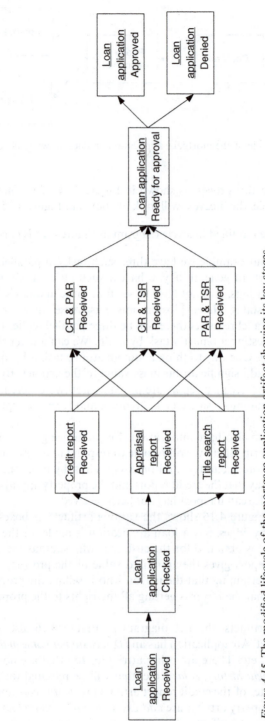

Figure 4.15 The modified lifecycle of the mortgage application artifact showing its key stages

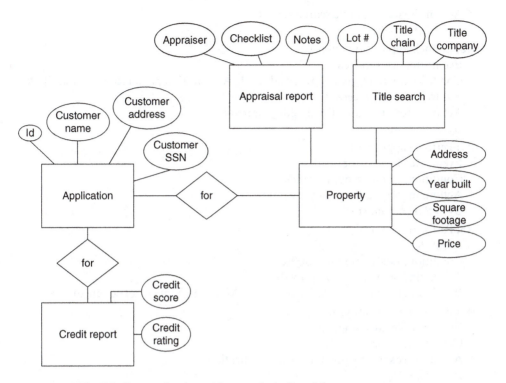

Figure 4.16 The ER diagram for the artifacts – a logical model

Now, we are in a position to describe the ECA rules for this application. The rules (R1–R10) are listed below.

ECA rules
   R1: Start
      Event: Application received
      Condition: None
      Action: Invoke(check_application)
      By: Agent

   R3: Get credit report
      Event: Application_checked_OK
      Condition: Not(Credit_report_ received)
      Action: Invoke(Get credit report)
      By: ABC service

   R4: Get property appraisal
      Event: Application_checked_OK
      Condition: Not(Appraisal_report_ received)
      Action: invoke(Get appraisal report)
      By: XYZ service

   R5: Get title search report
      Event: Application_checked_OK
      Condition: Not(Title_search_report_ received)

Action: Invoke(Get title search report)
By: AAA service

R6: Launch application approval
Event: Report_received
Condition: Credit_report_received and Appraisal_report_received and Title_ search_report_ received
Action: Move to state "Ready_for_approval"
By: Automatic

R7: Perform approval 1
Event: Ready_for_approval
Condition: Loan amount <500K
Action: invoke(Perform_approval_1)
By: VP or Manager

R8: Perform_approval_2
Event: Ready_for_approval
Condition: Loan amount ≥ 500K
Action: invoke(perform_approval)
By: VP or (Manager where Qualification(Manager, Years of experience) > 5)

R9: Perform Notification 1
Event: Approval_complete
Condition: Approval_OK
Action: Invoke(Perform_approval_ notification)
By: Agent

R10: Perform Notification 2
Event: Approval_complete
Condition: Not(Approval_OK)
Action: Invoke(Perform_denial_ notification)
By: Agent

Upon examination, we can check that these rules enforce the desired ordering sequence among the activities, despite the fact that an explicit control flow is not speci-fied. Instead, it is derived implicitly by the rules. Also, note that, in general, the ordering of the rules does not matter since they are declarative.

Discussion of the Artifact-Centric Approach

As you can see this is a very different paradigm for designing process-based applications as compared to the earlier approaches we have seen. It certainly adds a lot of flexibility to the design process. To make changes to the process, we can change rules. For example, to change the loan amount cut-off requirement for a manager to approve a loan in rule R7, we could change the associated condition with it to "loan amount < 750K." Similarly, we could also change the requirement for the qualifications of the manager in the "By:" section of this rule.

Another change one could make might be related to the sequencing between the appraisal, credit report, and title search activities. At present these activities may be done in any order with respect to each, and also in parallel with each other. A process designer might decide that the credit report should be obtained first and only if the credit report is OK would it make sense to proceed with the other two activities.

Exercise 7: How will you revise the set of rules (R1–R10) so as to capture this requirement?

Exercise 8: Describe the above process model by a conventional control flow modeling approach, and compare the two models.

Execution Semantics and Further Extensions

The execution semantics of the ECA rules is concerned with how the rules are actually fired. It may occur that two rules become applicable for firing at the same time. In such a situation, firing both of them together could cause interference. In our example above, we saw that rules R3–R5 became eligible to fire at the same time and firing them together did not cause any problems, since the actions produced by them could run concurrently.

However, there may be situations where rule interaction might occur. Say, there is a rule R3' as:

R3': Exempt credit report
   Event: Application_checked_OK
   Condition: Credit_report_received in last 90 days
   Action: Exempt(Get credit report)
   By: Automatic

This rule basically exempts the applicant from a credit report, and hence it should take precedence over rule R3. Hence, it is necessary to have a mechanism whereby R3 can be prevented from executing if R3' is satisfied. One way to deal with this is by associating priorities with rules. Thus, if rule R3' has a higher priority than rule R3, then when both become eligible only the higher priority rule will execute.

In general, a rule is triggered when the event stated in the rule occurs and there is a running process instance whose variable values satisfy the conditions of the rule. It becomes eligible for firing after it is triggered. When a set of rules becomes eligible for firing, then an algorithm must select which rules from that set can be fired and whether they can all fire together or in a certain sequence. When a rule fires, an action is performed. The action is done by the system (i.e. automatically) or by an actor. For a non-system action, in addition, the actor who will perform the task will also have to be determined based on attributes such as Name, ID, Years of experience, Skills, etc. For a rule to be fully eligible, a full match must occur. Once a match of a rule occurs with a specific process and resource instance, it is called a binding.

It may be the case that a certain rule is triggered and the condition part of the rule is satisfied with the variables of the artifacts; however, the "By:" part might not be satisfied, since no suitable resource is found to perform the task. In this case, a partial binding is said to occur and this instance is "parked" in a queue until a resource becomes available. It may also occur that multiple resources are available for a process instance. In such a case any resource may be selected randomly, or some algorithm may be applied to make the selection (e.g. the resource with the minimum workload – to balance the resource load, or the junior most resource – to minimize the cost of processing, etc.).

Various extensions of this approach are also possible. Thus, other terms may be added to the ECA rule structure to include a location, a time interval, and any additional equipment that would be required for performing the selected action. For example, a more general rule would look like:

Rule 9′: Perform Notification 1
   Event: Approval_complete
   Condition: Approval_OK
   Action: Invoke(Perform_approval_ notification)
   At: Office Premises, 5th floor
   During: M-F, 9-5
   Using: Outlook electronic mail and FedEx 1-day mail

In this way it is possible to impose restrictions on location, time intervals, and physical resources that are needed.

Chapter Summary

The fit, flow and sharing dependency patterns are due to Zlotkin [13]. Both the approaches described in this chapter, PDM and artifact-based modeling, are data-centric approaches in that the main focus is on data objects or data artifacts. The PDM approach is more direct, while the artifact approach is based on lifecycles of artifacts and ECA-style declarative rules. Both these approaches are less intuitive than the control flow-based modeling discussed in Chapter 2, yet they offer alternative ways of understanding processes from different perspectives. There are not many tools that support these approaches other than research prototypes (from universities and research labs). This suggests that they have not gone mainstream yet. Another drawback of these methods is that they do not handle loops well. Nevertheless, the ideas and concepts introduced in these approaches are interesting and useful to study, and can help in gaining a deeper insight into a process.

A major work on Product data models is the thesis of Irene Vanderfeesten [11]. This thesis looks at PDM comprehensively and also develops some tools for creating them. PDM has roots in earlier work of Reijers et al. on product-based workflow design [8], and in document-centric workflows [12]. Issues of data flow validation in the context of workflow modeling and coordination have also been discussed in [5, 9]. In more recent work [2], new guidelines for designing PDM models based on techniques for activity composition and evaluation of alternative designs have been proposed. Another study that analyses dependency issues related to the data flow perspective in much detail was conducted by Sun et al. [10].

A large body of work on artifact-centric approaches was done at IBM Research. Business artifacts were first introduced by Nigam and Caswell [6], who showed that business operational models can be constructed using a collection of lifecycles of all artifacts and their interaction. Liu et al. [3] developed the idea of the business operational model further by adding nine operational patterns for constructing the model and a method for model verification. This led to the concept of business artifacts as a way to build process models [1]. A Framework for implementing artifact-centric business processes in the context of a service-oriented architecture is described in [7]. An approach for monitoring artifact-centric business models is presented in [4].

The artifact-centric approach is both data-centric and declarative in nature as a way of modeling processes. Declarative approaches based on rules lend themselves more easily to changes, as compared to strictly control flow approaches, because rules may be modified to change the model. They are also better at dealing with exceptions, since rules can be created for the exceptional situations. In the next chapter, we shall study modeling techniques that help create models that are flexible and variable.

References

1. K. Bhattacharya, R. Hull and J. Su. A Data-Centric Design Methodology for Business Processes. In: J. Cardoso, W. M. P. van der Aalst (eds) *Handbook of Research on Business Process Management*. Science Publishing, Hershey, PA, USA, 2009.
2. H. A. Reijers and I. Vanderfeesten. Designing like a pro: the automated composition of workflow activities. *Computers in Industry*, Vol. 75, pp. 162–177, 2016.
3. R. Liu, K. Bhattacharya and F. Y. Wu. Modeling Business Contexture and Behavior Using Business Artifacts. In: J. Krogstie, A. L. Opdahl, G. Sindre (eds) CAiSE 2007 and WES 2007. *LNCS*, Vol. 4495. Springer, Heidelberg, pp. 324–339, 2007.
4. R. Liu, R. Vaculín, Z. Shan, A. Nigam and F. Wu. Business Artifact-Centric Modeling for Real-Time Performance Monitoring. In: S. Rinderle-Ma, F. Toumani, K. Wolf (eds) BPM 2011. *LNCS*, Vol. 6896. Springer, Heidelberg, pp. 265–280, 2011.
5. D. Muller, M. Reichert and J. Herbst. Data-Driven Modeling and Coordination of Large Process Structures. In: R. Meersman, Z. Tari (eds) *Proceedings of the 15th International Conference on Cooperative Information Systems (CoopIS'07)*, Vol. 4803. Springer, Heidelberg Darlinghurst, Australia, 2007.
6. A. Nigam and N. S. Caswell. Business artifacts: an approach to operational specification. *IBM Systems Journal*, Vol. 42, No. 3, pp. 428–445, 2003.
7. K. Ngamakeur, S. Yongchareon and C. Liu. A Framework for Realizing Artifact-Centric Business Processes in Service-Oriented Architecture. In: S. Lee, Z. Peng, X. Zhou, Y. S. Moon, R. Unland, J. Yoo (eds) Database Systems for Advanced Applications. DASFAA 2012. *Lecture Notes in Computer Science*, Vol. 7238. Springer, Berlin, Heidelberg, 2012.
8. H. A. Reijers, S. Limam and W. M. P. van der Aalst. Product-based workflow design. *Journal of Management Information Systems*, Vol. 20, No. 1, pp. 229–262, 2003.
9. S. Sadiq, M. Orlowska, W. Sadiq and C. Foulger. Data Flow and Validation in Workflow Modelling. In: *Proceedings of the 15th Australasian Database Conference*, Vol. 27, Australian Computer Society, Inc. Springer, Heidelberg Darlinghurst, Australia, 2004.
10. S. X. Sun, J. L. Zhao, J. F. Nunamaker and O. R. L. Sheng. Formulating the data-flow perspective for business process management. *Information Systems Research*, Vol. 17, No. 4, pp. 374–391, 2006.
11. I. Vanderfeesten. Product-based design and support of workflow processes. Ph.D. thesis, Eindhoven University of Technology, 2009.
12. J. Wang and A. Kumar. A Framework for Document-Driven Workflow Systems. In: W. M. P. van der Aalst, B. Benatalla, F. Casati, F. Curbera (eds) Business Process Management. BPM 2005. *Lecture Notes in Computer Science*, Vol. 3649. Springer, Berlin, Heidelberg.
13. G. Zlotkin. *Organizing Business Knowledge—The MIT Process Handbook*. In: T. W. Malone et al. (eds). The MIT Press, Cambridge, MA, USA, p. 20, 2003.

5 Modeling for Variation and Flexibility
Dealing with Change

Introduction
Notions of Flexibility
Approaches for Flexibility
Fragment (or Subprocess) Configuration using Standard Patterns
Template and Rules
A Declarative Approach – Declare
Declare Tool – Language and Architecture
Chapter Summary

Introduction

We have seen in the previous chapters how one can create models from the control flow
and data flow perspectives. These models tend to be very precise in terms of steps that
are required and the exact order in which they must be performed. While this works
well for certain applications where the process is very well defined, there are also other
applications where the process is not well defined. *Real world processes are not rigid,
they evolve and change with time.* Organizational policies also change with time and
they necessitate changes in process design. As they say, change is the only constant
in life!

In this chapter we ask, how do we adapt business processes to change? Of course, we
can make changes to both the control flow and data flow approaches, but each change
necessitates further checking and verification to be sure that the change is correct. Even
the smallest change made to a process may introduce an error, sometimes a subtle one.
It would be nice if we did not have to check a process model for correctness every time
a minor change was made to it. In addition, a process model may have many variants
of the same basic model. Different variants may apply in different scenarios depending
upon parameters like the order size, customer status, loan amount, etc. It would help if
several related models could be integrated into one model so that there is no unwieldy
proliferation of process models. We start with some general notions of flexibility and
then introduce three concrete approaches. These three approaches are later discussed in
further detail: Fragments; Templates and rules; and Declarative approach.

Notions of Flexibility

Consider an auto (or home) insurance company PEICO that has one way of dealing with small claims of $250 or less and another way of dealing with larger claims of more than $250. Perhaps PEICO has a single process that checks the amount of the claim at a decision or XOR node and then branches off along two separate paths depending upon the size of the claim. This check may apply to one or more parts of the process because some parts may be common to both small or large, claims. Say at some time along the way PEICO modifies its policy to redefine small claims as all claims of $500 or less. In this case, a process designer or modeler will have to check the process and modify it at every place where this check is made to distinguish a small claim from a large claim. This can be tedious and lead to errors. Hence, there is a need for ways to design process models that are flexible.

The two different paths taken by small and large claims can be considered as two variants of the same underlying process that handles insurance claims. A company may decide to make two separate process models for these two types of claims (Model 1 and Model 2). When a new claim arrives it would be labeled as small or large, and handled by Model 1 or Model 2 accordingly. This is a feasible approach, but it can lead to a plethora of process models over time that would be hard to manage. Hence, other approaches merit consideration.

Consequently, the goal of the various approaches we present in this chapter is to develop models that can deal with different variants of what is essentially the same underlying process (e.g. an insurance claim process) in a flexible framework. The task of selecting an actual path for a specific case based on its case data and other factors is called configuration. Thus, by other factors we refer in particular to the context of the company. Based on the workload at any given time, a company may decide to process cases differently than normal. If the workload is high, PEICO may decide to omit one approval out of the regular two. A car rental company we shall call We-Rent that usually performs a car wash before renting out cars may decide to skip the car wash when their load is high or when some workers are absent. It may even decide to replace the regular car wash with an express car wash. The ability to change a model on the fly in response to exigencies is called process flexibility.

In general, a flexible process modeling approach should allow you to design a process that considers a variety of factors such as case data, workload, resource availability, time of day, weather conditions, etc. This is called *designing for variability*. Note that the case data is a case-specific feature, while the other data are non-case specific features that pertain to the context of the company or to external factors. The task of creating a specific model from the actual values of the non-case-specific factors is called *process configuration*. Given a process model, a higher-level configuration may be made on a seasonal basis if certain patterns of traffic and workload arise in different seasons by specifying the value of seasonal parameters to the process model. Further configuration can be performed even at a monthly, weekly, or daily basis.

Perhaps by now it does not bear repetition that control flow-based workflows are rigid. Every detail must be precisely specified. On the other hand, a flexible workflow is one that allows room for making changes in an easy way and ensuring that the changed workflow is correct. One way to think about such workflows is shown in Figure 5.1, which gives two scenarios that offer a generic way to think about flexibility. The dark background represents the space of all possibilities, while the white area is a specific process model within that space.

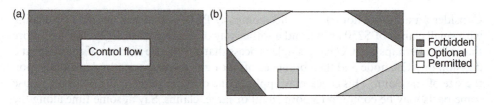

Figure 5.1 Aspects of flexibility (adapted from van der Aalst, Pesic, and Schonenberg, 2009): (a) control flow-based approach; (b) a flexible approach

Figure 5.1(a) gives the scenario where a strictly control flow-based approach is used. The outer rectangle shows the space of all possible ways in which a set of tasks may be combined to create a process model. However, the inner rectangle shows the actual control flow that has been specified for the process. On the other hand, Figure 5.1(b) shows the flexible approach. In this approach, we specify the forbidden areas within the space of possibility in black, the permitted areas in white and the optional areas in gray. By optional, we mean that these combinations of tasks are permitted under certain situations. An example of an optional task may be a task that is done under normal circumstances but may be omitted when the workload is very high. Thus, a loan application that requires two approvals may be processed with just one approval if a deadline has to be met. A car rental company that normally washes a car before it is rented out may omit this step, or perform it selectively if resource availability is scarce.

Flexibility may be introduced in different stages of a process lifecycle (see Table 5.1). The main stages in a process are: *design time* (when a process model is designed); *configuration time* (when the process model is adjusted based on contextual factors); *instantiation time* (when an instance of a process model is further adjusted based on contextual and case-related factors and started); and *run time* (when a process is actually running). Process flexibility implies that changes may be made to a process in any of these stages. Of course, it is easiest to make a change in the design stage because the process has not been finalized. Yet at configuration time, a process model that allows flexibility may be configured according to certain parameters or conditions. For example, a patient visit process for an outpatient clinic may be configured to include the subprocess "Check flu vaccination status" during the fall and winter seasons only. Thus, if a patient made a visit during this time, they would be asked if they wanted to get a flu vaccine, and if so it would be given to them. This subprocess would not be needed during spring or summer.

In a similar way, changes may be made to a process at instantiation time. When a process is instantiated, certain initial data pertaining to the case are available. The data can be used to make changes to the process. For instance, in a surgery process patient information such as age may be used to determine whether the patient should be given a tolerance test. This can be achieved by having a rule like: "If the patient is older than 75 years, then give a tolerance test before surgery." This would be an additional task in the process, and the surgery would commence only if the patient passed the test. A different example in the context of a customer online order, say, at Orders-R-Us, may require that if a customer has a gold-star rating, then no credit check would be performed for them for all credit orders up to $5000. Thus, the process would be modified accordingly.

Table 5.1 Classification of flexibility by phase and mechanism (adapted from van der Aalst, Pesic, and Schonenberg, 2009)

	Defer	*Change*	*Deviate*
Design time	Postpone to run time	N/A	N/A
Configuration time	Postone configuration decision	Modify process model at configuration time	Deviate from a configuration constraint
Instantiation time	N/A	Modify model based on customer, time of day, other attributes	N/A
Run time	N/A	Change model for a running instance	Skip or redo a task in violation of specs

Changes can also be made at run time to a process. In the above example where a tolerance test is required to be given to all patients who are older than 75 before surgery is performed, it is possible that the doctor who examines the patient may decide to waive the test if she feels that the patient is healthy and strong enough to endure the test. This is an example of a *deviation* (see Table 5.1) since it was not permitted by the model, yet the doctor is overruling or making an exception to the normal requirement based on her professional judgment. Alternatively, she may replace the standard tolerance test by a simpler test that takes less time. Of course, it is important to note, however, that these changes can only be made if the person making the changes is authorized to do so. This issue of authorization will be addressed in Chapter 8.

Approaches for Flexibility

Having established the need for process flexibility, in this chapter we shall introduce some approaches for flexibility and then discuss them in detail in the subsequent sections. To motivate the problem, we return to the PEICO Insurance company.

Example 1: PEICO receives claims from customers who have suffered losses to their property. PEICO reviews each claim in a systematic manner and determines the payment according to their policies. The main stages in the process are: *receive claim, validate claim, review damage, receive (or assess) damage report, determine settlement, approve settlement*, and *make payment*. Some of these stages may require multiple steps, such as multiple reviews or approvals. On the face of it, this is a simple process. However, the model for this process gets complicated because of various policies of the company. Some of the elements of their policy (P1–P7) are:

- P1. If the amount of the claim (or loss) is less than $500K then only one assessor is needed, but if it is higher, then two assessors are required.
- P2. One manager is required to approve claims of less than $100K; a manager and a senior manager for claims under $500K; and a manager and a VP for still higher claims.
- P3. If a claim is marked urgent, then the payment is made before the second approval.
- P4. If the claim is marked expedite, then the two approvals should occur in parallel.
- P5. For a loss of $250K or higher, the first reviewer should have 10 or more years' experience.

- P6. For a loss of $500K or more, the second assessor must be an expert.
- P7. If the loss amounts to $250K or more, the second reviewer should fill a *long form*.

Figure 5.2 describes this process. After the claim is received it is checked by an agent to ensure that it is complete and covered by the policy of the customer. Researchers and practitioners of BPM call such a process a *spaghetti process* because it reminds them of spaghetti, by virtue of the fact that it often has many intertwined branches and criss-crossing paths, and it can become very difficult to understand.

Exercise 1: Count the number of task nodes, control flow nodes, and edges in the claims process of Figure 5.2. Suggest how you might redesign it to make it more easily readable.

Observe that for the claims process of Figure 5.2, each process instance goes through the same phases of *receive, validate, assess, approve,* and *payment.* From a modeling standpoint, we can think of each phase as corresponding to a subprocess or a fragment. In all processes, the same phases are performed with many common tasks, but there are differences in detail. The goal of modeling for flexibility is to find better ways of describing processes such as this one. Such processes are unwieldy and we'll study approaches for managing them. We shall return to this example of Figure 5.2 later in this chapter, after introducing some techniques.

Some generic approaches to model flexibility that we shall discuss in this chapter are:

- fragment (or subprocess) configuration using standard patterns
- templates and rules: apply rules based on case data to fragments and *across fragments* in an end-to-end process to determine ordering relationships and make decisions on whether to *skip* tasks, *defer* tasks, etc.
- declarative approach (Declare).

Fragment (or Subprocess) Configuration using Standard Patterns

Different types of standard patterns can be used to introduce flexibility in a process model, as follows:

- **Constrained-OR:** This complex pattern allows any *m-of-n* branches (or more) to be selected for execution in parallel.
- **Ad hoc or any order:** We can specify the tasks that are to be performed but not enforce an ordering among them, i.e. the tasks may be done in any order.
- **Pockets of flexibility with restrictions**.

These patterns represent different degrees of flexibility, as we shall illustrate in our more detailed discussion of these various approaches below.

Constrained-OR

As explained in Chapter 2, the OR pattern is an inclusive OR as opposed to an exclusive OR (XOR). This is a flexible pattern that allows any combination of outgoing branches to be selected at the split node. However, it can be constrained so as to allow exactly *m*

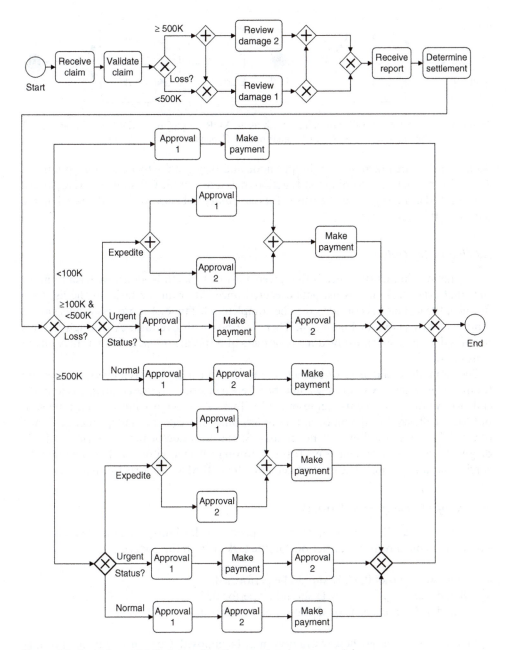

Figure 5.2 A single model that describes the complete insurance claim process

out of the *n* outgoing branches emanating from an OR split node. A special example of the constrained OR pattern is a 1-of-2 constrained OR, as shown in Figure 5.3. An OR join or OR split node is represented by an asterisk inside the diamond block. Notice how this pattern can behave both as an XOR and AND. In Figure 5.3(a), only the upper branch is taken at the OR split node and it activates the OR join node. In Figure 5.3(b),

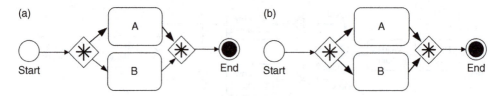

Figure 5.3 A constrained OR can behave both as an XOR and as an AND: (a) constrained OR behaving like an XOR; (b) a constrained OR behaving like an AND

both branches are taken at the OR split node and they both activate the OR join node. The OR join behaves according to the action that occurs at the OR split. The OR pattern is also called a smart gateway because of its capability to behave differently based on the nature of the application.

Ad Hoc or Any Order

The main idea in this structure is that given a list of tasks to be done, we wish to make sure that every task in this list gets executed once. After all the tasks in the list have finished, the instance is considered to be complete. This type of a process model can be represented as shown in Figure 5.4. There is a box with five tasks A through E. This denotes that each task must be done regardless of a specific order, so long as they all are completed.

Such a model could arise when there are no dependencies between tasks, i.e. they are totally independent. An example could be where a customer representative has to make calls to five different clients (represented by Tasks A through E) in a given time slot, but these calls could take place in any order. Since the calls are independent of each other, their exact ordering does not matter. Similarly, a doctor may prescribe multiple diagnostic tests to a patient (say, Tasks A through E in Figure 5.4) but they may be carried out it any order. The current version 2.0 of BPMN supports this pattern.

Pockets of Flexibility with Restriction

A set of tasks, say, B, C and D, comprise a "pocket of flexibility," and the idea is that we can impose constraints or restrictions on the tasks within the "pocket," e.g.

- only two of tasks B, C, D should be performed.
- B and *exactly one* of C or D should be performed.
- B and *at least one* of C or D should be performed.

Figure 5.5 shows how these restrictions may be imposed. Currently, there are no standard languages for representation of these restriction patterns. Perhaps future versions of BPMN will provide it.

Template and Rules

This approach is a further generalization of the above methods. It allows a user to define a basic process model (called a *template*) and then apply rules to modify it through

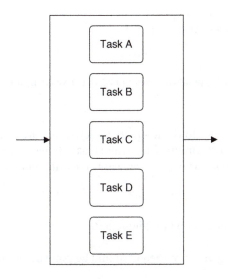

Figure 5.4 An ad hoc subprocess fragment with five tasks

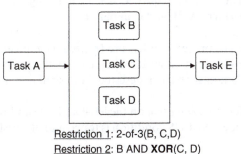

Restriction 1: 2-of-3(B, C,D)
Restriction 2: B AND **XOR**(C, D)
Restriction 3: B AND **OR**(C, D)

Figure 5.5 Pockets of flexibility

various transformation operations. The idea here is that a template would represent a simple process model that contains all the essential elements or tasks that must be performed in every variant of a process. It is like a highest common factor among the variants. Now, *if a process has many variants it is not necessary to make a model for each variant.* Instead we can create a set of rules using primitive change operations that can allow us to *realize or materialize each variant at run time by applying the primitive operations to the template if certain conditions are satisfied.* This is also called *process variant configuration.* In addition to modifying the control flow of a template by applying primitive operations, it is also possible to specify resource requirements of a task.

Exercise 2: What are the pros and cons of such an approach versus just storing realized versions of all process variants?

Example 2: Consider that a template consists of four sequential tasks, A, B, C and D, in a process as shown in Figure 5.6. We can also think of this template as a *region of*

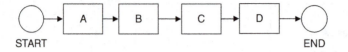

Figure 5.6 A base model template upon which operations are applied to derive a variant

flexibility. In this approach, we could apply rules to the template to determine ordering relationships among the tasks in the region of flexibility. Rules can be based on case and contextual data, e.g. *amount of a claim, customer status, resource use and availability, the time of day*, etc.

Thus, examples of rules could be (say in the context of Figure 5.6):

- **R1:** If task A is finished by 11 a.m. on a given day, then C should be done before D, else D should occur before C
- **R2:** If the customer has gold-star status, then skip task B
- **R3:** If task A was performed by a manager, then skip task C
- **R4:** If task A was performed by an agent, then require task C by a manager
- **R5:** If case_status is urgent, then perform A, B, and C in parallel.

By applying such rules, various different process models are realized as you can see in Figure 5.7. However, this flexibility does not come for free! The challenge in this approach lies in coming up with a rules language that can describe the desired semantics. The general structure of a rule is:

If (LHS), then (RHS) where LHS refers to a *condition* on the left-hand side and RHS to a *step or an action* on the right-hand side. The LHS condition is tested and, if satisfied, the action on the RHS is performed.

Exercise 3: Check that each of the example rules above in English satisfies the generic rule structure.

Now we would like to express them in a more formal way by having a standard syntax for writing LHS and RHS. The general structure for a condition is: attribute (operator) value. The operator can be =, <, ≤, >, ≥, etc. Thus, we could say if task_A. finish_time < 11 a.m., or customer_status = "Gold", etc. Similarly, the actions on the right can be expressed more formally using certain primitive action functions like **Do, Skip, Do_Seq, Do_Par**, etc.

Hence, we may rewrite the five rules above in a more formal way as:

- If **EAV**("customer," status, *S*) && *S* = "Gold" then **Skip**(task_B)
- If **Do**(task_A, Role) && Role = "manager" then **Skip**(task_C)
- If **Do**(task_A, Role) && Role = "agent" then **Do**(task_C, "Manager")
- If **EAV**(caseID, Status, *S*) && *S* = "urgent" then
  Do_Par(task_A, task_B)
- If **EAV**(task_ID, Finish_time, F) && F < 11 am then **Do_Seq**(task_C, task_D) Else
  Do_Seq(task_D, task_C)

These formal representations of the rules facilitate consistency and accuracy. In writing these rules we use primitives for condition testing and action functions (with appropriate arguments). The **Skip** function omits a task, while the **Do** function has the form **Do**(*task, role*), i.e. a certain task should be performed by a role. The **Do_Par** and **Do_Seq** functions perform the tasks in the corresponding order of parallel or sequence respectively. When a **Do**(*T, R*) function appears on the left-hand side as a condition, it is a test to see if a task T was performed by role R. Finally, the **EAV** function represents the entity-attribute-value triple. As shown above, an entity like a customer (or task, case, etc.) can have various different attributes like name, address, status, payment information, etc. A value can be attached to each attribute. When an EAV function appears on the left-hand side, it is used as a test to check if the entity has a certain value for an attribute. When on the right-hand side, an EAV function assigns a value to an attribute of an entity.

While actual literal string values are within quotes, a variable name such as S, F, Role, etc. starts with an upper case alphabet letter and is not quoted. Numeric values do not have to be in quotes. Entity, attribute, and role names start with a lower case letter and are not quoted. If an upper case letter is used as the first letter then it will be interpreted as a variable name. In the first example above, we are using variable S to check if the status of a customer is "gold." The set of action functions listed above is not exhaustive and it can be expanded by a user.

This approach offers several advantages. First, *it incorporates business policy into process design dynamically*. If a policy changes, only the corresponding rules have to be modified, while the process template can remain the same. Process variants derived from this process template will be automatically reconfigured to adapt to policy changes without human intervention.

In addition, an end user does not have to create a large number of process variants beforehand, and manually determine which schema to execute when a case (e.g. a new insurance claim) arrives. This approach leads to holistic process design by also

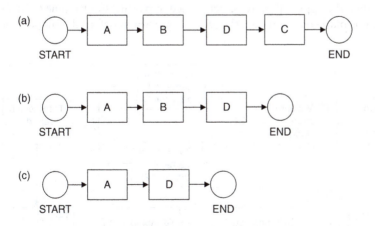

Figure 5.7 Various process models realized by applying rules R1–R3 to the template of Figure 5.6: (a) Task A finished after 11 a.m. (Rule R1); (b) customer has gold-star status (Rule R2); (c) customer has gold-star status and Task A was done by a manager (Rules R2, R3)

considering data and resource issues. Workflow research has mostly focused on the modeling of the control flow of a process, while other key aspects like data flow and resource needs are neglected. In general, a holistic process model requires additional information like resource needs (e.g. equipment and facilities) for task completion and data values of parameters associated with a task, etc. This approach integrates the modeling of resource and data needs of various tasks as well into the process description.

Thus, the essence of this approach is: **process template** + **rules** = **process variants**. The rules create specific change operations (e.g. insert or delete a task) based on the actual case data and then apply them to the process template to generate a variant. Naturally, this leads to considerably more flexibility than conventional approaches and is suitable in a constantly changing environment, as well as for resource-intensive or ad hoc workflows.

Example 3: Recall the spaghetti insurance claim process of Figure 5.2 for PEICO, which was hard to understand. Now we will try to express the same process in a different way using the idea of templates and rules. To do so, we have extracted a base template from that process as shown in Figure 5.8. This template simply shows the main tasks that were present in that process along with the default roles that perform them and the control flow relationships among them. However, note that this template does not say anything about the various conditions associated with the claim amounts or, for that matter, the urgency levels (normal, expedite, urgent). Yet, it shows us the main tasks that were present in that process.

Now to capture the additional details we will supplement the base process with a set of rules. An example rule set is shown in Figure 5.9. The rules are written in the formal syntax introduced above and are explained next. Thus, if the loss claimed is less than $500K, then only one reviewer (or adjuster) is required (Rule R1); however, if the loss is more than $250K, then the adjuster should have more than ten years of experience (R7) and must fill the "long" form (R9). Further, if the loss is more than $500K, the second adjuster should be classified as an expert (R8). After a settlement is assessed, either one or two approvals are required before payment is made, depending upon the amount of loss (R4, R5, R6). The other two rules deal with the urgency status of the case. If it is marked expedite, then the approvals may be performed in parallel to save time (R2). On the other hand, if it is marked urgent then the second approval is deferred until payment

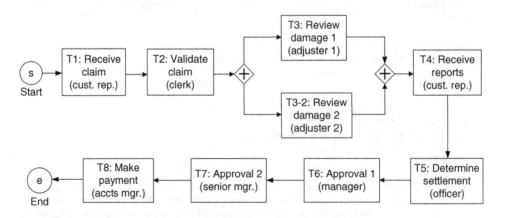

Figure 5.8 The base process template for the insurance claim process of Figure 5.2

R1: If loss < $500K, **then Skip**(review 2)
R2: If case_status = expedite **then Do_Par**(approval1, approval 2)
R3: If case_status = urgent **then Do_Seq**(payment, approval2)
R4: If loss < $100K, **then Skip**(approval2)
R5: If $100K ≤ loss < $500K, **then Do**(approval1, "Manager") && **Do**(approval2, "Senior Manager")
R6: If loss ≥ $500K, **then Do**(approval1, "Senior Manager") && Do(approval2, "VP")
R7: If loss ≥ $250K, then Do(review1, Reviewer1) && EAV(Reviewer1, experience, X) && X ≥ 10
R8: If loss ≥ $500K, **then** Do(review2, Reviewer2) && EAV(Reviewer2, status, "Expert")
R9: If loss ≥ $250K, **then** Do(review1, Reviewer1) && EAV(review1, type, "Long")

Figure 5.9 Rules to be applied to the process template of Figure 5.8

is made (R3). You can check for yourself that this approach does indeed capture the same process as in Figure 5.2, but in a different way.

Clearly, by applying rules to the template based on different case data, we obtain different process variants. For example, Figure 5.10 shows two variants, V1 and V2, derived from the process template in Figure 5.8. In part (a), the loss is $200K and it is marked expedite, while in part (b) the loss is $300K and it is marked urgent. We can see that these two variants are identical in most parts and only have minor difference in policy. As noted above, this approach leads to a separation of the essential process structure from the company's policy. For the most part, barring drastic changes, if there are minor policy changes only the rules can be modified while leaving the base process template intact.

Exercise 4: Compare the **template + rules** design of the insurance claim process with the spaghetti process of Figure 5.2. Which one is more easily understandable? What are the pros and cons of the two approaches?

Exercise 5: Say an additional step called *"Get customer Feedback"* is added by PEICO in their process at the end. Show the new design of the process using the spaghetti process approach and the "templates + rules" approach.

Informally, the basic criteria for differentiating business logic (or business rules) from process logic is that rules are more dynamic (e.g. the approval procedure is different depending upon the damage and the urgency status), while process logic is relatively static and hardly changes over time. The purpose of these examples was to motivate the need for configuring process variants by separating the business policy from the process model schema. The motivation behind this method is to reduce the redundancy between process models that are only *slightly* different from each other, to make process models more adaptive to business policy changes, and to efficiently retrieve the desired model for a specific case. Thus, process templates are used to abstract process logic for similar cases, and rules to better handle dynamic requirements.

Exercise 6: How can a process template be determined for a given process?

Exercise 7: How will you check if a set of rules to be applied to a base template is correct?

The "templates + rules" method is a hybrid method in that it retains some aspect of a control flow in the template and superimposes declarative rules on it. Next, we shall look at a purely declarative approach for process design.

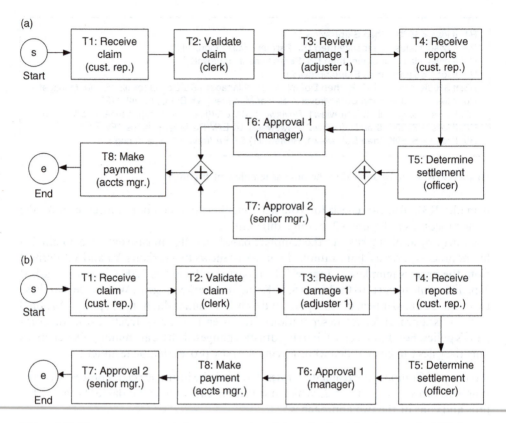

Figure 5.10 Two process variants from process template and rules: (a) process variant V1 (loss = $200K, status = expedite); (b) process variant V2 (loss = $300K, status = urgent)

A Declarative Approach – Declare

Declare builds on some of the ideas discussed above to describe process models in a declarative way. It is based on writing constraints that apply to the model. It is also a step in the direction of greater flexibility. In effect, it restricts the space of possibilities for a process model. As opposed to stating what must be done (or what is permitted) it describes what cannot be done. This enables a lot of flexibility at execution time. A key step towards declarative modeling was the Declare framework, a declarative constraint-based workflow management system. The idea is that given a set of tasks to be performed for a process, we impose constraints on their behavior. Any process instance that does not violate any constraint is a valid one. Thus, a key feature of this approach is that we declare what cannot be done (the dark region in Figure 5.1) explicitly. The remaining region of Figure 5.1 is permitted or optional.

This framework uses a modeling language called **ConDec** to express constraints among activities in a workflow. There are four main types or categories of constraints:

- *existence constraints* to indicate how many times an activity must occur in a workflow instance (at least, at most, exactly, position, absence, error)

- *relation constraints* to indicate the ordering relationship between the occurrences of a pair of activities in an instance (no order, order – simple, alternate, chain)
- *choice constraints* to show the alternative activities that may be selected in a workflow instance (simple, exclusive)
- *negative relations* to specify prohibited relations among activities in a workflow instance (not co-occurrence),

Figure 5.11 shows the screenshot of the first screen you see after you launch Declare and select New from the Model menu. By clicking on the + button next to the diamond, a user can create new tasks or activities and edit their names. When you double-click on ConDec a new "create a constraint definition" screen appears, as shown in Figure 5.12 in its fully expanded form. Here you can select a template for the kind of constraint you wish to define. After a template is selected, another window pops up where more parameters need to be provided, such as the activity name(s), desired ordering between them, etc. The detailed definition window for the response(A,B) template is shown in Figure 5.13.

The constraint templates are organized into four groups in Figure 5.12. We'll discuss each group of constraints next. An *existence constraint* may state that an activity A may occur at least, at most or exactly a certain number of times (e.g. 0, 1, 2, 3). We can also specify the position in which A might occur. Thus, *init(A)* denotes that A must be the first activity of an instance, while *last(A)* denotes that A must be the last one. We can also specify that A must be absent or not exist. Finally, it is possible to state that an error should be generated if A occurs.

For the *order relation constraints*, we must specify the occurrence sequence between a pair of activities, say A and B. In the *simple order* constraints, every occurrence of A could be followed by an *eventual* occurrence of B (response), every occurrence of A could be preceded by at least one occurrence of B (precede), or A and B may be in response and precedence relation (called succession). These templates are described in Table 5.2 Variations of the simple order are *alternate order* (where a pair of A and B occurrences must alternate) and *chained order* (where an A occurrence is *immediately* followed or preceded by a B occurrence).

In the *choice constraints*, it is possible to specify that only 1 out of n (say, 2, 3, etc.) activities may occur in a workflow instance. In general, one can require that exactly (at least) m out of n activities (where $m < n$) may occur in a workflow instance. To specify

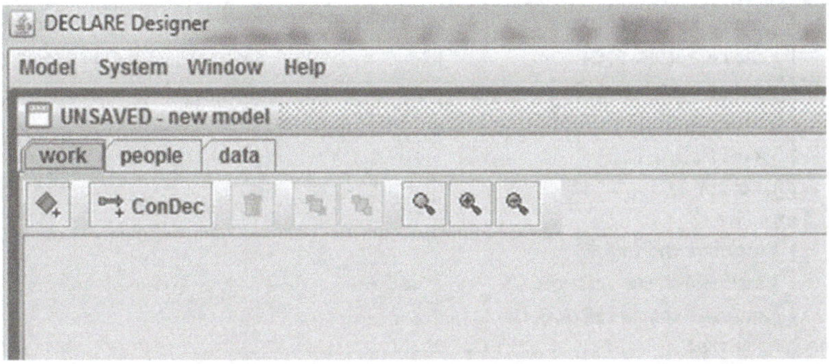

Figure 5.11 Main screen of Declare

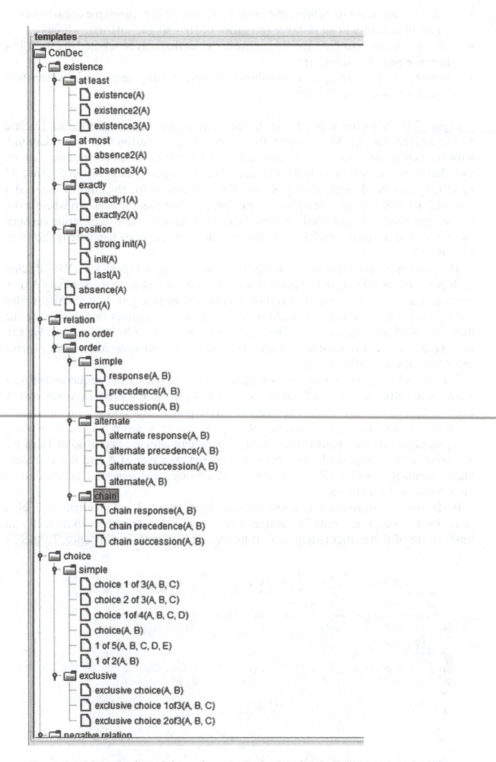

Figure 5.12 A screenshot of the various constraint patterns in Declare

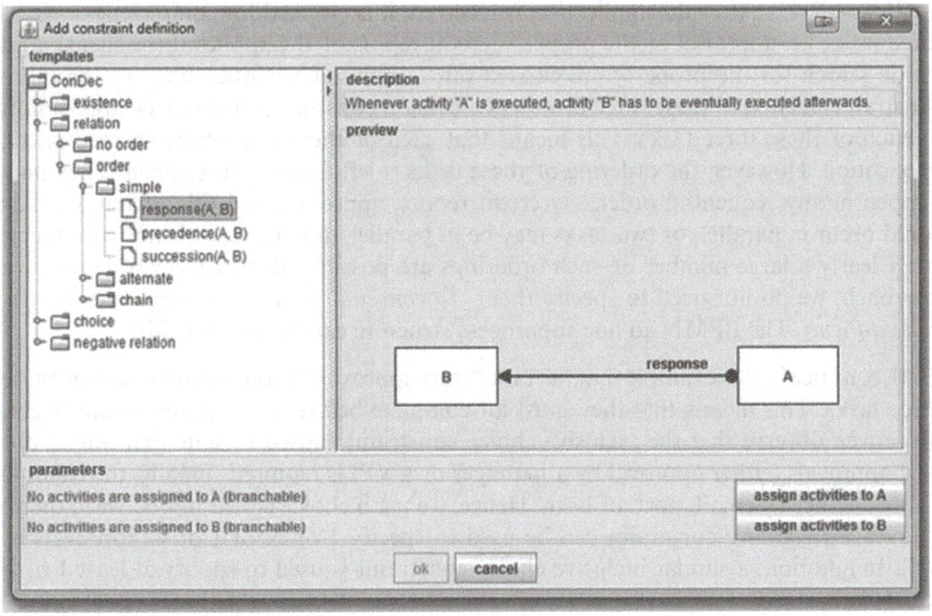

Figure 5.13 Specifying a response(A,B) relationship in Declare

Table 5.2 Response, precedence, and succession constraint templates

Pattern name	Representation	Meaning
Response	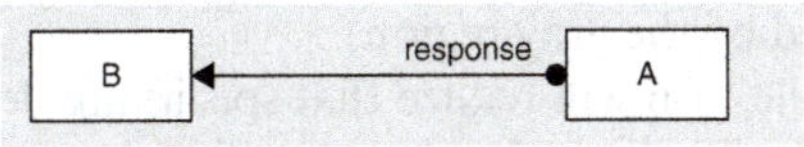	Whenever A happens B must happen
Precedence	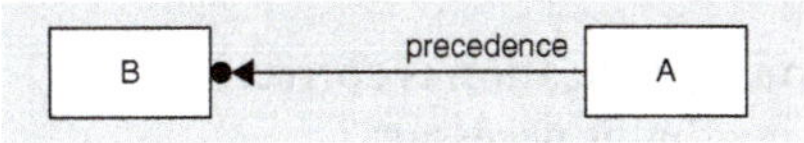	B must be preceded by A
Succession:	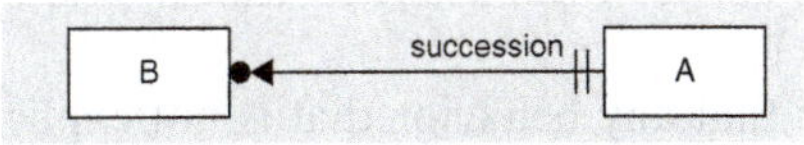	Response and Precedence

exactly *m* out of *n* activities, the exclusive choice operation is used, while for at least *m* out of *n*, the inclusive choice operator is used.

Finally, a *negative relation* may specify non-co-existence between two activities – say A and B, i.e. that activities A and B cannot co-exist.

Exercise 8: Explain how non-co-existence is different from an exclusive choice between A and B.

It is also possible to specify that the relation between A and B is not chained, i.e. they may not occur in immediate sequence.

102   *Modeling for Variation and Flexibility*

Example 4: Figure 5.14 shows an example in the context of the loan application process for Loans-R-Us. After the application is received, it is checked for completeness. Next, three tasks, i.e. appraisal of the property, credit report of the applicant (or client), and a title search for the property are carried out *in any order*. Notice how we show the constraints related to these three tasks as succession constraints from check application to each of these three tasks. This means that each of these tasks must succeed check application. However, the ordering of these tasks is left entirely unspecified. They may happen in any sequential order, say credit report, appraisal, and title search, or they could occur in parallel, or two tasks may be in parallel and one in sequence with them, etc. Clearly a large number of such orderings are possible. But by using a declarative approach, we do not need to specify them. *To convey this idea in an imperative way is quite difficult.* The BPMN ad hoc subprocess structure can be used for this.

Also, notice in this example that the task "start approvals" is preceded by each of these three tasks. This means that they must all complete before start approvals can begin. Moreover, observe that the exclusive choice constraint is used to state that only 1 out of 2 approvals (either approval by a manager or a VP) is required. Finally, the client is notified either by email, post, or both. Hence, we use a choice constraint between them. The *exclusive choice* constraint can be used to specify 1 of 3, or 1 of 4, approvals as well. In addition, a similar inclusive choice constraint is used to specify at least 1 of *n* constraints.

Let us pause to reflect on what we have described using Declare. We have specified the various activities, their existence types (i.e. number of occurrences), their (non-)occurrence relationships, and also the set of permitted alternatives among two or more activities. If we refer back to Figure 5.1, we can see that in this declarative manner we have specified both what is required or permitted, and what is forbidden (the white and black regions, respectively). In addition, we have also specified what is optional, e.g. by stating that an activity can occur at most once, we are making it optional in that it may occur 0 or 1 times (denoted by the gray region).

When you consider for a while, you will realize that specifying declarative workflows is not always an easy thing to do. In particular:

- How will you verify that your specification is correct?
- Have you specified everything that is necessary?
- Have you missed a relation between two activities that should or should not occur?

It is important to remember that any behavior that is not explicitly prohibited by a constraint is allowed. Hence, you may allow a large number of behaviors without realizing it. It is difficult to verify that they are all valid and acceptable. Consequently, this is an extremely liberal design approach at the other end of the flexibility spectrum from the control flow-based approach.

Exercise 9: Describe the insurance claim process for PEICO and the online ordering process for Orders-R-Us in Declare.

Declare Tool – Language and Architecture

Declare is an example of a tool based on a declarative language. At the heart of Declare is a collection of constraint templates. The Declare system provides for multiple languages

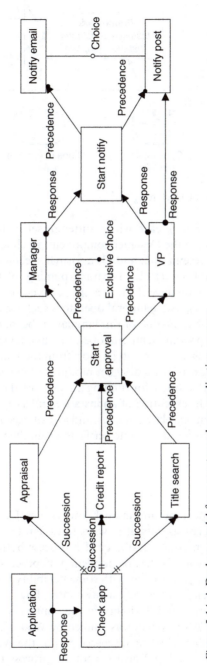

Figure 5.14 A Declare model for a mortgage loan application process

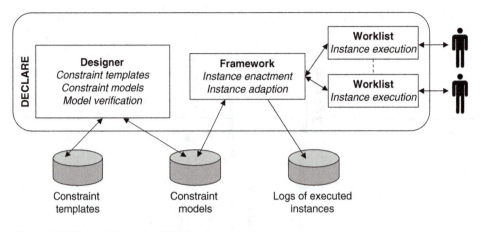

Figure 5.15 The architecture of Declare

(e.g. ConDec and DecSerFlow), each with a different set of templates. Templates are defined on the system level in the Designer component. Each template has: (1) a unique name; (2) a graphical representation; and (3) a formal specification of its semantics in terms of Linear Temporal Logic (LTL). The underpinnings of Declare lie in a language called Logical Temporal Language. LTL is a special type of logic which, in addition to classical logical operators, uses temporal operators such as: always, eventually, until, and next occurrence. A full discussion of this language is beyond the scope of this work. However, it is a way of expressing temporal operators in a logical framework.

An architecture for the Declare prototype tool (from the University of Eindhoven) is shown in Figure 5.15. It consists of a designer module to build a model using constraint templates and a framework module for running an instance. The latter module interacts with worklists that track the execution of an instance and assigns tasks to roles or users accordingly. The constraint templates, models, and logs of execution instances are stored in a database. Declare also has a separate verification module that checks a model for correctness.

Chapter Summary

Process flexibility is an important topic in workflow systems. Declarative process descriptions based on rules and constraints offer ways to design flexibility, as we saw in this chapter. There is a major need for flexibility of a process both at design time and run time. We created a framework for flexible modeling of processes and discussed hybrid approaches that combine a control flow with some flexibility features, and also a purely declarative approach which is not based on any control flow.

Work on issues of change and flexibility in the context of BPM goes back to the late 1990s [13, 21]. The WASA system was studied by Weske [21] and the ADEPT system by Reichert and Dadam [13]. As discussed in [2], the ADEPT project ran for a decade with the vision to develop a next-generation process management technology that would be considerably more powerful and flexible than the technology of that time. Some of their goals were to achieve ease-of-use for end users and system developers, high flexibility through the support of ad hoc deviations at the process instance level,

quick implementation of process changes through process schema evolution, and correctness guarantees enabling robust execution of implemented processes [2]. This group
published several papers on approaches for dealing with change and schema evolution [1, 14, 18]. They point out that making changes to a process model or a running
instance is non-trivial, and can introduce many kinds of anomalies related to missing
data, deadlocks, multiple instances, etc. and discuss correctness criteria for doing so [15].
They also develop algorithms for dealing with such situations and show their correctness. Many of the ideas about flexibility were consolidated into a book [14] that was
published in 2012.

The idea of pockets of flexibility is described by Sadiq et al. [17]. Van der Aalst et al.
introduced the notion of configurability of a process model [5, 19] with the goal of introducing flexibility. Their idea is to make certain tasks or control nodes configurable, i.e.
they can be turned ON or OFF (at design time or run time), thus changing the behavior of the process depending upon certain conditions related to workload, staffing, etc.
This approach was applied to EPC diagrams to make them configurable (C-EPCs), and
a reference language for configuration was described in [16]. Similar methods for configuration can be applied to other modeling languages as well. Models that are configurable
from multiple perspectives are discussed in [8]. The template and rules approach was proposed by Kumar and Yao [7]. A fine survey of business process modeling for variability
that is based on a systematic framework appears in [9]. Several additional approaches
and techniques for handling variability are discussed there.

The work on Declare was conducted in the thesis of Pesic [12] and is published
in [11, 20]. Papers and links to prototype versions of Declare are accessible at [4]. More
recent work that evaluates Declare and also presents empirical results is discussed in [6].
Another constraint-based approach for managing business process variants in a similar spirit to that of Declare is described by Lu et al. [10]. For a discussion of Logical
Temporal Language (LTL), see [3].

The approaches discussed here are in prototype stages and in university products. To
the best of our knowledge, they are not being supported by commercial tools. We expect
this will happen soon.

References

1. C. Ayora, V. Torres, M. Reichert, B. Weber and V. Pelechano. Towards run-time flexibility for process families: open issues and research challenges. *Business Process Management
Workshops*, pp. 477–488, 2012.
2. P. Dadam and M. Reichert. The ADEPT project: a decade of research and development for
robust and flexible process support. *Computer Science – R&D*, Vol. 23, No. 2, pp. 81–97, 2009.
3. E. M. Clarke, O. Grumberg and D. A. Peled. *Model Checking*. The MIT Press, London, UK,
1999.
4. C. Haisjackl, I. Brba, S. Zugal, P. Soffer, I. Hadar, M. Reichert, J. Pinggera and B. Weber.
Understanding declare models: strategies, pitfalls, empirical results. *Software and System
Modeling*, Vol. 15, No. 2, pp. 325–352, 2016.
5. Declare. www.win.tue.nl/declare/research/.
6. F. Gottschalk, W. M. P. van der Aalst, M. H. Jansen-Vullers and M. L. Rosa. Configurable
workflow models. *International Journal of Cooperative Information Systems*, Vol. 17, No. 2,
pp. 177–221, 2008.
7. A. Kumar and W. Yao. Design and management of flexible process variants using templates
and rules. *Computers in Industry* (CII), Vol. 63, No. 2, pp. 112–130, 2012. (PDF)

8. M. L. Rosa, M. Dumas, A. H. M. ter Hofstede and J. Mendling. Configurable multi-perspective business process models. *Information Systems*, Vol. 36, No. 2, pp. 313–340, 2011.
9. M. L. Rosa, W. M. P. van der Aalst, M. Dumas and F. P. Milani. Business process variability modeling: a survey. *ACM Computer Survey*, Vol. 50, No. 1, Article 2 (March 2017), 45 pages, 2017.
10. R. Lu, S. W. Sadiq and G. Governatori. On managing business processes variants. *Data and Knowledge Engineering*, Vol. 68, No. 7, pp. 642–664, 2009.
11. M. Pesic, M. H. Schonenberg, N. Sidorova and W. M. P. van der Aalst. Constraint-based Workflow Models: Change Made Easy. In: F. Curbera, F. Leymann and M. Weske (eds) Proceedings of the OTM Conference on Cooperative Information Systems (CoopIS '07), *Lecture Notes in Computer Science*, Vol. 4803. Springer-Verlag, Berlin, Germany, 2007, pp. 77–94.
12. M. Pesic. Constraint-based workflow management systems: shifting control to users. Ph.D. thesis, TU Eindhoven, 2008.
13. M. Reichert and P. Dadam. ADEPTflex-supporting dynamic changes of workflows without losing control. *Journal of Intelligent Information Systems*, Vol. 10, No. 2, pp. 93–129, 1998.
14. M. Reichert and B. Weber. *Enabling Flexibility in Process-Aware Information Systems – Challenges, Methods, Technologies*. Springer, Heidelberg, Berlin, Germany, 2012.
15. S. Rinderle, M. Reichert and P. Dadam. Correctness criteria for dynamic changes in workflow systems: a survey. *Data and Knowledge Engineering*, Vol. 50, No. 1, pp. 9–34, 2004.
16. M. Rosemann and W. M. P. van der Aalst. A configurable reference modelling language. *Information Systems*, Vol. 32, No. 1, pp. 1–23, 2007.
17. S. Sadiq, W. Sadiq and M. Orlowska. Pockets of Flexibility in Workflow Specification. In: Proceedings of the 20th International Conference on Conceptual Modeling (ER '01). *Lecture Notes in Computer Science*, Vol. 2224. Springer-Verlag, Berlin, Germany, pp. 513–526, 2001.
18. B. Weber, M. Reichert and S. Rinderle-Ma. Change patterns and change support features: enhancing flexibility in process aware information systems. *Data and Knowledge Engineering*, Vol. 66, No. 3, pp. 438–466, 2008.
19. W. M. P. van der Aalst, M. Rosemann and M. Dumas. Deadline-based escalation in process-aware information systems. *Decision Support System*, Vol. 43, No. 2, (March 2007) pp. 492–511, 2007.
20. W. M. P. van der Aalst, M. Pesic and H. Schonenberg. Declarative workflows: balancing between flexibility and support. *Computer Science: Research and Development*, Vol. 23, No. 2, pp. 99–113, 2009.
21. M. Weske. Formal Foundation and Conceptual Design of Dynamic Adaptations in a Workflow Management System. In: R. Sprague (ed.) *Proceedings of the 34th Annual Hawaii International Conference on System Science (HICSS-34)*, IEEE Computer Society Press, Los Alamitos, CA, USA, 2001.

6 Verification of Business Processes

Introduction

In previous chapters, our focus was on process modeling. We saw that a process model captures business requirements accurately and formally. Thus, it facilitates interoperability in the sense that, if one designer makes the model another can understand it in an unambiguous way. If you are involved in some stage of a process in a company, by looking at the complete process diagram you can gain an understanding of the full process and how your work fits into it. We also saw that a process is built by combining tasks with basic control flow building blocks like ANDs and XORs. Each of these structures has a split and a join node (e.g. AND-split, AND-join, etc.). If these structures are combined properly it produces a correct process. But if they are not combined in the right manner then the process model is incorrect.

Our focus in this chapter is on understanding the properties of correct process models and learning how to check whether a given model is correct. While it is important that process models precisely capture business requirements, it is clearly also very important to check that the models we design are correct. A process that is deployed into normal operations before being properly checked and verified could fail to execute properly and cause considerable loss to a business. *The goal of process verification is to identify and point out erroneous processes to the process designer.* Ideally a process verification tool should be able to diagnose and pinpoint exactly where the error lies so that the designer can make the correction in that part of the process.

We will see in this chapter that a correct process model is one with no structural flaws, such as deadlocks, dead-end paths, incomplete terminations, etc. Therefore, it is very important that the correctness of workflows be verified systematically before the process models are implemented. We first introduce structured and unstructured workflows and then move on to notions of correctness. Next, we discuss issues in the verification of unstructured workflows. A formal verification approach based on satisfaction of structural balance equations is described later. Finally, we turn to examine verification issues in the context of data-centric approaches and where data is modeled along with control flow.

Structured Workflows

One accepted notion of correctness relies on the idea of structuredness. A *structured* (or *block-structured*) *workflow* is one in which each split control element (e.g. AND, XOR) is matched with a join control element of the same type, and such split-join pairs are also properly nested. As an example, consider the process model in Figure 6.1. In this model, notice that each AND-split is matched with a corresponding AND-join, and an XOR-split is matched with a corresponding XOR-join. Also observe in this figure how a loop can be created by combining an XOR-join and an XOR-split. Hence, as you would expect the number of AND-splits is equal to the number of AND-joins and the number of XOR-splits is equal to the number of XOR-joins.

However, not all workflows are structured; in general, some unstructured workflows have more expressive power than structured ones, and are also correct. Thus, the requirement of structuredness is restrictive.

Exercise 1: Give a simple example of a process model that is incorrect.

Exercise 2: Given a process model, describe three rules you will apply to check whether it is correct or not.

Unstructured Workflows

Unstructured workflows are different from structured ones in that the splits and joins are not matched with each other. Consider the workflow in Figure 6.2.

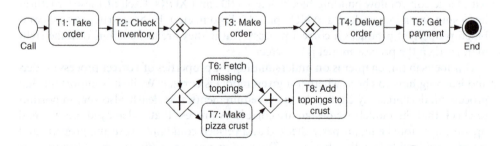

Figure 6.1 An example of a structured workflow model

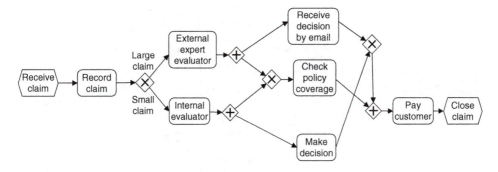

Figure 6.2 An insurance claim processing workflow (notice the crossover of edges)

Exercise 3: Explain briefly what the workflow in Figure 6.2 does. Why is this workflow unstructured? How many AND-splits, AND-joins, XOR-splits and XOR-joins are there in this workflow? Is this process correct? Explain your answer.

This workflow processes an insurance claim. A new claim is received and recorded. Then, if it is a small claim it is sent to an internal evaluator who makes a decision. If the claim is large, then it is sent to an external evaluator who makes a decision and communicates it to the insurance company by email. For both types of claims, in parallel with the decision making, an employee in the company also checks whether the damage is covered by the insurance policy of the client. After this, the client is paid and the claim is closed.

This is an unstructured process because the splits and the joins are not matched. Notice also how two edges cross each other. Of course, you could go around the "close claim" event (i.e. the end event) and then avoid the crossing lines, but it would be awkward. Normally a process should not extend outside the boundaries set by the start and end events. Such crossover of a pair of edges will typically happen in an unstructured process only. It will never occur in a structured process.

Exercise 4: Can you convert the unstructured process of Figure 6.2 into an equivalent structured process? Show how you would do it.

Exercise 5: Show why crossing edges (as in Figure 6.2) will never arise in a structured process.

One way to prevent a crossover of edges is shown in Figure 6.3. Does anything in particular strike you about the process in Figure 6.3? Which diagram do you find to be more readable, Figure 6.2 or Figure 6.3? Check for yourself to make sure that the process of Figure 6.3 does indeed have identical execution paths to the process in Figure 6.2. In Figure 6.3 there are two separate branches, the upper and lower branches, for large and small claims respectively, that emerge from the AND-split node after the claim is recorded. You can see that in this figure, the AND and XOR splits and joins are perfectly matched and hence this is a structured process. Be sure to note that in Figure 6.3, the task "Check policy coverage" is repeated twice. It appears in the upper part of the figure for large claims and also again for small claims.

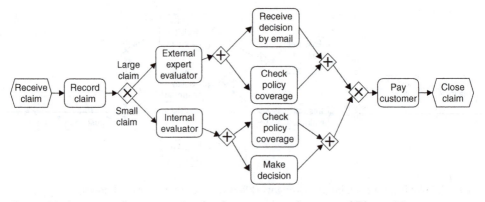

Figure 6.3 A structured representation for the unstructured process of Figure 6.2

Exercise 6: Do you think it is an error if a task is repeated? What is the disadvantage of a repeated task?

Having introdcued the ideas of structured and unstructured processes, we now turn to look at formal notions of process correctness.

Formal Notions of Correctness

In the process modeling literature, a well-known notion of correctness is based on the concept of soundness. Before discussing *soundness*, we will introduce the idea of a valid execution path. A valid execution path is one that includes the start task, the end task(s)  and other tasks such that the correct behavior is observed at every control flow node for the execution path from start to end. A well-behaved process is one in which all possible execution paths are valid.

A **valid execution path** VP is a set of tasks Ti and control flow nodes ASi, XSi, AJi and XJi such that:

- There is a start task and an end task in the path.
- At an AND-split node AS_i in VP, all outgoing edges of AS_i are activated.
- At an XOR split node XS_i in VP, exactly one outgoing edge of XS_i is activated.
- At an AND join node AJ_i in VP, all incoming edges of AJ_i are activated (i.e. there are no deadlocks).
- At an XOR join node XJ_i in VP, exactly one incoming edge of XJ_i is activated (no lack of synchronization).

A valid execution path is also called a process instance. The definition of soundness is based on the idea of a valid path.

Definition 1: A sound process model is one where the following three conditions are satisfied:

(1)   *Option to complete*: It should always be possible to complete a running process instance that is proceeding according to the process model. This condition guarantees the absence of deadlocks and livelocks, as we explain presently.

(2)   *Proper termination*: All execution paths that include a given task are valid. It should not be the case that for some execution instance, the end of the process is reached when there is still some unfinished work remaining in the instance.

(3)   *No dead task*: Every task should lie on at least one valid execution path from an initial start task (or event) to a final (or end) task. This means that every task contributes towards the completion of the instance.

A sound process is also called a *correct* or *well-behaved process*. These terms are used somewhat interchangeably. As discussed above it is easy to check for correctness in a structured process model because there is a strict *one-to-one correspondence* between split and join control flow nodes. However, in an unstructured workflow this is not true. This lack of structuredness may cause structural flaws that may lead to problems in execution. We will next discuss scenarios where problems can arise in process models and techniques for checking correctness of models.

Deadlocks, Livelocks and Multiple Instances

When we say that a process (or a process pattern as in Table 6.1) is well-behaved, it means that all possible execution paths in the process are correct from start to end. In particular, it means that at an AND join node, all incoming branches will be activated while at an XOR join node, exactly one incoming branch will be activated. Pause to consider what would happen if only one incoming branch out of two or more is activated at an AND join node, or say two or more are activated at an XOR node. These two situations are shown in Figures 6.4 and 6.5 respectively.

In the case of a deadlock (Figure 6.4) since only one outgoing branch is activated at the XOR node, thus both branches cannot synchronize at the AND node and further execution of the process does not proceed. Hence, we say the process is "stuck" at the AND node and the process model is incorrect.

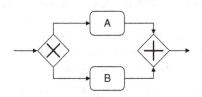

Figure 6.4 Deadlock

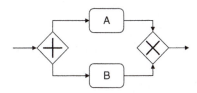

Figure 6.5 Multiple instances

For the multiple instance case (Figure 6.5), an AND-split is matched with an XOR-join. At the AND-split, two branches are activated for tasks A and B. However, at the XOR-join only one branch needs to be active for the join connector to be triggered.

Strictly speaking both these scenarios are incorrect. However, in many situations multiple instances are allowed, and they even serve a practical purpose. The semantics of an XOR join node can be one of the following:

(1)   *Single execution*: The XOR join node is executed only once after whichever branch is done first. The other incoming branches are discarded when they finish. Thus, in Figure 6.5, if A finished first, then activity B and its results are ignored. In a strict sense, the activity B represents unfinished work and it is a sign that the process instance did not terminate properly.

(2)   *Multiple executions*: Whenever any of its incoming branches is done, the join-choice element is executed. This may create multiple instances. In Figure 6.5, this means that after A and B finish, execution will continue past the XOR-join both times. As an example, consider that you are applying for a job and they have asked you to submit three letters of reference by a certain deadline. Just to be on the safe side you may decide to contact four references and ask them to send letters on your behalf. However, as soon as three reference letters have been received your application would be considered complete and the process can continue. You wonder what will be done with the fourth letter if it arrives later. What do you think?

Well, when the fourth letter arrives, it may be discarded. Alternatively, if a decision has not been reached on your case when the fourth letter arrives it may be added to your application to provide more information about you to the hiring department. Process modeling languages like BPMN do not provide much support for these sorts of situations. Application developers have to add support themselves for dealing with such situations on a case-by-case basis.

Another situation that is similar to a deadlock is *livelock*, as illustrated in Figure 6.6. Here we have a loop, but there is no way to exit the loop because the Exit condition from the loop never becomes true. This indicates a problem in the process design. It is syntactically correct but semantically incorrect. This means that the logic of the process has to be modified so that it will always get out of the livelock after a maximum number of iterations. Perhaps a step can be added after task A such that after a certain number of iterations through the loop, the exit condition will always become true.

Exercise 7: Say the loop of Figure 6.6 is such that the process always exits this loop after performing task A once, and it never really gets to task B. Is this a correct process? Why or why not? If not, then how would you fix this process?

Next we shall revisit structured and unstructured workflows.

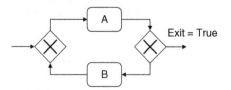

Figure 6.6 A livelock occurs when the process gets stuck in the A–B loop forever

Converting an Unstructured to a Structured Process

Since structured workflows are easier to understand, despite their lesser expressive power than unstructured ones, it is natural to ask: What kinds of unstructured processes can be converted into equivalent structured ones? Let us consider some scenarios of unstructured workflows and see how they can be converted into structured ones by applying simple rules.

One pattern or structure that arises frequently in unstructured workflows is improper nesting. An example of an improper nesting is shown in Figure 6.7. The dashed edges simply mean that other tasks may occur along these edges. Notice how there are two XOR split-join pairs: C1S-C1J and C2S-C2J. Because C2J lies in a branch from C1S to C1J, we say that the two split-join pairs are *improperly nested* with each other and denote it using the $\vert_\vert$ symbol as (C1S-C1J) $\vert_\vert$ (C2S-C2J). Nevertheless, C1S-C1J (and C2S-C2J) correspond with each other because there are two (or, in general, more) branches that split at C1S and meet at C1J. Such split-join pairs are called corresponding pairs. We define corresponding pairs as follows:

Definition 2: Corresponding control flow elements. A split element s corresponds to a join element j, if two *minimal* paths, starting along two different outgoing edges of s, first join at j.

Recall that in a structured process, this kind of improper nesting does not arise and, in general, one structure would be fully nested inside another (see Figure 6.8).

Figure 6.8 shows an equivalent representation for the structure in Figure 6.7. Now, how can we check if the two processes are equivalent? One way to verify a process is of course to enumerate each possible execution sequence and check if it is correct,

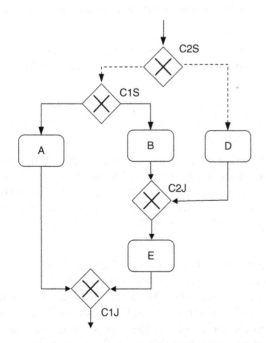

Figure 6.7 An improperly nested structure with XOR-splits and XOR-joins

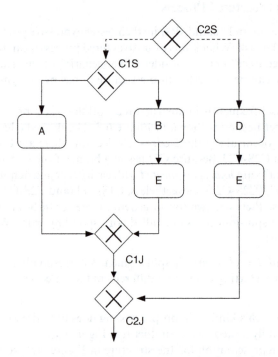

Figure 6.8 An equivalent representation for the improperly nested structure of Figure 6.7

but this method will work only for small process models because of the computational complexity. One well-known notion of what it means for two process models to be equivalent is called trace equivalence.

Definition 3: Trace Equivalence. Two process models are said to be trace equivalent if all the valid execution paths in model 1 have an exactly identical valid execution path in model 2, and vice versa.

Exercise 8: Are the two structures in Figure 6.7 and Figure 6.8 trace equivalent? Check for yourself by tracing all execution paths in the two structures. Also note how the two XOR split-join structures are *properly nested* here.

Example 1: Figure 6.9 shows a workflow with pairs of three split and three corresponding join control elements: (C1S, C1J), (C2S, C2J), (C3S, C3J) as per Definition 2. Note that (C1S, C2J) is not a corresponding pair because it is dominated by (C1S, C1J), and, hence, not minimal. There are many improper nesting relationships in this process, also denoted as follows: (C1S, C1J) $^{[}_{]}$ (C2S, C2J); (C1S, C1J) $^{[}_{]}$ (C3S, C3J); and (C2S, C2J) $^{[}_{]}$ (C3S, C3J).

First, we can transform the improper nesting between (C1S, C1J) and (C2S, C2J) using this technique: *"push" the activities that lie between two join-choice nodes up, and thus create a structured mapping.* This allows us to derive workflow wf2 of Figure 6.9(b). In wf2, only one improper nesting between (C3S, C3J) and (C1S, C1J) remains. Again, this improper nesting can be similarly transformed to obtain the process model shown as workflow wf3 in Figure 6.9(c). It is easy to check that this is a fully structured process

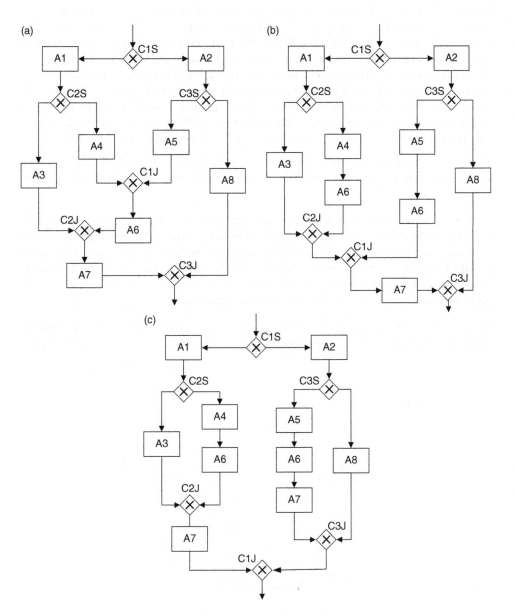

Figure 6.9 Steps in mapping an unstructured workflow wf1 into a structured workflow wf3: (a) workflow wf1; (b) workflow wf2; (c) workflow wf3

model. You can verify for yourself that the model in Figure 6.9(a) is equivalent to the one in Figure 6.9(c). Also, note that the "push up" technique works only when all the control nodes are of XOR type.

We can generalize the special case of XOR type nodes above to arbitrary combinations of split and join node types, i.e. where the control flow nodes are either XOR or AND as shown in Figure 6.10. In this figure, there are two split-join pairs that are nested together.

Each split or join can be either a XOR or an AND; and even in a pair such as split1 and join1 in Figure 6.10, *split 1* may be of a different type than *join 1*. Since each control flow node can have two patterns, either XOR or AND, and there are four such nodes in this figure, there is a total of 16 combinations of such nesting patterns. These 16 patterns are listed in Table 6.1. In this table, we can see that there are two patterns that are well-behaved: the one with all XOR splits and joins (pattern 1) and the one with all AND splits and joins (pattern 8). As you can see, there are many cases that lead to deadlocks and multiple instances. Note that we do not introduce OR connectors in this discussion because their semantics are very complicated, as explained in previous chapters.

Exercise 9: Consider the process model shown in Figure 6.11. Is this a correct process? Is it structured or unstructured? If the latter, then is there an equivalent structured representation for it?

One can check and verify that these two patterns are indeed correct. The remaining 14 patterns in Table 6.1 have two kinds of issues, deadlocks and multiple instances. Column 6 of Table 6.1 shows the correctness issue of each pattern: it is well-behaved, a deadlock occurs, or multiple instances occur. The last column shows whether an equivalent structured transformation can be found for the pattern. It is evident that structured equivalents exist only for very few unstructured patterns.

Exercise 10: Show that a process with one start node and one end node created by arbitrarily nesting only XOR splits and XOR joins in any manner will be correct. Is this

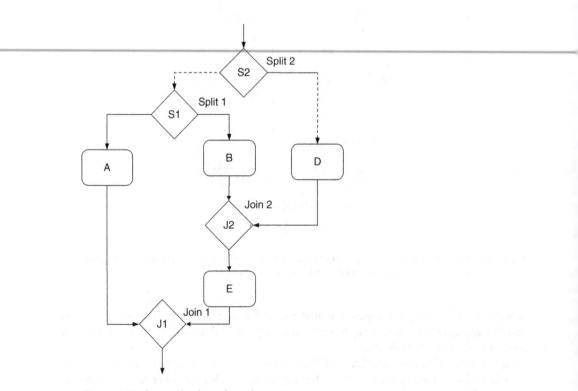

Figure 6.10 Generalization of nesting patterns

Table 6.1 First-order improper nesting and mismatched pairs and their behaviors

Type	Split 1	Join 1	Split 2	Join 2	Correctness issues	Structured transformation
1	XOR	XOR	XOR	XOR	Well-behaved	Yes
2	XOR	XOR	XOR	AND	Deadlock	No
3	XOR	XOR	AND	XOR	Multiple instances	No
4	XOR	XOR	AND	AND	Deadlock	No
5	AND	AND	XOR	XOR	Deadlock	No
6	AND	AND	XOR	AND	Deadlock	No
7	AND	AND	AND	XOR	Multiple instances	No
8	AND	AND	AND	AND	Well-behaved	No
9	XOR	AND	XOR	XOR	Deadlock	No
10	XOR	AND	XOR	AND	Deadlock	No
11	XOR	AND	AND	OR	Deadlock	No
12	XOR	AND	AND	AND	Deadlock	No
13	AND	XOR	XOR	XOR	Multiple instances	No
14	AND	OR	OR	AND	Deadlock	No
15	AND	OR	AND	OR	Multiple instances	No
16	AND	OR	AND	AND	Multiple instances	No

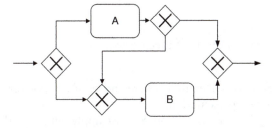

Figure 6.11 An example process

also true for a process that consists only of AND splits and AND joins in any manner? Try to justify your answer.

Exercise 11: Consider the improper nesting example of Figure 6.12 which is similar in structure to Figure 6.10, but here all the split and join nodes are AND connectors. Is this process well-behaved? Can you find an equivalent structured representation for it?

Next, we shall see that there are some special unstructured patterns and processes whose structured equivalents exist.

More Complex Nesting Patterns

As another example of unstructured-to-structured mapping, consider Figure 6.13. In this example, both XOR and AND control flow structures are present. The process with an overlapping structure in Figure 6.13 is clearly unstructured. An overlapping structure is one that exhibits vertical (or horizontal) symmetry, and there are symmetric crossover

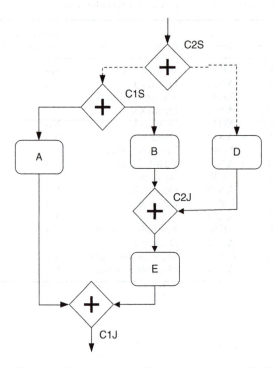

Figure 6.12 An example of improper nesting with AND connectors

paths among its components. However, we will analyze it here and see if it is possible to convert it into an equivalent structured representation.

Figure 6.13 is an example of a $(s, j)^l_1\{(u, v), (x, y)\}$ process. We apply our method to analyze this workflow by finding all paths between an AND split ($C2S$ or $C2S'$) and the corresponding AND join ($C2J$) nodes. Next, we find combinations where all paths within a combination are in parallel with each other, and exclude the other combinations of paths. Obviously, DI and GJ, and FI and EJ are two pairs of *exclusive* paths, and can be eliminated. However, there are two other combinations with two *parallel* paths in each. These are shown along with the final structured mapping in Figure 6.14. Hence, an equivalent structured representation does indeed exist.

Exercise 12: If we modify Figure 6.13 such that there are three overlapping patterns instead of two, then does a structured representation still exist? If so, show it and explain the general principle that can be applied here for converting the unstructured process to a structured one.

Exercise 13: Figure 6.15 shows another unstructured process. How many execution paths are there in this process? Is it sound? Justify your answer.

Next, we shall describe a formal approach for checking correctness of a process. It is based on mathematical programming and the material is slightly advanced. However, you can skip this section without loss of continuity.

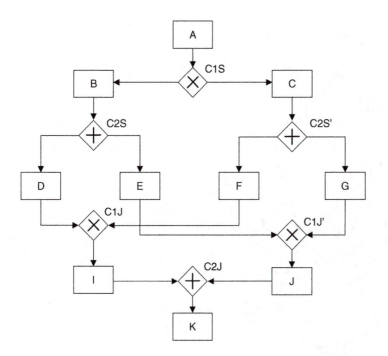

Figure 6.13 An overlapping structure

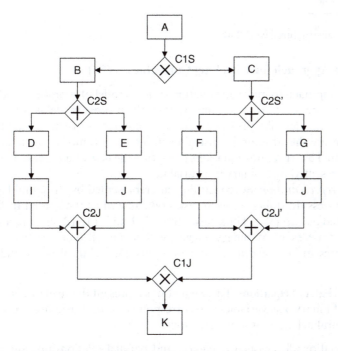

Figure 6.14 An equivalent structured representation for the process in Figure 6.13

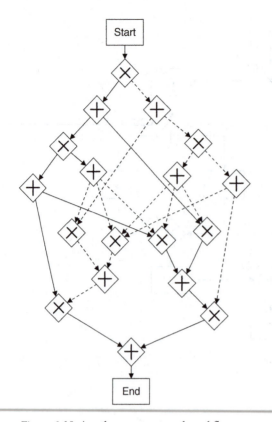

Figure 6.15 Another unstructured workflow

A Formal Verification Approach for Checking Correctness (***)

Here, we will dicuss an approach to make an equation system model of a process model and then show how it can be solved to determine whether the process model is correct. The basic idea is that we can describe the full process model in terms of structural balance equations that capture the structural constraints in the process model. Structural constraints are represented by structural equations to capture the flow of a process. Each node in a process is represented by a binary 0–1 variable.

Structural constraint representation. SC constraints are represented by structural balance equations of a process. In doing so, each task node as well as the special tasks, start and end, are treated as variables. Thus, task "Start," "End," T1, T2, etc. are also variable names. These variables are all binary integers with a value 1 to denote that the corresponding task is present in an execution path or an instance of the process, and 0 to denote it is absent.

Definition 4: **Structural balance equations**. These equations represent the structural relationships among a set of binary task variables that correspond to actual tasks in a process and describe the structural behavior of a process model.

For example, the equations for sequence, choice, and parallel relationships among tasks are shown in Figure 6.16.

Structure	Representation	Constraint equation
Sequence	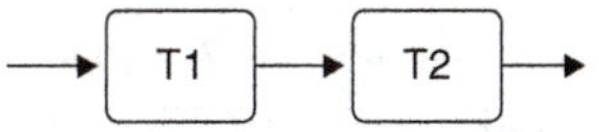 T1 → T2	$T2 = T1;$
Choice-split	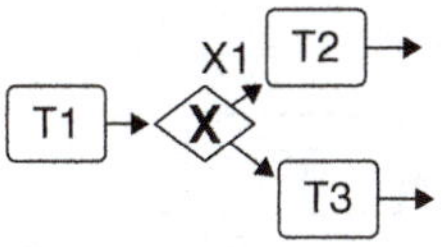 T1 → X → X1 T2 / T3	$X1 \leq T2 + T3;$ $X1 \geq T2; X1 \geq T3;$
Choice-join	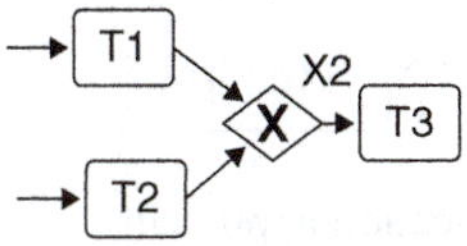 T1 / T2 → X → X2 T3	$X2 \leq T1 + T2;$ $X2 \geq T1; X2 \geq T2;$ $T1 + T2 \leq 1$
Parallel-split	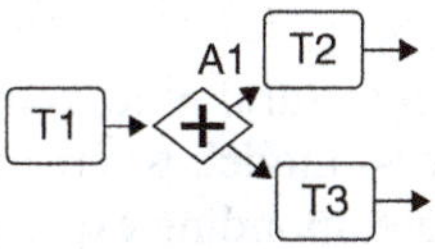 T1 → + → A1 T2 / T3	$A1 \geq T2 + T3 - 1;$ $A1 \leq T2; A1 \leq T3;$
Parallel-join	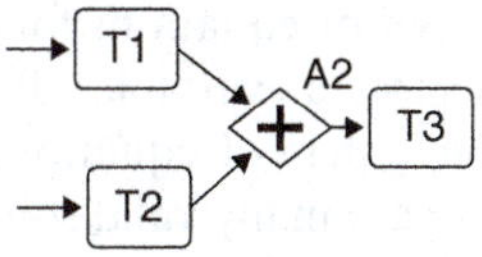 T1 / T2 → + → A2 T3	$A2 \geq T1 + T2 - 1;$ $A2 \leq T1; A2 \leq T2;$

Figure 6.16 Structural balance equations for process modeling structures

Definition 5: A **complete structural process model** is one that includes:

- one equation that captures the link of each task Ti (or connector Xi, Ai) to its preceding task(s) and/or connector(s) unless Ti is the first task in the process; and
- one equation that captures the link of each task Ti (or connector Xi, Ai) to its succeeding task(s) and/or connector(s) unless Ti is the last task in the process.

Exercise 14: Check if the equations in Figure 6.16 represent the behavior of each structure correctly. Explain your answer. You can create all possible scenarios of execution paths and check if the equations are correct for all scenarios.

Definition 6: A solution of a structural process model is of the form:

$\forall$ Ti $\in$ T, Ti $= 0$ or 1,
$\forall$ Xi $\in$ X, Xi $= 0$ or 1, and
$\forall$ Ai $\in$ A, Ai $= 0$ or 1

Such a solution identifies the tasks that are included in an instance (i.e. the corresponding Ti $= 1$) and the associated X and A (i.e. the corresponding Xi or Ai $= 1$) connectors. Thus, for a choice split node if T1 $= 1$, then T2 $+$ T3 $= 1$; however, if T1 $= 0$, then they must both be 0.

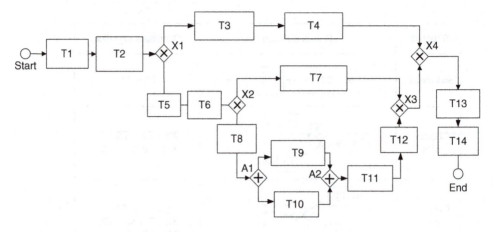

Figure 6.17 A process model to illustrate the verification approach

Definition 7: A **correct solution** of a complete structural process model is one that consists of a valid executable instance of the process model, where each connector that is part of the solution behaves according to its corresponding expression in Figure 6.16.

By applying this approach, we can create a set of equations for a process model that consists of tasks, and AND and XOR connectors as variables. If we assign a value of 1 to the first task in the process and solve the system of equations, we can find a valid solution for a correct process. In general, there are many valid solutions.

Example 2: Now, let us illustrate this approach with an example. Figure 6.17 shows a process diagram in BPMN syntax. The corresponding 0-1 integer optimization formulation for this process model is shown in Figure 6.18 after simplifying the general constraints in Figure 6.16. This formulation consists of an objective function and a set of constraints. By setting the value of the start node to 1 and posing an objective to maximize the value of the "End" node, we are checking if a valid solution exists. If it does, then an optimization program will produce a value of 1 to indicate that this node is activated and produce suitable (0 or 1) values for other nodes to indicate whether they are active or not. A solution of 0 would indicate that the formulation is incorrect and we must check it.

Now we can solve this formulation using an optimization tool like CPLEX from IBM (or open source optimizer LPSolve) and obtain a solution as follows:

T1, T2, T3, T4, T13, T14, X1, X4 ,'End' = 1; all other variables are 0.

This solution tells us what tasks appear in a valid instance of the process. Once we know the tasks, then we can easily determine the exact execution path of the process instance that corresponds to the solution. You may like to verify that this is indeed a valid instance. Now, to check, say, if a solution exists that includes task T7, then we may add a constraint "T7 = 1" to the formulation of Figure 6.18. By adding this constraint, we are forcing a solution that produces an instance that includes T7 (if one exists). On solving the revised formulation we obtain a solution as follows:

T1, T2, T5–T7, T13, T14, X1–X4, 'End' = 1; all other variables are 0.

```
                    Maximize 'End'
    Such that:

    Start. Start = 1;          S9. X2 = T7 + T8;
    S1. T1 = Start;            S10. A1 = T8; T9 = A1; T10 = A1;
    S2. T2 = T1;               S11. T9 + T10 = 2*A2
    S3. X1 = T2;               S12. T11 = A2;
    S4. X1 = T3 + T5;          S13. T12 = T11;
    S5. T4 = T3;               S14. X3 = T7 + T12;
    S6. T5 = X1;               S15. X4 = T4 + X3;
    S7. T6 = T5;               S16. T13 = X4;
    S8. X2 = T6;               S17. T14 = T13;
```

Figure 6.18 A formulation for the process model in Figure 6.17

Table 6.2 Additional structural constraints

Constraint	Meaning	Formal specification
Mandatory (Ti)	Task Ti must be executed.	$Ti = 1$
Prohibited (Ti)	Task Ti must *not* to be executed.	$Ti = 0$
Co-exist (Ti, Tj)	Both or none of Ti and Tj are executed.	$Ti = Tj$
Choice ($T1, T2, \ldots, Tn, m$)	Exactly m of $T1, T2, \ldots, Tn$ should be executed.	$T1 + T2 + \cdots + Tn = m$
Exclusion (Ti, Tj)	At most one of Ti or Tj can be executed.	$Ti + Tj \leq 1$

Notice that this is also a valid instance of the process in Figure 6.17. In this way, by forcing a node(s) to appear by adding a constraint, we can check to ensure that every node in the model does appear in some solution instance. If a solution is not found, then it means that there is no valid solution that includes that node(s). Such a process is not sound. Recall from condition 3 of soundness (see Definition 1) that a sound process must not have any dead task.

In general, a user may add a variety of constraints to check for satisfaction of various conditions. Some standard types of constraints can be expressed as patterns, as described in Table 6.2.

Exercise 15: Make an optimization model like the one in Figure 6.18 for the example process shown in Figure 6.18. Solve it using a tool like CPlex or Solver. Try to produce several different instances of this process model and check for yourself if they are correct.

Verification in Data-Centric Approaches

So far we have only focused on the control flow of a process, disregarding the data flow that occurs between tasks. It is also important to check that our design is correct from a data flow perspective. The key idea here is that every task has the input data that is necessary for it to run. An application for a credit card or loan cannot be evaluated until the credit score for the applicant is available. Therefore, the task to determine the credit score must be completed before the evaluation can start. An opposite sequence in the control flow will not make sense. Hence, as a general rule, the control flow and the data flow must synchronize with each other in a consistent way. *If the control flow in a process by itself is correct but the data flow is not, such a process is clearly incorrect.*

The methods for preventing data flow errors are discussed next. They are discussed in the context of various data-centric methods we discussed in previous chapters. However, it is important to realize that they apply to all processes, and are widely applicable.

PDM (and Document-centric) methods. In these methods that are directly based on flows of data, it is important to prevent three types of errors in particular.

Missing data errors. This occurs when a data item that is required for further steps in a process was not generated by a previous step. Thus, in a mortgage loan application the social security number (SSN) of an applicant may have been omitted. This means that a credit report cannot be created and further processing of the application is stalled. Hence, it is important to check to make sure that each operation in a PDM has the correct inputs and outputs.

Redundant data. Data redundancies arise when there is excessive information, e.g. when all the data items that are available may not be necessary to carry out the process instance. For a mortgage loan application, we may have the driver's license of an applicant along with her SSN. However, both these data items are not needed for a credit report. This is not such a problem in general, except when there is a redundancy that leads to conflicting data values as we discuss in the next case.

Conflicting data. Data conflicts can arise when data becomes inconsistent. This could occur for various reasons. A user may be asked to fill two different forms for a loan application and the SSN she provides may not match in the two documents, perhaps simply from human error. This is a case of a mismatch. A price of an item on an online website catalog that is shown to the user may differ from its price in the ordering database because they may not have been updated. Sometimes a data field is derived from another data field. Say, the derived item $d3 = d1 + d2$. It may transpire that d1 is modified but d3 is not automatically updated. This would lead to an inconsistency as well.

In a PDM model, it is necessary to prevent these kinds of anomalies.

Example 3: Figure 6.19 shows a simple PDM model. Initially, two input attributes d1 (highest qualification) and d2 (years of experience) are sought from a candidate to

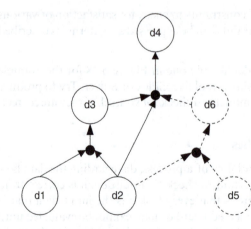

Figure 6.19 A simple PDM model to illustrate verification issues

determine d3 (eligibility of a candidate for an exam). Next, d3 and d2 are used to determine d4 (exam level). However, on deeper investigation it is realized that to determine exam level, another metric, d6 (that is derived from age and years of experience), is also needed. Hence, the PDM model is modified to include d6 as another input for d4 and, further, d5 (age) is also required from the applicant. The changes made to the initial model are shown in dotted lines. In this way, by focusing on data needs of tasks at different levels of the PDM model and tracking their dependencies it is possible to make a complete and correct model. Once a correct data model is obtained, it can be mapped into a control flow model.

Artifact-centric process models. These models must be verified by ensuring that:

- The logical data model is correct and captures all the artifacts and attributes
- The rules are correct, consistent and complete
- The invocation of services is correct.

Thus, one can make sure that the design indeed conforms to the actual requirements. Some formal techniques have been developed to ensure correctness also.

Ensure reachability. Every rule will be executed under some combination of conditions. This is hard to guarantee. Perhaps there is no VP in the company and all managers have experience of less than five years. Then the following rule may not fire and an application for under $500K may not be approved.

R7: Perform approval 1
Event:
Condition: if application *a* in state "ready for approval" and loan amount <500K
Action: invoke(perform_approval)
By: VP or (manager m where qual(m, years of experience) > 5).

Deadlock Prevention. The execution should not reach a stage where it gets stuck and no further progress is made. This could happen for instance when Rule 1 causes Rule 2 to fire and vice versa. In this case the execution will simply bounce between two rules and not proceed further.

Termination. The execution of the rule set for a given artifact-centric application with a finite number of artifacts and stages should eventually terminate in a finite number of steps.

Verification Issues with Control Flow and Data

It is very important to understand the interactions between control and data flow. We shall give some illustrative examples and then discuss some lessons that can be learned from them.

Example 4: An online orders company Orders-R-Us has a process as follows. They receive two types of orders (prime and non-prime) on their website and then calculate a base price for the order. Next, the order is sent in parallel to shipping and accounting departments. The shipping department will pack it accordingly, depending upon whether it has to be shipped by two-day mail for prime and regular mail for non-prime orders. In parallel, the accounting department will calculate a discount for prime customers and perform an authorization check for non-prime customers. Non-prime customers are not entitled to a discount. Finally, the system will calculate a delivery date for non-prime customers and the package will be shipped by regular mail. On the other hand, for prime customers the system will optimize the route for two-day shipping.

The process diagram for this process is shown in Figure 6.20. If we check the control flow of this process in isolation, then we will notice that it is incorrect because the process

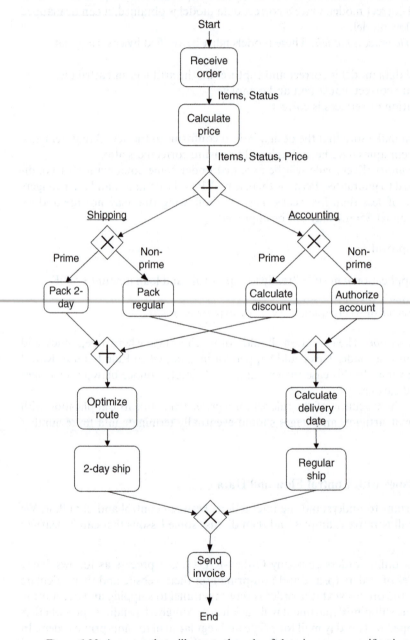

Figure 6.20 An example to illustrate the role of data in process verification

will deadlock along certain paths. However, if we consider the data flow as well, then we realize that this process is correct because the branches taken at the two XOR-split nodes will be consistent. This means that using the same data to make decisions at different XOR nodes can constrain the process in such a way that it behaves correctly.

Example 5: Travel-by-Us is an agency that makes travel bookings for international customers. This involves making flight bookings for customers and processing their visa applications. The visa processing can take two to four weeks and the traveler may not get a flight booking if she waits for the result of the visa application. Hence, the normal practice is to book the flights and send the visa application in parallel. If the visa is granted, then the agent issues the ticket for the booking; otherwise, the flight is cancelled. Figure 6.21 shows a possible design for this process.

Notice how, if we consider the control flow alone, the process is strictly incorrect. This is because in the case when the visa application is denied, only one branch reaches the

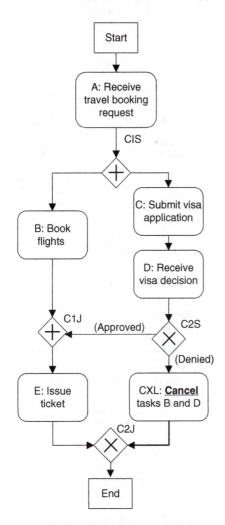

Figure 6.21 The travel agency process design

AND-Join node, and the process still terminates, leaving "unfinished work." But if we consider the semantics of the process carefully, we realize that the unfinished work – i.e. the travel bookings – have been compensated for, if the visa application is denied, by being cancelled. Thus, the behavior of the process is correct. Another alternative design for this process is shown in Figure 6.22(a).

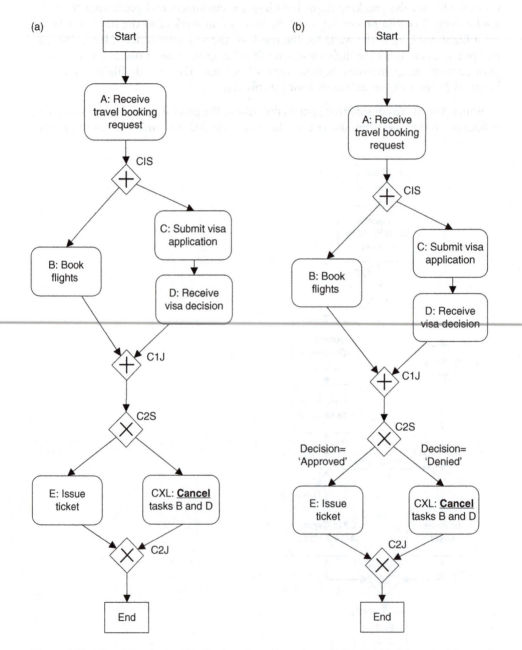

Figure 6.22 Alternative designs for the travel agent process of Figure 6.21: (a) control flow only; (b) control flow and data flow

Check for yourself that the revised process of Figure 6.22(a) is strictly correct semantically if we look at the control flow alone. There is one structured AND pattern followed by a structured XOR pattern. However, if you enumerate the execution paths through this process, you will realize that there is one valid path that might not make semantic sense:

Submit visa application – Receive decision – Issue ticket

The problem in this path, clearly, is that we would like to get the ticket issued *only if* the visa decision is positive. Therefore, we should prevent the path where the visa decision is negative and the ticket is still issued from arising since this scenario does not make any sense. The way to correct this problem is to simply add the decision condition on the XOR-split node as shown in Figure 6.22(b). Here, the data produced by a previous activity, i.e. the decision ("approved" or "denied") is used to constrain the control flow. This shows the importance of considering the data flow and control flow in conjunction.

Chapter Summary

In this chapter, we first examined techniques for verification of control flows in a process applying concepts likes soundness, deadlocks, livelocks, and multiple instances. We also described a formal algorithm for verification and illustrated it with examples. We also discussed techniques for verification of process models based on PDM and artifact-centric models, and covered verification considerations that arise when the control flow and data flow interact in a model. In particular, we highlighted the importance of analyzing a process in terms of both control and data flow to be sure that it is indeed correct.

In an early work by Kiepuszewski et al. [9], a restrictive group of workflows were defined as structured workflows, which never lead to structural flaws. The possibility of mapping an unstructured workflow to a structured one through equivalence preserving transformations was also explored through examples. A graph reduction technique is proposed by Sadiq et al. [17]. This technique can detect structural conflicts through a reduction process, but it gives no details about the causes of these conflicts, and, therefore, does not provide aid for further improvement. Later, these efforts were extended by Liu and Kumar [13], who developed a more general framework to describe and understand structured workflows. Much of our discussion in this chapter is based on that work. Structured process models are appealing because they are easier to comprehend and less error-prone than unstructured ones, as shown by an empirical study [11].

Woflan [21] is a verification tool from the University of Eindhoven. A lot of information about this tool is available on the Woflan home page [22], from where it can also be downloaded. Woflan uses standard Petri net-based analysis techniques. However, the analysis results are presented in such a manner that end users can understand the output of Woflan. There are three parts: parser, analysis routines, and user interface. A Petri net which models a workflow process definition is called a workflow net (WF net). Woflan verifies if, in fact, the process corresponds to a workflow net and it also checks for the soundness property. If the process is not sound, then Woflan produces diagnoses. The Woflan diagnostics are related to boundedness, potential deadlocking scenarios, and coverability property of the Petri net. However, Woflan cannot accept processes modeled in BPMN or other business languages. Dijkman et al. [5] have developed a technique to convert BPMN models into Petri nets and perform semantic analysis on them. Techniques to diagnose common errors that occur in real-world industrial processes along with empirical results are described by Roy et al. [16].

RPST (Refined process structure tree) was introduced by Vanhatalo et al. [20]. It produces a fine-grained decomposition of a process model by parsing it. The authors exploit the notion of a fragment as a connected single-entry, single-exit (SESE) structure that has exactly one entry and one exit node. An RPST is a tree of the canonical fragments of a process model, i.e. trivial, polygon, bond, and rigid. An RPST can be computed in linear time. Region trees [8] impose a hierarchy of regions as an overlay structure on a process model. They are built using region-growing rules and serve as a mechanism for analyzing and checking soundness of process models based on the idea of region-reducibility.

In a subsequent work, Polyvyanyy et al. [14] show the conditions under which an acyclic BPMN process model can be converted into a structured form. Their characterization is based on the properties of the RPST of the process model. They have given an algorithm for converting a unstructured process to a structured equivalent, and also developed a tool called **bpstruct**. This tool may be accessed from the University of Tartu [1]. Another approach to convert BPMN unstructured process to a semi-structured process is proposed by Eshuis and Kumar [7]. This algorithm creates structured processes with dependency links and dummy tasks, hence they are called semi-structured.

The formal process verification approach based on an integer programming optimization model discussed earlier in this chapter is described in detail in [6], and the **Diagflow** tool that implements this algorithm is accessible at [3]. The **CPLEX** optimizer can be obtained from IBM [2] and the **LPSolve** is an open source program. There has also been work on weaker notions of correctness where strict soundness is sacrificed to allow greater flexibility in modeling. These ideas are based on *relaxed soundness* [4]; *lazy soundness* [15]; and *partial synchronization* [10]. However, these approaches have not gained much traction in the real world.

Verification of process models that describe both control flow and data are discussed by Sidorova et al. [18]. Methods for detecting and resolving data dependency constraint conflicts are developed in [19]. Lin and Sadiq [12] describe an approach to model data dependency constraints in a process and enforce them in a consistent and systematic way in a database system.

References

1. BPStruct—A Tool for Structuring BPMN Models. http://sep.cs.ut.ee/Main/Bpstruct.
2. CPLEX Optimizer. IBM Corporation. www-01.ibm.com/software/commerce/optimization/cplex-optimizer/.
3. Diagflow Tool. http://is.ieis.tue.nl/staff/heshuis/DiagFlow/.
4. J. Dehnert and P. Rittgen. Relaxed Soundness of Business Processes. CAiSE, *LNCS* 2068, Springer-Verlag Berlin, Heidelberg, pp. 157–170, 2001.
5. R. M. Dijkman, M. Dumas and C. Ouyang. Semantics and analysis of business process models in BPMN. *Information and Software Technology*, Vol. 50, No. 12, pp. 1281–1294, 2008.
6. R. Eshuis and A. Kumar. An integer programming based approach for verification and diagnosis of workflows. *Data & Knowledge Engineering*, Vol. 69, No. 8, pp. 816–835, 2010.
7. R. Eshuis and A. Kumar. Converting unstructured into semi-structured process models. *Data & Knowledge Engineering*, Vol. 101, pp. 43–61, 2016.

8. R. Hauser, M. Friess, J. M. Küster and J. Vanhatalo. An incremental approach to the analysis and transformation of workflows using region trees. *IEEE Transactions on Systems, Man, and Cybernetics*, Part C, Vol. 38, No. 3, pp. 347–359, 2008.

9. B. Kiepuszewski, A. H. M. Hofstede and C. Bussler. On Structured Workflow Modeling. In: B. Wangler, L. Bergman (eds) Proceedings CAiSE'2000. *LNCS*, Vol. 1789. Springer-Verlag, Berlin, Heidelberg.

10. A. Kumar, A. K. Sen, M. H. Sundari and A. Bagchi. Semantic notions of weakly correct AND/XOR business workflows based on partial synchronization. *IEEE SCC*, pp. 128–135, 2011.

11. R. Laue and J. Mendling. The impact of structuredness on error probability of process models, Information Systems Technology and its Applications (UNISCON). *Lecture Notes in Business Information Processing*, Vol. 5. Springer, Berlin, Heidelberg, pp. 585–590, 2008.

12. J. Y. C. Lin and S. W. Sadiq. A business process driven approach to manage data dependency constraints. *ICEIS*, 2010, pp. 326–339.

13. R. Liu and A. Kumar. An Analysis and Taxonomy of Unstructured Workflows. In: Third International Conference on Business Process Management (BPM 2005), Nancy, France. *Lecture Notes in Computer Science*, Vol. 3649, pp. 268–284 Springer-Verlag, Berlin, Heidelberg, 2005.

14. A. Polyvyanyy, L. G. Bañuelos and M. Dumas. Structuring acyclic process models. *Information Systems*, Vol. 37, No. 6, pp. 518–538, 2012.

15. F. Puhlmann and M. Weske. Investigations on Soundness Regarding Lazy Activities. In: S. Dustdar, J. L. Fiadeiro, A. P. Sheth (eds) *Proceedings of the 4th International Conference on Business Process Management (BPM'06)*. Springer-Verlag, Berlin, Heidelberg, pp. 145–160, 2006.

16. S. Roy, A. S. M. Sajeev and S. Sripathy. Diagnosing industrial business processes: early experiences. *FM*, pp. 703–771, 2014.

17. W. Sadiq and M. E. Orlowska. Analyzing process models using graph reduction techniques. *Information Systems*, Vol. 25, No. 2, pp. 117–134, 2000.

18. N. Sidorova, C. Stahl and N. Trčka. Soundness verification for conceptual workflow nets with data: early detection of errors with the most precision possible. *Information Systems*, Vol. 6, No. 7, pp. 1026–1043, 2011.

19. S. X. Sun, J. L. Zhao, J. F. Nunamaker and O. R. L. Sheng. Formulating the data-flow perspective for business process management. *Information Systems Research*, Vol. 17, No. 4, pp. 374–391, 2006.

20. J. Vanhatalo, H. Völzer and J. Koehler. The refined process structure tree. *Data & Knowledge Engineering*, Vol. 68, No. 9, pp. 793–818, 2009.

21. H. M. W. Verbeek, T. Basten and W. M. P. van der Aalst. Diagnosing workflow processes using Woflan. *The Computer Journal*, Vol. 44, No. 4, pp. 246–279, 2001.

22. Woflan Tool. www.win.tue.nl/woflan/doku.php.

7 Process Evaluation

Introduction

In this chapter, we shall discuss how to evaluate processes by applying various techniques. First, we explain several KPIs that can be used for understanding the performance of a process. Next, we show how basic queuing theory can be applied to analyze process performance, and the value of simulation as a tool for process analysis. Later, we discuss complexity metrics that measure how difficult a process is to describe. It is important to recognize that tasks in a process instance are performed by actors or resources that operate within a social context. Hence, we shall cover techniques for computing metrics that capture the nature of the interaction among actors in their social network. Finally, we turn to metrics for comparing how similar a process is to another process.

KPI – Key Performance Indicators

An important way to evaluate a process is by means of key performance indicators. These indicators can be used to evaluate a process in terms of *time, cost, quality, and flexibility*. Together, time, cost, quality, and flexibility constitute what is called the "Devil's Quadrangle," as we saw in Chapter 2. This comes from the fact that these objectives tend to conflict – in trying to improve one objective, we might hurt another one. For example, in trying to improve quality we may incur greater cost and the process may take longer to run.

Some KPIs for time are:

Process throughput time or flow time (average, minimum, maximum). This is a measure of how long an instance takes to complete in minutes (or hours or days).

Process throughput rate (average, minimum, maximum). This is a measure of the number of instances of a process that were handled in a unit of time, e.g. per hour, day, or week.

Process throughput rate per resource (average, minimum, maximum). This is a measure of the number of instances of a process that were handled in a unit of time by a resource, e.g. per hour day, or week.

Process instances (or cases) running late by more than 5 percent. It is important to track the number (and percentage) of instances that are running late. This is an important metric from the viewpoint of customer satisfaction. Late running process instances should be reported to a responsible person, like the process owner, on a daily basis. Additional information, like tasks of the instance that have been delayed and the resources associated with the tasks, is also useful.

Average delay for instances that are late. This measure can give us an idea about the length of delay of instances. If this value is large over several reporting periods, then some action may be necessary. Ultimately, management must decide what kinds of delays are acceptable. Some delays are naturally to be expected during rush periods, e.g. car rental lines become longer around Thanksgiving and Christmas time when more people travel.

Further, splitting the *total service time* experienced by a customer for a service into *waiting time* and *working time* is helpful, i.e.

Total service time = waiting time + working time

This can help to identify whether the delays are arising due to shortage of resources or from longer working times. The latter could occur from a variety of factors, such as higher complexity of cases, new staff being trained, etc. It is also important to compare the value of these metrics in the current period (e.g. day, week, month, quarter, year) with the same period historically. So, the current quarter may be compared against the same quarter in the previous year, the current month against the corresponding month in the previous quarter, and so on.

The minimum and maximum values of the various measures help to identify *outliers*. Outliers can often serve as "red flags" or alerts. When an instance finishes very quickly or takes an inordinately long time, it can alert a manager to some abnormal situation. Both scenarios raise cause for concern, and a manager ought to look into such cases carefully. An instance that finishes very quickly may represent incomplete or poor quality of service, while one that takes much longer than expected may underline both service and quality issues.

The **cost** of running a process instance is also an important consideration in evaluating a process. A major component of cost is the amount of time devoted by various employees in serving each customer. A simple way to calculate the direct cost is by using the hourly rate of each actor involved in the process instance and multiplying that by their time spent on the instance in hours, and summing it over all actors who worked on the instance. There are indirect costs also in every organization that must be accounted for separately by suitable cost allocation. Naturally, if a process can be partially or fully automated, then the amount of actor time needed is reduced and the cost will decrease. This is why companies are trying hard to automate their processes, especially those parts of the processes that are of a routine nature.

Another way to lower costs is by outsourcing or offshoring some tasks. Thus, for a loan approval process it is likely that a property appraisal being done in-house within a lending company or bank may be outsourced to a third party to cut down costs. Sometimes, merging two tasks into one can make the process more efficient, as we saw in Chapter 2.

Other KPIs relate to *revenue improvement, quality*, and *customer satisfaction*. The revenue KPI is the fee charged per process instance. A bank charges fees for various types of products and services, such as mortgage processing, funds transfer, underwriting a loan, originating a letter of credit, etc.

A *quality-related KPI* is the *number of errors* that occur in a process for every 1000 instances. This can be calculated from looking at historical logs. If an incorrect value is entered into the system while processing a customer loan application (say, a salary of $100,000 instead of $200,000), it could result in the loan application being denied. Later, when the error is discovered, the application will have to be processed all over again. This will cause delay in processing and also hurt both quality and customer satisfaction. KPIs can be tracked through a dashboard, as shown in Figure 7.1. This dashboard shows the status of mortgage applications. There are 72 instances in progress, of which 5 are overdue, 1 is at risk and 66 are on track. It also shows that the average instance duration is 2 hours and 14 minutes. In addition, it also gives the turnover rate of instances by day in a graph below. Through this interface, a manager can explore further and get more information about the instances that are overdue and at risk.

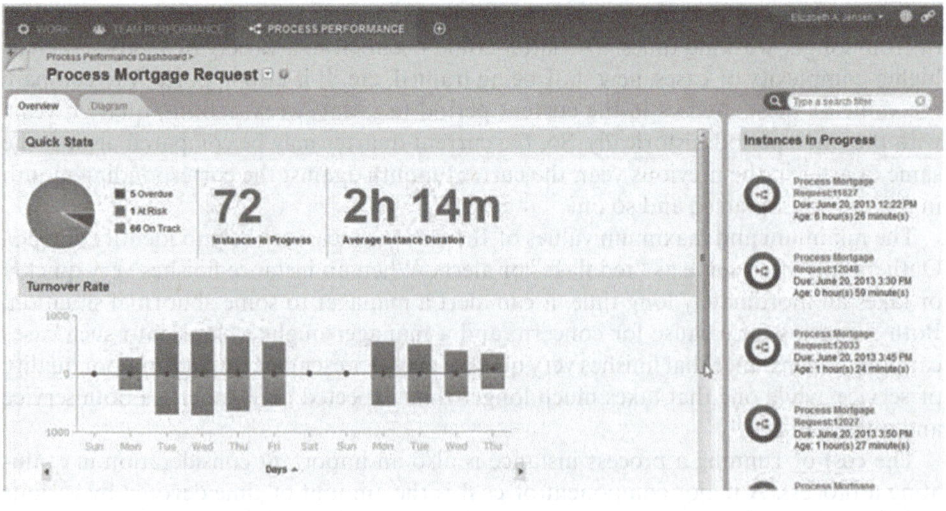

Figure 7.1 A KPI dashboard

Source: www.ibm.com/developerworks/bpm/bpmjournal/1506_harris/1506_harris-trs.html.

Queuing Analysis

Overview

The approaches that may be used to analyze a process are both analytical and simulation based. A common analytical approach for understanding the behavior of service times is queuing theory. This theory assumes a certain arrival rate, and also a service time distribution pattern of process instances in a service provider organization, e.g. customers arriving at a bank ATM machine or a supermarket checkout counter. Figure 7.2 shows a queue where customers arrive at the rate of λ per hour, and there is one server with a service rate of μ per hour. An "M/M/1" queue is one where the arrival times (the first M in the expression) are distributed following a "memoryless" *Markovian process* and the service times (the second M in the expression) are also similarly distributed. This arrival pattern is also said to represent a *Poisson distribution*. The '1' in the expression denotes that there is one server (or service station) available. An M/M/n queue denotes a service where there are *n* service stations and the customers (or process instances) may go to the first available server. An M/G/1 distribution is one where the arrivals follow a Poisson distribution but the service times follow a general distribution that indicates an arbitrary probability distribution. If the latter is a normal distribution, it can be characterized by the mean service time and its variance. Queues also have a *service order* or *service discipline* such as First-come-first-serve (FCFS), Last-come-first-serve (LCFS), Last-come-first-serve preempt resume (LCFS-PR), etc. However, here we shall assume the service discipline is FCFS that is most common.

M/M/1 Models

The analysis for M/M/1 queues is as follows. First, we define the *utilization* or *traffic intensity* (ρ) as the ratio of the arrival rate (λ) to the service rate (μ) as:

$$\rho = \frac{\lambda}{\mu}$$

It is important to note that ρ must be less than 1. If not, then the queue at the service facility will build indefinitely. The probability that at any given time there will be *n* customers in the system is given by $p_n = \rho(1 - \rho)^n$.

Next, the mean number of customers in the system is expressed as:

$$N = \frac{\rho}{1 - \rho}$$

The mean number of customers in the queue N_q is given by $N - \rho = \frac{\lambda^2}{\mu(\mu - \lambda)}$

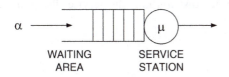

$$\alpha \longrightarrow \boxed{\text{|||||}} \mu \longrightarrow$$

WAITING AREA   SERVICE STATION

Figure 7.2 A task in a process can be modeled as a queue

From the above formulas, it is clear that if ρ is close to 1, then N will be very large. Finally, the total time for a customer in the system (waiting time + service time) on average is expressed as:

$$T = \frac{1}{\mu - \lambda}$$

Again, it is evident that if the arrival rate approaches the service rate, then the total time for a customer in the system becomes very large. A typical value for ρ is about 60 to 70 percent for offering good service. Now, the waiting time in the queue T_q is given by:

$$T - \text{average service time} = \frac{1}{\mu - \lambda} - \frac{1}{\mu} = \frac{\lambda}{\mu(\mu - \lambda)}$$

Example 1: Consider a service station where applications for insurance claims are received. Note the "service station" is used figuratively to represent a face-to-face service at an office or phone service. Assume that the arrival rate for this service is 10 customers per hour (i.e. one every 6 minutes) and the service rate is 15 customers per hour (i.e. 4 minutes per customer). If both the arrival and the service durations follow a Poisson distribution, then we can apply the formulas above. Thus,

Utilization, $\rho = 10/15 = 0.67$

$$\text{Mean number of customers} = \frac{\rho}{1 - \rho} = 2$$

Total time in the system, $T = 1/5$ hours $= 12$ minutes. This includes the average service time of four minutes and an average waiting time of eight minutes.

Markov distributions are commonly used because they are often quite accurate in modeling various real-world phenomena and are easy to compute. General distributions are not always easy to analyze because they do not have closed-form solutions. In many cases, simulation has to be applied, as we shall discuss below. We shall also give references to Queuing theory so you can look up results for various types of queues yourself.

Little's Law

Another useful result from Queuing theory is called Little's Law. It says that:

$$N = \lambda \cdot T$$

where, N is the long-term average number of customers in a system.

The nice feature of Little's Law is that it is a general law that is not influenced by the arrival process distribution, the service distribution, the service discipline, or anything else.

Sequential Queues

A sequential process can be thought of as a network of *s service stations in series*. If we model each station as an M/M/1 queue, then each individual queue can be analyzed

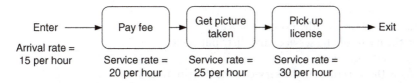

Figure 7.3 Three service stations in series at a DMV office

independently of other queues with an arrival rate λ. Further, if μ_i is the service rate for the ith server, then:

Utilization of ith server $\rho_i = \lambda/\mu_i$

Now, the probability of n_i jobs in the ith queue $= (1 - \rho_i) \cdot \rho_i^{ni}$

Hence, the joint probability of queue lengths is:

$$P(n_1, n_2, n_3, \ldots, n_M) = (1 - \rho_1)\rho_1^{n_1}(1 - \rho_2)\rho_2^{n_2}(1 - \rho_3)\rho_3^{n_3}\ldots(1 - \rho_M)\rho_M^{n_M}$$
$$= p_1(n_1)p_2(n_2)p_3(n_3)\ldots p_M(n_M)$$

Notice that this joint probability of queue length is the product of the individual probabilities at each queue.

Moreover, the average number of jobs in the system

$$= \text{Number of jobs at queue } 1 + \text{Number of jobs at queue } 2$$
$$+ \cdots + \text{Number of jobs at queue } s$$
$$= \frac{\rho_1}{1 - \sigma_1} + \frac{\rho_2}{1 - \rho_2} + \cdots + \frac{\rho_s}{1 - \rho_s}$$

Example 2: At a department of motor vehicles (DMV) facility, to renew a license a customer first queues up in the line to pay the renewal fee. Then she moves to a second line to get her photograph taken. Finally, she moves to the third line for picking up her license. The arrival rate of customers is 15 per hour and the service rates are, respectively, 20, 25 and 30 per hour at the three stations. Figure 7.3 shows the workflow of this process.

It should be noted that treating each service station in series as a M/M/1 queue is an approximation because the distribution of the traffic inflow into a subsequent service station may be shaped by the service rate of the previous queues. By applying the formula above, we can determine the total number of customers in this system.

Exercise 1: Calculate the average service time and waiting time at each station in Figure 7.3. What is the total length of time a customer can expect to spend on a trip to the DMV?

Analysis of M/G/1 Queues

If the arrivals follow a Markovian distribution, but service times follow a general distribution, the mean queue length N_q is given by the following formula:

$$N_q = \rho + \frac{\rho^2 + \lambda^2 Var(S)}{2(1 - \rho)}$$

Where

- λ is the arrival time of the Poisson process
- $1/\mu$ is the mean of the service time distribution S
- $\rho = \lambda/\mu$ is the utilization
- *Var(S)* is the variance of the service time distribution S.

For the mean queue length to remain finite, it is necessary that $\rho < 1$ as otherwise jobs arrive faster than they leave the queue.

Now, if we write T for the mean total time a customer spends in the system, then $T = W + \mu^{-1}$ where W is the mean waiting time (time spent in the queue waiting for service) and μ is the service rate. Now, applying Little's Law, we can derive W as:

$$W = \frac{\rho + \lambda\mu \, Var(S)}{2(\mu - \lambda)} + \mu^{-1}$$

Finally, we can express mean waiting time simply as:

$$W = \frac{N_q}{\lambda} = \frac{\rho + \lambda\mu \, Var(S)}{2(\mu - \lambda)}$$

Simulation

An alternative way to model processes is by simulation. Simulation is a systematic methodology to mimic the behavior of a process or a scenario by means of a model. By simulating a business process or a workflow using realistic parameters, we can expect to predict somewhat approximately how it will perform when the process is actually implemented in our organization. It cannot be exact because a model can never capture the minute details, and complexities and vagaries of the real-world situation. Nonetheless, the simulation exercise based on a reasonably accurate model can help us to determine the number of actors we should have at various service stations, the likely service times and waiting times, cost of the operation, etc. In this way, a simulation model can be used to answer a variety of questions about a current process or a proposed modification to an existing process. Some kinds of questions that can be posed are:

How will the proposed modification affect the KPIs of the current process?
What will be the effect of the changes on the resource utilization?
Will the changes lead to any bottlenecks?
How and where should resources be reallocated to accommodate the changes?
What kinds of savings in time, cost, etc. can we expect from making the changes?

By running a simulation, one can increase one's level of confidence and also assure others in the organization that the proposed changes are indeed reasonable.

The basic idea is to create a software model of a process model, and simulate actual running instances of the process. In the simulation, the user must specify values of important parameters like arrival rate, service rates for each task or service station, resource requirements, available resources and their capabilities, hourly costs, etc. Then it is possible to run a simulation for a certain length of time and produce results for various KPIs or metrics of interest. The best way of gaining an appreciation of simulation is by studying how a simulation tool works. Next, we shall describe the BIMP simulation tool.

BIMP Process Simulation Tool

BIMP is a web-based tool that can read a BPMN model file created, say, in Signavio. Then you can specify certain parameter values related to the service time of each task and the availability of resources. Finally, you can run the model for a certain number of process instances and get the results of the simulation.

This tool allows you to simulate complex real-world business processes in large-scale scenarios. It was designed and implemented by Marlon Dumas and his colleagues at the University of Tartu. The BIMP simulator is a Google code project. The prototypes are available as part of the modeling platform of the BPM Academic Initiative. The main screen of the BIMP simulator is shown in Figure 7.4, organized into sections. In the top section, a user can specify the inter-arrival time between incidents in terms of one of the following distributions: *Fixed, Normal, Exponential, Uniform, Triangular, Log-Normal, Gamma* and *Histogram.* Of course, for the chosen distribution, the corresponding parameter values are also provided. A user can specify the

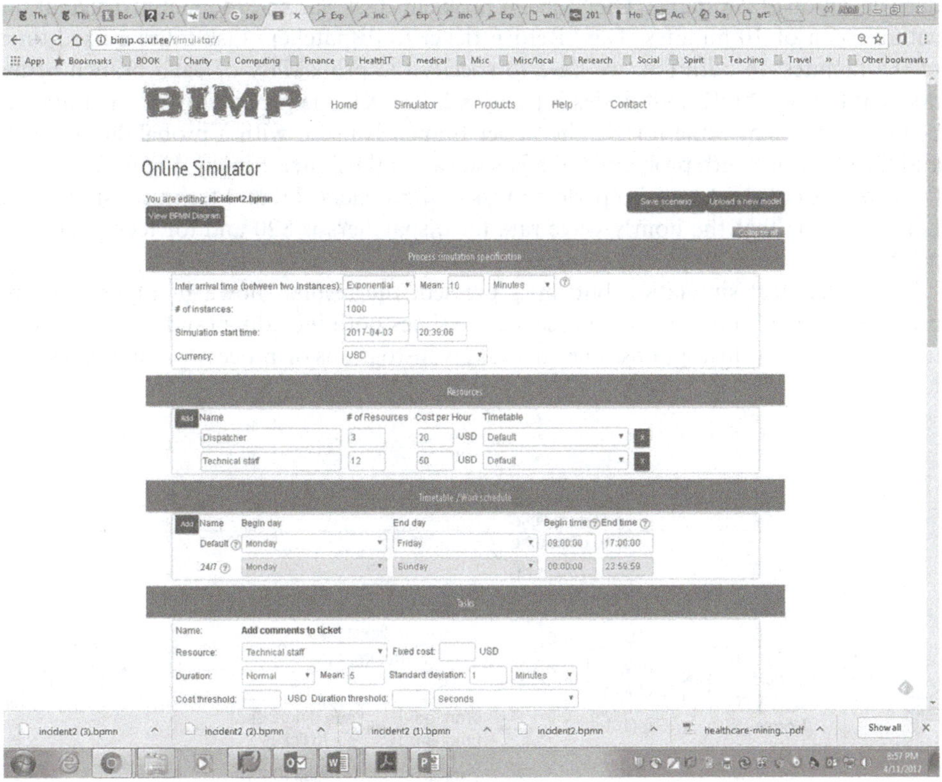

Figure 7.4 The main interface of BIMP simulator

number of instances to be simulated, a start time, and a currency in the top section of the screen.

In the next section, one can specify the types of resources, the number of resources of each type available and their hourly wage rate. It is also possible to define a work timetable or schedule. By default, the work timetable is Monday through Friday, from 9 a.m. to 5 p.m. The tasks section allows a user to provide some basic information for each task (only one task is shown in Figure 7.4 as an example), which consists of the distribution pattern for the task duration and its parameter values. Optionally, it is also possible to specify a fixed cost for a task, a cost threshold and a duration threshold. The last section for gateways requires a user to specify the probabilities of each outgoing path of the XOR gateway being taken as shown.

Example 3:   We shall illustrate this tool with the example process shown in Figure 7.5 to describe a help desk or an incident resolution facility to resolve software problems and issues. In this process, a ticket is received by a dispatcher (D) who assigns it to a technical staff (TS) member for review. Based on her understanding of the issue, she may add some quick comments and then pass it on to another technician (via the dispatcher). Alternatively, she may decide to work on the problem herself, add diagnostic notes pertaining to what she did, and then pass it on to another resource (via the dispatcher).

Figure 7.5 also shows the distributions of service times of various tasks. Thus, the "Assign incident task" has a normal distribution with a mean of 5 minutes and standard deviation of 2 minutes. The "Review problem" task has an exponential distribution with a mean of 10 minutes. The "Return ticket to dispatcher" task takes a fixed time of 0.5 minutes. In addition, we have to specify the probability of each branch being taken at the two XOR-split nodes X1 and X2. For X1, the probability of each branch being taken is 0.5, while for X2 the upper branch is taken with a probability of 0.75 and the lower one with probability 0.25 as shown in the figure. Finally, Figure 7.5 shows the two types of workers who perform tasks: dispatchers (D) and technical staff (TS). Let us assume that the hourly wage rate for dispatchers is $20 and for technical staff it is $50.

When the start simulation button is pressed, the results shown in Figure 7.6 are produced. The results show the process cycle times both including (and excluding) off-timetable hours as histograms. They also show histograms of process waiting times and

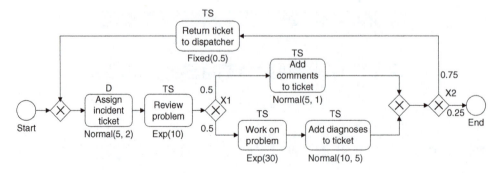

Figure 7.5 An incident resolution process

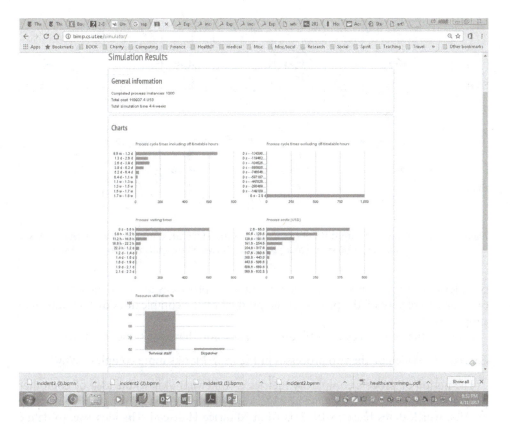

Figure 7.6 The results produced by BIMP simulator

process costs. In addition, the resource utilizations are also provided along with more detailed instance- and activity-level statistics.

This example illustrates how a simulation tool can provide valuable information that can help the management of an organization to make the right business decisions.

Exercise 2: Recreate the simulation we just described yourself. Then vary the number of dispatchers from 2 to 4 and the number of technical staff from 10 to 12 in your model and rerun the simulation each time. How does this affect the process cycle time and waiting time? Based on the results, discuss how you would change the resource allocation for this process to get better results.

Process Complexity Metrics

The next set of metrics we shall discuss relates to the complexity of a process. *Workflow complexity* is defined as the degree of difficulty or cognitive effort involved in describing, analyzing, and understanding a process. It can be characterized in terms of: the number of tasks; the intricacies of connections between them; and the types of structures such as choice, parallel, and loop. One intuitive idea of complexity is that it is related to the number of different pathways that can arise in a process since each pathway adds more

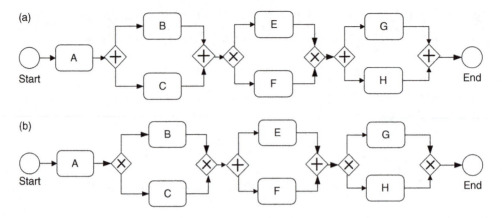

Figure 7.7 Two processes with different kinds of control structures: (a) a process with two AND splits and one XOR split; (b) a process with two XOR splits and one AND split

complexity to the process. Also, when multiple subprocesses are in sequence in a process, the complexity of the process is the product of the complexities of the individual subprocesses.

Examine the two processes in Figure 7.7. They both have the same set of activities.

Exercise 3: Which of the two processes in Figure 7.7 looks more complex? Why?

The notion of process complexity metrics is somewhat akin to the idea of computer program complexity metrics. One notable work in the context of program complexity metrics, which dates back to 1977, is from Maurice Halstead. His idea was to define metrics like program length, volume, and difficulty of coding in terms of the number of operands (e.g. different variables and constants used in a program) and operators that correspond to various operations like +, −, =, etc. The formulas for computing the metrics were based on both the unique and total counts of the operators and operands. Although business processes are also programs, in that they describe procedures for performing a series of related activities, the analogy is not a very direct one. Hence, new methods like the ones we shall discuss next are needed to evaluate the complexity of a process.

A very simple metric for computing the process complexity is called *NOAC, or the number of activities and control-flow elements in a process*. Thus, given a process, we can simply add up all the activities and the control flow structures in it together. In doing so, a split-join pair is counted only once. The problem with this metric is that it does not make any distinction between different activities and types of structures. Another metric is called the McCabe's cyclometric complexity (MCC) metric. In this metric, the complexity of individual control flow structures is computed, and then these values are added together.

Complexity of Control Flow Structures

A more accurate metric was developed by taking into account the different levels of complexity of the various control flow structures by Cardoso and his colleagues.

Their approach in devising this metric is based on analyzing the complexity of each structure separately. They argue that certain structures will create more "mental states" and hence are more complex than other structures. Next, we shall describe how this approach is used to calculate the complexity of each structure.

AND-split control flow complexity: For an AND-split structure, the complexity is simply 1 because all outgoing paths are taken at the split-node s.

$$CFC\text{-}AND\text{-}split(s) = 1$$

XOR-split (and Loops) control flow complexity: For an XOR-split structure, the complexity is computed as the fan-out of (i.e. the number of branches emanating from) the structure. Thus, the function CFC-XOR-split(s) computes the control flow complexity of an XOR-split node *s* as follows:

$$CFC\text{-}XOR\text{-}Split(s) = fan\text{-}out(s)$$

The rationale for this expression is that the process designer must consider each of the alternative paths separately in determining the correct design. Loops are also treated like XOR splits because they are created by using an XOR-split structure. In general, a loop may occur any number of times (theoretically infinite) and this can create a very large number of unique traces or paths, but in practice the number of repetitions is small.

OR split control flow complexity: The OR split control flow structure is the most complex one because *any combination of the outgoing branches* can be taken at the split node. Recall that this structure is modeled by a gateway in BPMN. The number of possible outgoing paths, then, is exponential in the fan-out of the split-node. Thus, a designer must consider the implications of all these combinations being pursued and ensure that the process design would still be correct. This also shows why using this structure with a fan-out of more than 2 is usually not advisable in view of its exponential complexity. The complexity of this structure is defined as:

$$CFC\text{-}OR\text{-}split(s) = 2^{fan\text{-}out(s)} - 1$$

Thus, the overall complexity of a process is obtained by adding the individual complexities of these three types of structures. As noted above, loops are treated like XOR structures for calculating complexity. Sequential structures are assumed to not add to the complexity metric.

Exercise 4: Figure 7.8 shows an online order process that we saw in Chapter 2. Calculate the complexity of this process by applying the NOAC and Carodoso metrics.

These metrics are approximate and should be taken with a grain of salt. They are more like rules of thumb that can provide some general idea for making rough comparisons across process models.

Social Network Analysis

A business process is a collection of tasks that work together to produce a goal. As we have mentioned before, the resources that perform different tasks for an instance

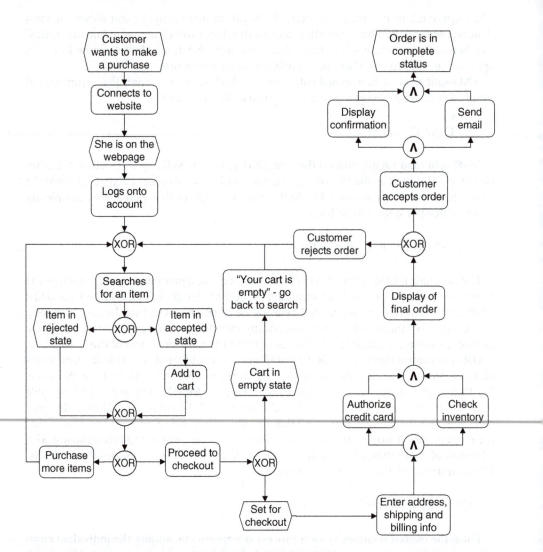

Figure 7.8 An example process to illustrate complexity calculation

should be suitably qualified. Moreover, they should work well together among themselves to lead to a better outcome. This is why an understanding of social network analysis methods is helpful for students of BPM.

Figure 7.9 shows an example of a social network of actors (or workers or resources). The nodes represent individual actors, and the edges show the distances between connected pairs of nodes. An edge from actor A (Ann) to actor B (Benn) indicates that A and B know each other or have had interactions with each other, say by working on the same process instance or case. Note that in general, the edges may also be directed (with arrows at the end), but if they are not directed as shown here it means they describe a two-way or symmetric relationship, i.e. if A knows B, then B knows A.

Next, we shall introduce and define a number of metrics that are used to analyze a social network. A network consists of *nodes*, and *edges* that connect a pair of nodes.

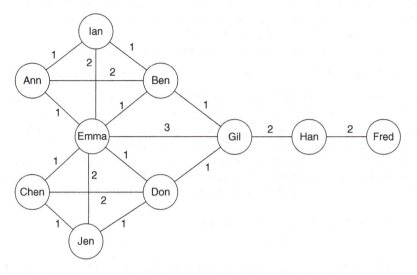

Figure 7.9 A conceptual graph representation of a social network

The *degree of a node* is given by the number of edges that are connected to it. We distinguish two types of metrics:

network-based metrics that measure features of the network or its sub-networks; and
local metrics which measure features of a particular node or edge in a network.

Network-based metrics include *size, density, cohesion,* etc. Typical local metrics include a number of node centrality measures, e.g. *node degree, betweenness* of a node, etc. Some metrics, e.g. closeness, can be defined both at the network level and local levels.

Next, we define some of these metrics more formally and illustrate them using Figure 7.9. Let us assume that we are given a network $G = (V, E, W)$ where V is the set of $|V|$ vertices (or nodes), E is the set of $|E|$ edges between a pair of vertices, and W is the weight of each edge, then:

Network Size is the total number of vertices in the network. The size of the network shown in Figure 7.9 is 10.

Density is defined as the ratio of the number of edges and the number of possible edges in the network, i.e. $\frac{2|E|}{|V|*(|V|-1)}$. The density of the network in Figure 7.9 is 0.38.

Closeness indicates how near a node is to all the others. We first compute all shortest paths between all node pairs in the network and calculate their average, i.e. $Avg_{i,j \in V}(d_{ij})$, where d_{ij} is the shortest path between a pair of vertices, say i and j. In Figure 7.9, the closeness of the network is 2.93. In a social network sense, closeness reflects how well an actor knows other actors.

Cohesion of network. This metric is defined as the minimum number of nodes needed to be removed from the network such that the network gets disconnected. The cohesion in Figure 7.9 is 1, as removing node "Gil" or "Han" will disconnect the network.

Clustering Coefficient (CC) measures the degree to which nodes in a graph tend to cluster together. If node v has k_v neighbors, then at most $k_v(k_v - 1)/2$ edges can exist among them. CC_v denotes the fraction of these edges that actually exist. Thus, CC_{Gil}

is calculated by first noting that Gil has four neighbors, Ben, Emma, Don, and Han. Among these four neighbors there can be a maximum of 6 links, but actually there are only 2 links among them. Hence, $CC_{\text{Gil}} = 2/6 = 0.33$.

CC is the average of CC_v over all nodes v, and in Figure 7.9, $CC = 0.672$.

Exercise 5. In Figure 7.9, find all the nodes that have a clustering coefficient of 1.

Hierarchy measures the degree to which the network approaches a perfect hierarchy, i.e. the degree to which all relations are unidirectional.

The degree of node "Emma" is 7 since it has 7 direct connections. *Betweenness of a node* measures the number of shortest paths that pass through the node. *Betweenness centrality of a node* is the number of shortest paths that pass through a node as a fraction of the total number of shortest paths that pass through all nodes. If there are N nodes in a graph, the Betweenness centrality of node N_i is calculated as:

$$\frac{\text{Number of shortest paths passing through node } N_i}{|V|(|V|-1)}$$

Where, $|V|$ is the number of vertices in the network (excluding N_i), and $|V|(|V|-1)$ is the total number of shortest paths between $|V|$ nodes. In the 10-node network in Figure 7.9, there are 28 (bidirectional) shortest paths that pass through Emma (and also Gil). Hence, each one has a Betweenness centrality of $28/72 = 0.39$. In fact, "Gil" is a "bridge," without which one set of nodes would be disconnected from another set. Hence, it is a single point of failure, and plays the role of *information broker*. It helps to keep the network unit intact. Han has the next highest Betweenness centrality of 0.11.

Exercise 6: Calculate the Betweenness centrality of all other nodes in this network by applying the above formula.

Gephi is a tool for interactive visualization and analysis of social networks. Figure 7.10 shows a rendering of the graph of Figure 7.9 in Gephi.

The Gephi tool is very easy to use. The format of the input file for our example graph is shown in Figure 7.11.

Process Similarity Metrics

Similarity is an objective measure of how close two process models are to each other. One formal notion of similarity is *trace similarity* or *trace equivalence*.

Trace equivalence (weak bi-similarity). Two process models are said to be *trace equivalent* if the set of traces that can be replayed on model P1 can also be replayed on model P2, and vice versa.

Example 4: Figure 7.12 shows two process variants where A, B, and C are in an exclusive relationship with one another. In variant 1 in Figure 7.12 (a) there is one XOR split where a choice is made between all three tasks. On the other hand, in variant 2 in Figure 7.12(b), first a choice is made between A and "not A" at the first XOR split node. If the "not A" path is taken, then a choice is made between B and C at the second XOR split node. From a trace equivalence point of view, both the processes are identical since only one task is selected; and all traces generated in variant 1 will have identical trace in variant 2, and vice versa. However, it is evident that *there is a subtle difference between the two variants, since in one case the decision is made in one stage, and in the other in two stages.*

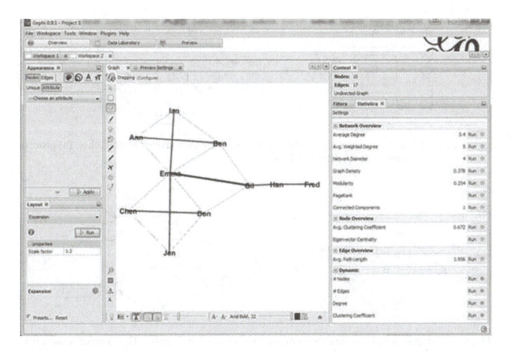

Figure 7.10 A social network graph in Gephi

```xml
<?xml version="1.0" encoding="UTF-8"?>
<gexf xmlns:viz="http:///www.gexf.net/1.1draft/viz" version="1.1"
xmlns="http://www.gexf.net/1.1draft">
<meta lastmodifieddate="2010-03-03+23:44">
<creator>Gephi 0.7</creator>
</meta>
<graph defaultedgetype="undirected" idtype="string" type="static">
<nodes count="10">
<node id="0" label="Ann"/>
<node id="1" label="Ben"/>
<node id="2" label="Chen"/>
<node id="3" label="Don"/>
<node id="4" label="Emma"/>
...
</nodes>
<edges count="17">
<edge id="3" source="1" target="0"  weight="2.0"/>
<edge id="4" source="1" target="4"  weight="1.0"/>
<edge id="5" source="4" target="0"  weight="1.0"/>
<edge id="6" source="4" target="2"  weight="1.0"/>
<edge id="7" source="4" target="3"  weight="1.0"/>
...
</edges>
</graph>
</gexf>
```

Figure 7.11 The input file for the graph of Figure 7.10

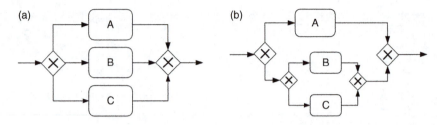

Figure 7.12 Two processes where tasks A, B, and C are exclusive with each other: (a) process variant 1; (b) process variant 2

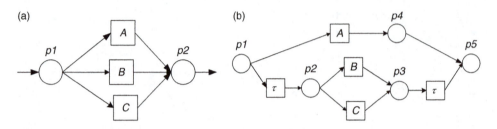

Figure 7.13 Equivalent Petri net models of the two processes in Figure 7.12: (a) process variant 1: (b) process variant 2

To explain this idea, we shall take a short detour into Petri nets. Figure 7.13 shows the equivalent Petri net representations for the two processes in Figure 7.12. Notice how in Figure 7.13(b) there are two transitions marked by the symbol τ. This symbol represents a silent transition. Thus, a trace that represents the selection of task B in Figure 7.13(a) is expressed as "B" while in Figure 7.13(b) is written as "τ-B-τ." If we show the silent transition in a trace, then it is evident that the two processes are not identical. The notion of weak bi-similarity does not include silent transitions and, hence, by this notion these two processes are identical.

Strong bi-similarity is a stricter standard of equivalence between two processes. In strong bi-similarity, two processes are equivalent if and only if, for every *transition* that occurs in process 1 there must be a corresponding *transition* in process 2, and vice versa.

Exercise 7: Figure 7.14(a) shows an unstructured process and Figures 7.14(b) and (c) show two different variants of this process. For each variant, say whether it is strongly bi-similar to the process in Figure 7.14(a), weakly bi-similar or neither. Justify your answer.

Similarity based on Process Profile

We can create a profile of a process by constructing a relationship matrix or REL. Table 7.1(a) shows a relationship matrix for the example log of Figure 7.15. The matrix is constructed by applying some simple rules as follows:

Sequence ($\rightarrow$): If task A always precedes task B in a log (and B never precedes A), then A, B are in sequence. This is written as A $\rightarrow$ B. A reverse sequence between A and B is expressed as B $\leftarrow$ A.

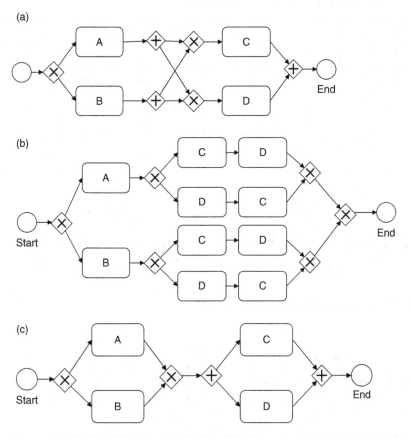

(a)

(b)

(c)

Figure 7.14 Three different representations of the same process: (a) an unstructured process; (b) the first variant representation of process in (a); (c) the second variant representation of process in (a)

Parallel (∥): If both tasks A and B appear in a log trace (i.e. either both are present or both are absent in every trace) but they can be in any order, then they are in a parallel structure.

Choice (# or X): If A appears in some log traces and B in others but both *never* appear together, then they are said to be in a choice relationship.

Note that in making this matrix, we disregard any loop structures. In a similar way, we construct an REL matrix for the reference process P2 shown in Figure 7.16. The matrix is shown in Table 7.1(b).

Notice that both P1 and P2 have the same set of tasks. By comparing the two matrices Rel(P1) and Rel(P2) one can get an idea of the differences between the two processes. Based on these matrices one can define similarity Sim(P1, P2) as:

$$\frac{\text{\# of (nonempty cells of Rel(P1)} = \text{corresponding nonempty cells of Rel(P2))}}{\text{Total number of unique elements in Rel(P1)and Rel(P2)}}$$

By applying this formula we can see that Sim(P1, P2) $= 36/42 = 0.857$. Note that the diagonal entries of the two matrices are empty. Moreover, in this case, the two processes

Table 7.1 Two relationship matrices Rel(P1) and Rel(P2)

(a) Profile of process P1								(b) Profile of process P2						
	A	B	C	E	F	G	H		A	B	C	E	F	G	H
A	-	→	→	→	→	→	→	A	-	→	→	→	→	→	→
B	←	-	‖	→	→	→	→	B	←	-	#	→	→	→	→
C	←	‖	-	→	→	→	→	C	←	#	-	→	→	→	→
E	←	←	←	-	#	→	→	E	←	←	←	-	‖	→	→
F	←	←	←	#	-	→	→	F	←	←	←	‖	-	→	→
G	←	←	←	←	←	-	‖	G	←	←	←	←	←	-	#
H	←	←	←	←	←	‖	-	H	←	←	←	←	←	#	-

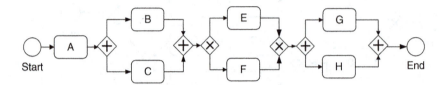

Figure 7.15 An example process P1 for profiling

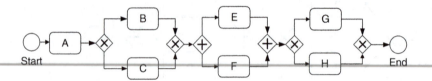

Figure 7.16 A second example process P2 for reference and comparison

have an identical set of tasks. In general, if the set of tasks in the two processes is different, the denominator in the expression above will be larger and the similarity will decrease.

Exercise 8: Calculate the similarity between process P1 and process P2 when task H in P2 is replaced by a new task J.

Exercise 9: Create a REL matrix for the process P3 in Figure 7.17. Do you notice anything special or different about the matrix for this process?

Exercise 10: Can you identify the pairs of tasks for which there are ambiguous relationships between the two tasks in the pair?

Well, if you work through this exercise you will realize that some pairs of tasks have two relationships between them for different execution instances. The interesting observation here is that in an *unstructured process,* ambiguous relationships between tasks *can arise.* In general, unstructured processes are subject to such ambiguities and that makes it harder to compare them with other processes.

The above measure of similarity discussed thus far is based on examining the structure of the process, i.e. the relationships among pairs of tasks. So, it is a *structural measure.*

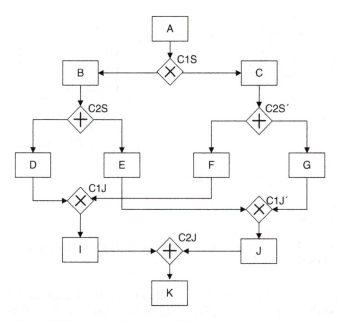

Figure 7.17 An example process P3

Next, we describe a more precise set of metrics for structural and behavioral precision and recall in the context of Petri nets.

Structural and Behavioral Similarity (Petri Nets) (***)

We shall now describe metrics for structural and behavioral precision and recall. These are useful in comparing how similar two models are. They are also useful in the context of process mining, as we shall see in Chapter 11. By comparing a mined model with a reference model, we can get an idea of how good the mining algorithm is.

There are two notions of similarity based on the structure and behavior of a process. They are easier to describe in terms of Petri nets (place transition nets) because, as noted previously in Chapter 2, Petri nets can also record the exact state of execution of a process by specifying the tokens in each place of the Petri net. It is not so easy to describe the state of a running process with respect to its BPMN model, since there is no notion of a "place." It should also be noted that each notion of similarity is measured in terms of two metrics: precision and recall, as we describe next.

Structural precision is calculated by determining causality relationships between pairs of tasks. Very simply, there is a causality relationship between tasks A and B, if the output of A is the input for B; i.e. completion of A can lead to the execution of B immediately afterwards. By comparing the number of pairs of causality relationships in a mined model with the corresponding number in a given reference model, it is possible to determine how close the mined model structurally is to the reference model. In the example of Figure 7.18(a) the causality relations are: $(A, B), (A, C), (A, D)$, $(A, E), (B, F), (C, F), (D, F), (E, F)$. Structural similarity is measured in terms of both precision and recall. In the definitions below, we refer to the mined model with a

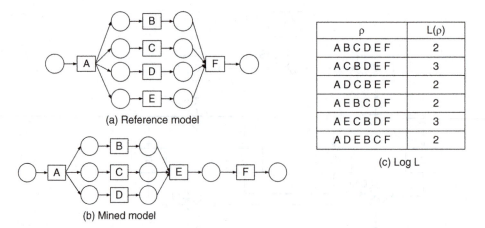

ρ	L(ρ)
A B C D E F	2
A C B D E F	3
A D C B E F	2
A E B C D F	2
A E C B D F	3
A D E B C F	2

(c) Log L

(a) Reference model

(b) Mined model

Figure 7.18 Example of a reference model, a mined model, and a log L: (a) reference model; (b) mined model; (c) log L

subscript "m" and the reference model (or the "true" or ideal model) with a subscript "r." The definition is based on the number of causality relations the mined and the reference models have in common.

Definition 1: (Structural precision and recall): Let $N_r = (P_r, T_r, F_r)$ and $N_m = (P_m, T_m, F_m)$ be respective Petri nets for the reference and mined models. Let C_r and C_m be the respective causality relations for N_r and N_m. The structural precision and structural recall are defined as:

$$S_p (N_r, N_m) = \frac{|C_r \cap C_m|}{|C_m|}$$

$$S_R (N_r, N_m) = \frac{|C_r \cap C_m|}{|C_r|}$$

The *structural recall* reflects the number of correct causality relations present in the *mined model* as a fraction of the total number of causality relations in the *reference model*. On the other hand, the structural precision reflects the fraction of *correct* causality relations present in the *mined model*. They are both measures of similarity and lie in the range [0, 1]. A value close to 1 means that the similarity between the mined and reference models is very high.

Given N_r and N_m as the two Petri nets shown in Figure 7.18, we can calculate the structural precision and recall metrics as follows:

$$S_P(N_r, N_m) = \frac{|\{(A, B), (A, C), (A, D), (E, F)\}|}{|\{(A, B), (A, C), (A, D), (B, E), (C, E), (D, E), (E, F)\}|} = \frac{4}{7} = 0.571$$

$$S_R(N_r, N_m) = \frac{|\{(A, B), (A, C), (A, D), (E, F)\}|}{|\{(A, B), (A, C), (A, D), (A, E), (B, F), (C, F), (D, F), (E, F)\}|}$$

$$= \frac{4}{8} = 0.5$$

The results ($S_R < S_p < 1$) reflect that the mined model is more concise than the reference model in terms of the structure.

The *behavioral similarity* metrics measure the similarity in behavior between two models, again in terms of precision and recall. These metrics analyze the event log to quantify how similar the behavior of, say, the mined model is to that of its reference model. This is done by replaying each trace against the two models and calculating how many transitions (or tasks) are enabled in each model at the occurrence of every event in the trace. The more enabled transitions the two models have in common, the higher is the similarity between them.

Definition 2: (Behavioral precision and recall): This definition uses the following parameters:

ρ: a trace in an event log.
$L(\rho)$: the number of occurrences of ρ in an event log.
N_r and N_m: the respective Petri nets for the reference and the mined models.
C_r and C_m: the respective causality relations for N_r and N_m.

Now, the behavioral precision and recall are defined as:

$$B_p(L, C_r, C_m)$$

$$= \left(\sum_{\rho \in L} \left(\frac{L(\rho)}{|\rho|} \times \sum_{i=0}^{|\rho|-1} \frac{|\text{Enabled}(C_r, \rho, i) \cap \text{Enabled}(C_m, \rho, i)|}{|\text{Enabled}(C_m, \rho, i)|} \right) \right) \Big/ \sum_{\rho \in L} L(\rho)$$

$$B_R(L, C_r, C_m)$$

$$= \left(\sum_{\rho \in L} \left(\frac{L(\rho)}{|\rho|} \times \sum_{i=0}^{|\rho|-1} \frac{|\text{Enabled}(C_r, \rho, i) \cap \text{Enabled}(C_m, \rho, i)|}{|\text{Enabled}(C_r, \rho, i)|} \right) \right) \Big/ \sum_{\rho \in L} L(\rho)$$

Where, Enabled(C_r, ρ, i): the *set* of enabled activities when parsing the next event (or task) after position i in trace ρ. For the example of Figure 7.18, which includes a trace $\rho =$ "AEBCDF," in the reference model (Figure 7.18(a)), Enabled(C_r, ρ, i) = {B, C, D, E} because this set of tasks is enabled after task A at position 1 is executed. Thus, the size of this set, |Enabled(C_r, ρ, i)| = 4. However, in the mined model (Figure 7.18(b)), Enabled(C_m, ρ, i) = {B, C, D}. Thus, the set $S1$ = Enabled(C_r, ρ, i) ∩ Enabled(C_m, ρ, i) = {B, C, D}. Hence, the size of set $S1$, |$S1$| = 3.

The behavioral precision reflects how much of the behavior of the *mined model* is also in the *reference model*. The behavioral recall reflects how much of the behavior of the *reference model* also occurs in the *mined model*. To appreciate the concept of behavioral precision and recall, let us revisit the example in Figure 7.18. It shows a reference model, a synthetic log (log L) of actual execution traces based on a reference model (Figure 7.18(a)), and a mined model (Figure 7.18(b)) generated from the log. For this example:

$$B_P(L, C_r, C_m) = (2/6 * (1/1 + 3/3 + 2/2 + 1/1 + 1/1 + 1/1) +$$
$$3/6 * (1/1 + 3/3 + 2/2 + 1/1 + 1/1 + 1/1) +$$
$$2/6 * (1/1 + 3/3 + 2/2 + 1/1 + 1/1 + 1/1) +$$
$$2/6 * (1/1 + 3/3 + 3/4 + 2/3 + 1/2 + 1/1) +$$

$$3/6*(1/1+3/3+3/4+2/3+1/2+1/1)+$$
$$2/6*(1/1+3/3+2/2+2/3+1/2+1/1))/14$$
$$=0.91.$$

And,

$$B_R(L, C_r, C_m) = (2/6*(1/1+3/4+2/3+1/2+1/1+1/1)+$$
$$3/6*(1/1+3/4+2/3+1/2+1/1+1/1)+$$
$$2/6*(1/1+3/4+2/3+1/2+1/1+1/1)+$$
$$2/6*(1/1+3/4+2/3+2/2+1/1+1/1)+$$
$$3/6*(1/1+3/4+2/3+2/2+1/1+1/1)+$$
$$2/6*(1/1+3/4+2/3+2/2+1/1+1/1))/14$$
$$=0.86$$

The results ($B_P = 0.91$ and $B_R = 0.86$) show that for the given log, the mined model is close to the reference model on both the precision and recall metrics.

Chapter Summary

It is important to realize that all similarity metrics give only an approximate idea of how similar two processes are. As we have seen above, different metrics will produce different results on the same set of processes. By looking at different metrics together, one can gain a better perspective. However, a similarity value of 0.9 does not really say that one process is 10 percent less similar than another and it is not quite clear what it means in objective terms. It is only an approximate measure. Sometimes a small change in the process model may produce large changes in structure and behavior that are not really reflected in the metric. Then it would not be appropriate to say that we have made only a minor change just because the similarity between the old and the new versions of the process is, say, 0.90.

Ross [18] is a well-known text for an introduction to queuing and probability. Laguna and Marklund have discussed concepts of simulation in their book [13]. In this text, ExtendSim (or Extend) software [8] is an accompanying tool that can be used to model discrete event, continuous, agent-based, and discrete rate processes. BIMP [2] is a free tool from the University of Tartu. Arena [1] is a well-known commercial simulation tool. It offers a flowchart modeling methodology to model any process in an easy and intuitive way without the need for writing custom code or for programming. Once the model is built and validated against actual operating data, you can use it to evaluate process changes, variations in market factors, or resources and equipment requirements quickly and easily. The Signavio software described in Chapter 2 also provides simulation capabilities. Another tool for simulation, called Disco, will be described in Chapter 11.

Complexity has roots in the work of Halstead [11], who had the objective of establishing an empirical science of software development. His work included concepts like program vocabulary, length, volume, difficulty, and effort. Work on complexity metrics in the context of business processes was done by Cardoso [4, 5]. Complexity is also related to coupling, cohesion and modularity [3, 17, 20]. Coupling measures the number of interconnections between activities in a process model. A higher value for it indicates a higher degree of coupling in the process, and thus greater complexity. Modularity reduces complexity in the sense that by separating a process into modules or subprocesses, it is possible to simplify the design and make it less complex. Cohesion is a measure of how well various modules fit together. Work on metrics related to quality appears in [19].

Network concepts are discussed in Newman [14]. There are many tools for analyzing networks. Among them, Pajek [7] is a well-known open source software for social network analysis. Gephi [9] is another easy to use, open source tool with powerful analysis and visualization features. NodeXL [15] is a free and open Excel add-in that makes it easy to explore network graphs. You can also install the igraph package in R-Studio [16] and perform various kinds of network analyses and visualization.

There are many notions of behavioral equivalence for processes which fall in the broader classes of concurrent systems [10, 12]. A common notion is that of bisimulation, and it is related to those of weak bisimulation and branching bisimulation. These notions are used for comparing process models. Behavioral similarity metrics that measure the similarity in behavior between two models in terms of precision and recall have been discussed in [6]. A similarity measurement technique based on creating a profile of a process using ordering, exclusiveness, and interleaving relations is discussed in [21]. This is a more advanced version of the method we described in the section "Similarity based on process profile."

References

1. Arena Simulation Software. www.arenasimulation.com/.
2. BIMP – The Business Process Simulator. http://bimp.cs.ut.ee/.
3. D. Braunnagel, F. Johannsen and S. Susanne Leist. Coupling and process modeling: an analysis at hand of the eEPC. *Modellierung*, pp. 121–136, 2014.
4. J. Cardoso. Evaluating the Process Control-Flow Complexity Measure. In: *ICWS, IEEE Computer Society*, pp. 803–804, 2005.
5. J. Cardoso. Approaches to Compute Workflow Complexity. Dagstuhl Seminar, "The Role of Business Processes in Service Oriented Architectures", Dagstuhl, Germany, 16–21 July 2006.
6. A. K. A. de Medeiros, A. J. M. M. Weijters and W. M. P. van der Aalst. Genetic process mining: an experimental evaluation. *Data Mining and Knowledge Discovery*, Vol. 14, No. 2, pp. 245–304, 2007.
7. W. De Nooy, A. Mrvar and V. Batagelj. *Exploratory Social Network Analysis with Pajek*. Vol. 27. Cambridge University Press, Cambridge, 2011.
8. ExtendSim. www.extendsim.com/.
9. Gephi. The Open Graph Viz Platform. www.gephi.org.
10. R. J. van Glabbeek. The Linear Time-Branching Time Spectrum (Extended Abstract). In: J. C. M. Baeten, J. W. Klop (eds) International Conference on Concurrency Theory (CONCUR). *Lecture Notes in Computer Science*, Vol. 458. Springer, Berlin, Heidelberg, pp. 278–297, 1990.
11. M. H. Halstead. *Elements of Software Science*. Amsterdam: Elsevier North-Holland, Inc., 1977.
12. B. Kiepuszewski, A. H. M. ter Hofstede and W. M. P. van der Aalst. Fundamentals of control flow in workflows. *Acta Informatica (ACTA)*, Vol. 39, No. 3, pp. 143–209, 2003.
13. M. Laguna and J. Marklund. *Business Process Modeling, Simulation and Design*. CRC Press, Boca Raton, 2013.
14. M. E. J. Newman. *Networks: An Introduction*. Oxford University Press, Oxford, UK, 2010.

15. NodeXL. https://nodexl.codeplex.com/.
16. R-Studio. www.rstudio.com/.
17. H. A. Reijers and J. Mendling. Modularity in Process Models: Review and Effects. In: M. Dumas, M. Reichert, M.-C. Shan (eds), Business Process Management—BPM 2008. *Lecture Notes in Computer Science*, Vol. 5240. Springer, Milan, Italy, pp. 20–35, 2008.
18. S. Ross. *Introduction to Probability Models*. Academic Press, Burlington, 2014.
19. I. T. P. Vanderfeesten. Quality metrics for business process models. *BPM and Workflow Handbook*, Vol. 144, pp. 179–190, 2007.
20. I. T. P. Vanderfeesten, H. A. Reijers, W. M. P. van der Aalst. Evaluating workflow process designs using cohesion and coupling metrics. *Computers in Industry*, Vol. 59, No. 5, pp. 420–437, 2008.
21. M. Weidlich, J. Mendling and M. Weske, Efficient consistency measurement based on behavioral profiles of process models. *IEEE Transactions on Software Engineering*, Vol. 37, No. 3, pp. 410–429, 2011.

8 Business Process Security

Introduction

Business processes in the real world often pertain to financial transactions such as approving and making payment for an insurance claim, an expense claim, a loan application, etc. Such processes are susceptible to fraud, since money is involved. Fraud is particularly rampant in healthcare, which is a $3 trillion industry in the US alone. Hence, it is necessary to have control mechanisms in place and to ensure that these controls are complied with from the start until the end of the process. These controls are established in the first place as part of company policy. A process in which the controls are in place is called a *secure process*, although there is no fool-proof guarantee of security.

In this chapter, we will discuss some fundamental principles of security and compliance in an organization, bearing in mind that there are many steps in a process instance that are performed by several individuals who occupy different roles or positions. A breach in security can occur at any step of a process instance or it may arise from interactions across steps. We shall consider process security in the context of compliance requirements, both external and internal, and control mechanisms. Internal compliance requirements relate to authorizations, rules, delegation, and revocation. External compliance requirements pertain to regulatory requirements imposed by governmental bodies.

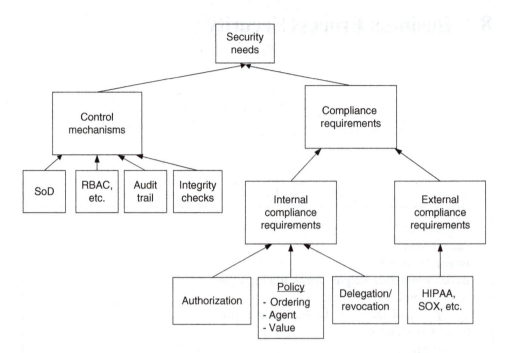

Figure 8.1 A roadmap

Authorizations are necessary to meet compliance requirements so that roles and individuals can only perform tasks that they are authorized to do. Further, an authorization may be delegated to other roles and individuals subject to certain conditions. We shall also discuss control mechanisms like integrity checks, separation of duties, audit trails, RBAC and its extensions as means to enforce security. Figure 8.1 gives a roadmap for this chapter in the context of a security framework.

Background

Sarbanes-Oxley legislation in the United States, and similar laws in other countries, has highlighted the importance of making business processes secure. It has made it mandatory for top officers of organizations to certify that suitable controls are in place to guarantee that processes are secure. Section 302 of the Sarbanes-Oxley Act requires that CEOs and CFOs must personally sign off on their company's financial statements, while Section 404 requires that appropriate processes and controls must exist for all aspects of a company's operations that affect financial reports.

Security is necessary in almost any business process where the exchange of money or goods is involved. Moreover, this would apply regardless of whether a system is fully automated, partially automated, or entirely manual. In the automated case, the computer system should have been tested thoroughly beforehand to make sure it operates correctly. In the manual case, the human worker must have the appropriate qualifications and authority to perform the task. In all cases, appropriate controls must be in place to prevent fraud or abuse of authority.

Control mechanisms are safeguards or countermeasures to avoid, detect, counteract, or minimize security risks to physical property, information, computer systems, and other assets. In general, controls are characterized as *preventive, detective*, or *corrective*. Preventive controls deter errors or fraud from occurring and incorrectly updating the records of an organization. Detective controls identify errors or fraud that have already occurred and/or updated records of an organization. Corrective controls can be applied as soon as an incident of fraud is discovered to minimize any further damage or loss. If a detection is made in real-time or near real-time, then it is likely that corrective action can be taken to stop the fraud or at least limit the extent of it. A corrective control would be one that implements a process to stop a bank transfer that has been illegally initiated by an employee. It could also be a mechanism to withhold salary and other payments due to an employee as soon as they perform a fraudulent action. Ideally, an organization should have all three controls in place.

Essentially, control relates to: Who is allowed to do what? In addition, there can be restrictions that relate to dollar amounts, location, timing, etc. Thus, a company policy may require that:

- An accounts manager may approve employee travel expenses only up to $2500.
- The approvals must be made while the manager is at the office.
- The approvals must be made during working hours.

This is an example of a compliance rule. *Compliance* requirements refer to the *minimum* (external and internal) security standards companies must adhere to. In addition to the Sarbanes-Oxley law mentioned above, other external requirements may pertain to the Health Insurance Portability and Accountability Act of 1996 (HIPAA) in the United States. This law specifies data privacy and security provisions for safeguarding medical information. Similarly, the Payment Card Industry Data Security Standard (PCI DSS) is a set of security standards designed to ensure that all companies that accept, process, store, or transmit credit card information maintain a secure environment.

Internal Control

Every organization must have an internal control system in place consisting of processes, policies, and procedures that satisfies its internal control objectives. It is also important to note that internal control is a separate and independent department from accounting. In fact, its job is to review all accounting transactions and ensure that they were performed as per the policies of the company. The Committee of Sponsoring Organizations of the Treadway Commission (COSO) is a joint initiative of various private-sector organizations that is dedicated to the development of frameworks and guidance on enterprise risk management, internal control, and fraud deterrence. The COSO Framework describes internal control as a process implemented by an organization's management that provides reasonable assurance that certain key objectives will be met, such as:

- reliable financial reporting
- efficient and effective operations
- compliance with laws and regulations.

The objective of reliable financial reporting is to ensure that all transactions are: valid (i.e. they did occur); properly authorized by the appropriate officer of the company in accordance with company policy; and recorded accurately (i.e. the transaction has been posted in the records in the correct account, with the right amount, date, and other relevant information).

In addition, the aim behind these objectives is also to safeguard assets and data from loss or theft, as well as to make business operations more efficient and effective through the information generated for making decisions. Clearly, a failure to record transactions accurately may well result in lost or stolen assets, thus inflicting much harm to the business operations.

Of course, an internal control system is never perfect and absolute, but is meant to be reasonable for helping meet its objectives. Just what is "reasonable" is rather subjective within any particular organization. It is the responsibility of an organization's management to identify risks and respond appropriately with control procedures for helping provide reasonable assurance.

Some inherent weaknesses in any system of internal control are management override of controls, collusion amongst people with incompatible duties, and human error. The cost of a control in relation to the amount of risk reduction can also be a prohibitive factor when designing an internal control. For these reasons, there is no fool-proof system of internal control. Remember that a well-determined and smart group of employees can always collude to defeat even the strongest internal control system an organization can put in place. The COSO Framework has identified five inter-related components of internal control for helping meet internal control objectives:

Control environment – The tone at the top of an organization; management's philosophy and operating style; the board of directors; management's commitment to integrity and ethics; management process; and human resource standards.

Risk assessment – Proper identification, response and management of risks that can impede or prevent operational objectives from being met.

Control activities – Processes, policies, and procedures that help address risks and meet objectives.

Monitoring – Review and response to how internal control is meeting risks and meeting objectives. This includes internal audit activities as well.

Information and communication – Gathering information about internal control, and communicating it to management and employees provides feedback on what is being done successfully and what is not, so that improvements can be made for managing risks and meeting objectives.

The control environment is the most important component or foundation of internal control. This is because it is management driven, and management are responsible for an organization's internal control. Hence, internal control begins with management and its attitude and objectives.

Finally, it is important to realize that internal control is not meant to be busy work, but is rather put in place to help meet specific objectives. It should be possible to explain why a control procedure is put in place by relating it to one or more control objectives in the given situation. To summarize, internal controls serve to: improve data collection and processing; enhance the reliability of information generated for decision-makers; safeguard assets and data from loss or theft; make operations more efficient and effective; and enable compliance with laws and regulations.

Basic Compliance Requirements and Principles

The first standard principle of control is **segregation (or separation) of duties**. The simplest illustration of this rule is: If you are an employee in a company, you may even be the CEO, you can still not approve your own business travel expenses. In a similar spirit, if you work in a bank and submit an application for a mortgage loan, you cannot approve your own loan application. In general terms, this principle can be interpreted to mean that *no single individual has the authority to execute two or more conflicting sensitive transactions*, especially if financial implications arise from it.

Exercise 1: Briefly explain the key idea that Figure 8.2 is trying to convey.

Figure 8.3 illustrates the *four-eyes principle*. It means that a certain activity, such as a decision, transaction, etc., must be approved by four eyes, i.e. at least two people. In Figure 8.3(a), an expense claim reimbursement process requires two approvals, one by the department manager and another by the accounts manager. In Figure 8.3(b), a loan application is approved by a loan officer and then by a credit manager. It is also possible that two approvals may take place in parallel instead of sequentially. For instance, if two vice-presidents have to approve a payment for $100,000 to a vendor, they may happen, in parallel, to speed up the process.

"Until we implement a complete segregation of duties solution the auditor said we will need to press the 'enter' key together"

Figure 8.2 Segregation of duties

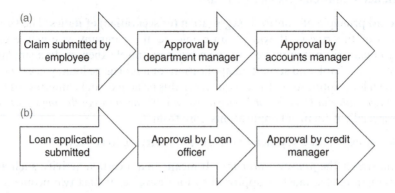

(a)

Claim submitted by employee → Approval by department manager → Approval by accounts manager

(b)

Loan application submitted → Approval by Loan officer → Approval by credit manager

Figure 8.3 The four-eyes principle: (a) an expense claim reimbursement process; (b) a loan application process

This principle is used to facilitate delegation of authority and increase transparency. As an example, the processes in the new business model of the United Nations Industrial Development Organization (UNIDO) are based on the four-eyes principle, which are facilitated by electronic approvals and workflows in the ERP system. This approach not only ensures the efficiency of processes by enabling fast decision making while ensuring effective control and monitoring, but also brings about cultural change. Staff members can perform these processes irrespective of whether they are based at headquarters or at any other location.

The four-eyes rule can be further extended to more individuals. For example, in some organizations it is required that *custody, authorization, recordkeeping,* and *reconciliation* functions be separated. Thus, for receipt of goods from a vendor, physical custody is kept by one person, the approval or authorization of the receipt is given by another, and the recording of the receipt is done by a third person. This ensures that the person receiving the shipment does not record it incorrectly. By separating receipt from recording, chances of fraud at delivery time are reduced. Moreover, there may be an additional requirement that the three individuals performing these tasks must be from different roles (say, an inventory clerk, a department supervisor, and an accounting clerk).

It is important to note that these control objectives not only apply to transactions but also to master data, which are used for processing transactions. Examples of master data are the employee database, customer database, vendor database, product database, price database, etc. This data tends to be of a fixed nature and changes only occasionally. Just as transactions must be properly authorized, validated, recorded, and accurate, so should master data. Further, meeting these control objectives over master data will also enhance the safeguarding of assets and data from loss or theft, as well as make business operations more efficient and effective through the information generated for making decisions.

Exercise 2: Should the individual who manages the pricing master database be allowed to prepare sales invoices? Explain.

Some companies require that the requester, authorizer, preparer of payment, and the one that releases it, all be different individuals. For extra-sensitive transactions, multiple approvals may be required instead of one at each stage, for example by having two approvers (say, a manager and a VP) instead of one.

Here are a few other examples of the four-eyes principle at work:

- Many legal and financial documents require the signatures of two individuals.
- Banks, casinos, and sensitive military areas often include *no-lone* (or never alone) zones: areas in which two people must be present and within each other's line of vision at all times.
- The Emergency War Orders (EWO) safe, which contains missile launch keys and codes, is locked by two padlocks with keys held by different launch officers.
- Some data management systems require that important record updates be approved by two separate people before the data is committed.

Although the four-eyes principle adds an element of security to any decision-making process, its effectiveness relies upon the ability, integrity, and diligence of the individuals involved. In a refinement of the basic principle, a random rotation of authorized individuals serves as the second pair of eyes, so that it cannot be known with any certainty which two individuals will be dealing with a given decision. Of course, we cannot prevent collusion between these two individuals.

In addition to separation of role requirements, ordering restrictions on roles may also be imposed. Thus, it may be necessary that a superior role (such as a manager or vice-president) may perform a task *after* a subordinate role (such as an engineer).

Application Level Controls

Application controls are checks that are specific to particular transactions and focus on proper data entry, processing, and output. These controls are summarized in Table 8.1 and are included in most industrial-strength applications.

In many enterprise applications such as SAP, upon entering a customer number on an input screen, the customer name is looked up and appears on the screen, and a full product description and price appear when a product code is entered. This kind of application control not only speeds up the process of preparing a sales invoice but also helps to ensure that valid data for a customer and item were entered in the first place. By applying these various checks, it is possible to improve the quality of the transaction-related data that are fed into a system. This leads to fewer errors and reduces the need for making corrections later.

If you consider a typical sales order process in any organization, it has to pass through various steps (or tasks) like order entry, order confirmation, pick goods, post goods issue, billing, and payment. At each step data has to be entered, and it is important to apply such checks to ensure the integrity of the data.

Segregation of Duties (SoD) and Audit Trails

In addition to segregation of duties, another control mechanism is an audit trail of all activities. To realize SoD, we create a *conflict matrix*. First, make a list of all transactions or activities that will occur in various processes of the business. Then, construct a square matrix where the transactions appear both in the rows and columns, as shown in Figure 8.4. Now, consider all pairs of transactions and identify the pairs where a likely

Table 8.1 Various types of standard checks that an application must perform

Field check	Ensures that the field is of the proper type: e.g. numeric, alphanumeric, credit card number, social security number, zip code, etc. A user is alerted immediately before the form is submitted.
Limit check/range check	Tests a numerical value to verify that it lies below a limit or within a permitted range. For example, an ATM withdrawal cannot exceed $200, an employee cannot work more than 50 hours in a week, and the value for the age of an employee must be between 18 and 75.
Reasonableness check	A test to ensure that the values of certain monetary fields are valid, e.g. a clerical worker does not make more than $100,000 in a company.
Sign check	Is the proper sign used for monetary amounts? Often in accounting applications, debits and credits are used to obviate the need for a negative sign.
Size check	The number of characters in a field can be limited. In the US, a zip code field must have 5, a social security field 9, telephone number 10, etc.
Completeness check	To ensure that all required data have been entered before a transaction is recorded or the record is updated. If a customer neglects to enter the CVV code for her credit card number while making an online purchase, she is prompted to do so.
Validity check	This check confirms that the data entered into a field for a transaction (or a master record) is related to some object that exists in the system. Thus, when an employee enters a time card, her employee ID should exist as a primary key in the employee database. Similarly, if a price change is to be made for an item in the pricing master database, then the product code for the item should exist in the database.
Zero-balance check	Compares numerical values to ensure they are equal, e.g. in an accounting application a transaction is entered as a debit with a corresponding credit of equal value, or vice versa.

conflict exists. An "X" in the matrix indicates that the corresponding transaction pair is conflicting. Thus, the first row of this matrix shows that the individual who creates or modifies the customer master records (row 1) should not be able to create or modify invoices (row 2) and credit memos (row 3), or post cash receipts.

In general, it is not desirable that a person who manages a master database also performs transactions related to the information stored in that database. Thus, when a sales invoice is prepared by, say, a sales clerk, a price lookup operation is performed by the system whereby the price of an item on the invoice is obtained from the pricing master database. If the sales clerk is also given access to the pricing master database, this individual could modify the price just before preparing the invoice (say, for a friend) and then change it back to the original value after the invoice is prepared. Hence, these two tasks should never be done by the same individual in an organization.

After this matrix is created, then assignment of permissions to roles in an organization must be made in such a way that a single role does not assume the permission to perform two conflicting types of transactions. In the context of Figure 8.4, the role that creates a customer master record is, say, a sales manager. However, the role that creates invoices for that customer is an accounts manager. By separating the roles in this way, it is possible to prevent fraud. Moreover, it is necessary to also ensure that a single user does not obtain access to two roles that in turn will allow access to two conflicting transactions.

Exercise 3: Create a conflict matrix for a mortgage department of a bank where some of the transactions are: receive application, review application, get credit report,

Figure 8.4 A conflict matrix

Source: EY white paper.

	1	2	3	4	5	6	7
1. Create/Modify/Delete customer pricing master/structure	—	X	X	X		X	
2. Create/Modify/Delete sales/service invoice		—	X	X		X	
3. Create/Modify/Delete customer credit memos			—	X		X	
4. Post cash receipts and apply to customer account				—		X	
5. Create/Modify/Delete customer master data					—	X	
6. Create/Modify/Delete sales orders						—	
…							

Column headers:
1. Create/Modify/Delete customer pricing master/structure
2. Create/Modify/Delete sales/service invoice
3. Create/Modify/Delete customer credit memos
4. Post cash receipts and apply to customer account
5. Create/Modify/Delete customer master data
6. Create/Modify/Delete sales orders
7. …

1. Create/Modify/Delete customer pricing master/structure

2. Create/Modify/Delete vendor master/structure

453	May 9 10.13 am	1, Main street	4555732	$100	Withdrawal

Figure 8.5 A sample log record of an ATM machine

obtain a title report, perform property appraisal, initial approval, final approval, send notification, and pay customer.

An audit trail maintains a full log of all transactions that occur and it is a powerful control mechanism, since it serves as a historical record of all activities. It can help to resolve any dispute by verifying the authenticity of every past transaction. The log must contain information like:

- log ID #
- time of transaction
- place of transaction
- ID of user that performed the transaction
- the amount of the transaction
- the type of transaction.

Figure 8.5 shows a sample log record of an ATM log. In addition, a picture or a video clip may also be added to the log record for still higher security. The log can be very helpful while investigating a discrepancy between the actual cash balance in the ATM at the end of the day and the expected balance based on the transactions that occurred that day. As another illustration of the value of an audit trail, the SAP R/3 system generates a document flow as shown in Figure 8.6. This is also an audit trail of the various tasks (order confirmation, delivery document, goods issue, invoice generation, and payment) that occurred in the sales order process. By clicking on a task, it is possible to see more details about the document like the time stamp, ID of the user who generated or approved the document, amount of the document, etc. In this way, it is possible to analyze and investigate a process in detail.

Policy Constraints

Yet another control mechanism consists of superimposing further constraints on a process model or an instance. This can further restrict what operations are explicitly permitted or prohibited within an organization and capture the policy more precisely. The constraints are expressed as parameterized constraint predicates or functions. At run time, a conformance checker can verify if these constraints are satisfied and it can highlight any violations.

In general, business requirements concern the following aspects:

- *ordering based*, i.e. about the execution order of tasks, and task inclusions and exclusions
- *agent based*, i.e. about the involvement of a role or a specific actor in a process case or instance
- *value based*, i.e. related to the attribute data values pertaining to objects such as dollar amounts.

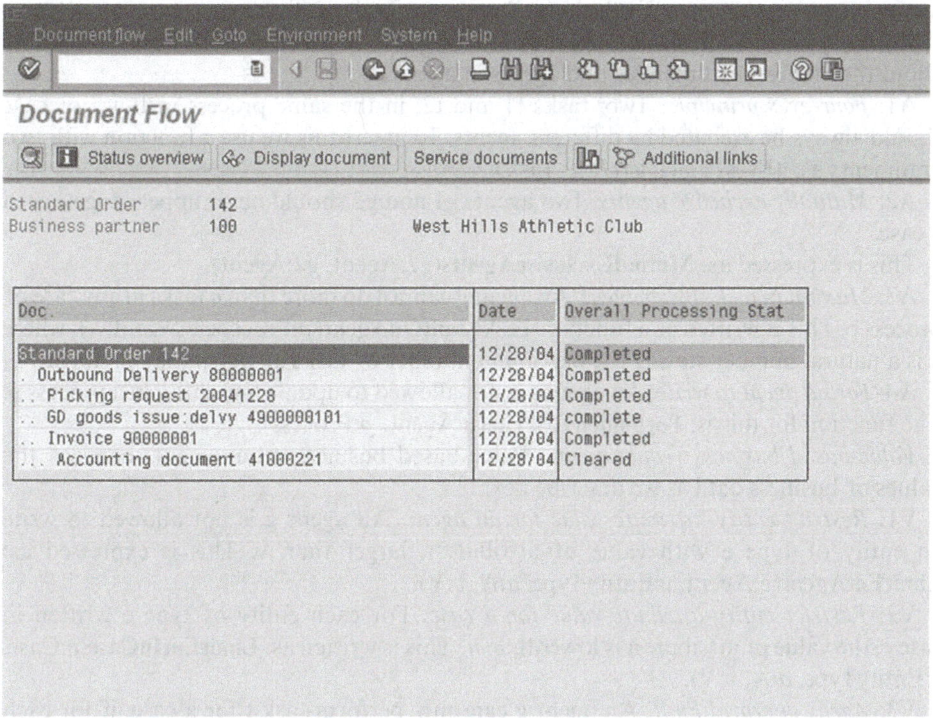

Figure 8.6 A document flow in SAP that serves as an audit trail

Source: SAP screenshot.

In general, these requirements may also be combined to enforce a policy. Next, we illustrate some generic classes of constraint predicates to represent policies. These predicates are illustrative but not exhaustive. In some examples, we refer to sets of attributes *A*, entity types *E*, and values *V*. We use the notation e. a = v to express that attribute *a* of object (or entity) *e* has value *v*.

Ordering based requirements. Ordering based requirements express constraints concerning the ordering of events and tasks in processes.

O1: Task precedence. A task t1 should always be performed before task t2 in any case of process p. Formally we can assert this requirement by means of a function of three arguments as: **TaskPrecedence**(*p*:Process, *t1*:Task, *t2*:Task).

O2: Restrict update operation. After task t1 for process p is performed in a case, no object of type x can be updated any more in that case. For example, an employee cannot change the travel expense form (or entity) after it has been approved. Again, we can assert this requirement by a function of three arguments as: **RestrictUpdate**(*p*:Process, *t1*:Task, *e*:EntityType).

O3: Maximum repetitions of a task in a case. In any case of a process p, task t1 cannot be executed more than *n* times. This is asserted by the function **MaxRepeatTask**(*p*:Process, *t1*:Task, *n*), where *n* is a natural number.

O4: Obligatory task in a process. This function specifies mandatory tasks as: **Mandatory**(*p*:Process, *t1*:Task).

O5: Strictly exclusive tasks. We can also require that two tasks do not appear together in any process instance as: **Exclusive**(*p*:Process, *t1*:Task, *t2*:Task)

Agent-based rules. Role- or agent-based business requirements express constraints about the involvement of roles and agents in a process.

A1: Four-eyes principle. Two, tasks t1 and t2, in the same process instance or case should always be executed by different agents. To assert this we use a function with two arguments as: **4EyesPrinciple**(*t1*, *t2*:Task).

A2: Mutually exclusive agents. Two agents g1 and g2 should never appear together in a case.

This is expressed as: **MutualExclusiveAgents**(*g1*:Agent, *g2*:Agent).

A3: Maximum tasks by an agent. An agent g cannot do more than *n* tasks in any case of process p. This is written as a function **TaskLimitOnAgent**(*p*:Process, *g*:Agent, *n*), where *n* is a natural number stating the maximum number of tasks an agent may perform.

A4: Forbid agent to write. An agent g is not allowed to update any entity in a process p. The function for this is: **ForbiddenToWrite**(*g*:Agent, *p*:Process).

Value-based business requirements. Value-based business requirements concern the values of business data as we describe next.

V1: Restrict entity-attribute-value for an agent. An agent g is not allowed to write an entity of type e with value of attribute a larger than v. This is expressed as: **LimitEntAgent**(*g*:Agent, *e*:EntityType, *a*:A, *v*:V).

V2: Restrict entity-attribute-value for a case. For each entity of type e written in case c, the value of attribute a is lower than *n*. This is written as: **LimitEntInCase**(*c*:Case, *e*:EntityType, *a*:A, *v*:V).

V3: Agent approval limit. An agent g can only perform task t for a case, if for each entity of type e written in that case, attribute a is less than v. For example, a bank vice-president can approve a loan up to a limit of $500,000. The function for this requirement is: **ApprLim**(*g*:Agent, *t*:Task, *e*:EntityType, *a*:A, *v*:V).

V4: Three-way match. In each case of a process p, if task t is executed, then entities of types e1, e2 and e3 belonging to the case should have the same value, e.g. the price on the invoice should match the price on the quotation and on the delivery notice. This is expressed as: **ThreeWayMatch**(*p*:Process, *t*:Task, *e1*:EntityType, *e2*:EntityType, *e3*:EntityType).

Next, we illustrate the use of these functions with a realistic example.

Through these predicates, it is possible to represent the business policy or rules of an organization.

A Case Study

We shall next use an example of a large international funds transfer at a bank to illustrate the above framework. Figure 8.7 shows the BPMN diagram for an administer account transfer process at Banks-R-Us. The process starts with a *customer representative* receiving an account transfer instruction (task t1) from a client, and recording the transfer instruction (task t2). Next, a *financial clerk* validates the instructions (task t3). If the validation reveals a problem, communication details of the invalid instruction are extracted (task t5). Otherwise, a *financial accountant* checks the transaction limit of the transaction (task t4). If the transaction amount exceeds the limit for the customer, the process starts the authorization subprocess consisting of tasks t7 and t8 (shown in dashed box on upper right). If the limit is not reached, or the transaction is authorized, the *banking specialist*

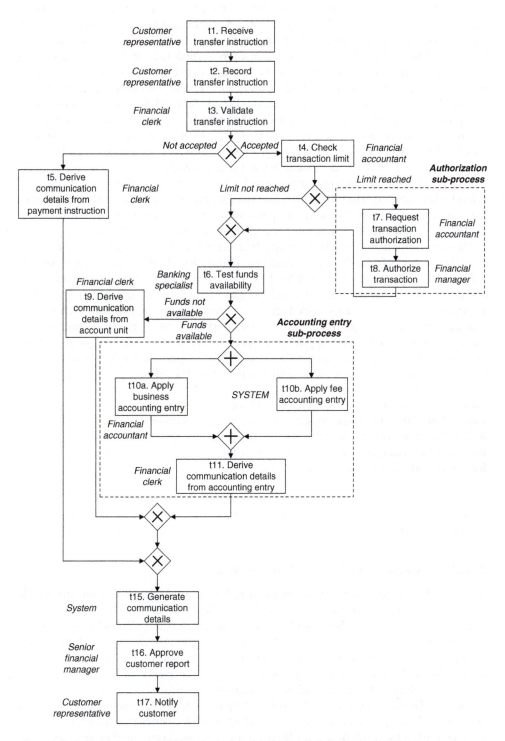

Figure 8.7 A formal representation of an administer account transfer request process

checks the availability of funds. If this check fails, communication details are derived from the account unit (task t9); if it passes, the Accounting Entry subprocess (shown in dashed box in center) is started, which applies the accounting entry and calculates a fee for it. In all cases, the results are collected in a report (task t15), and after it is approved (task t16), the customer is notified (task t17). If the report is not approved, it may need to be reworked (not shown in the figure), and tasks t15 and t16 would be repeated.

Thus, both t3 (validate transfer instructions) and t4 (check transaction limit) are decision points. A parallel structure is created in the "accounting entry" subprocess (if funds are available) for business accounting (t10a) and to apply a transaction fee (t10b). This process also involves the role of the *senior financial manager*, who supervises the financial manager, and heads a team including a financial accountant and a financial clerk. Table 8.2 shows the assignment of roles to tasks. Note, since the senior financial manager role is higher in the organizational hierarchy than the financial manager, financial accountant, and financial clerk, it inherits the permission to do everything its subordinate can do. We'll have more to say about role hierarchies in the section on "RBAC."

The organization has the following agents: agent-joe, agent-sue, agent-eric and agent-beth. These agents fulfill the roles within the organization. In this organization, we next define the business rules that must hold for the process. First, it is not permissible to update the entity cust-account after task t11 has been executed. Second, agent-joe and agent-sue are not allowed to work together in any case. Agent-eric is not allowed to execute more than 4 tasks. Last, tasks t8 and t10a in a case may not be executed by the same agent, and this also applies to tasks t8 and t10b. We need to implement these business rules in the system. Given the set of predefined business rule functions in the previous section, the process owner only has to specify the following functions:

Rule 1: RestrictUpdate(account-transfer, t11, cust-account)
Rule 2: MutualExclusiveAgents(account-transfer, agent-joe, agent-sue)
Rule 3: TaskLimitOnAgent(account-transfer, agent-eric, 4)
Rule 4: 4EyesPrinciple(account-transfer, t8, t10a)
Rule 5: 4EyesPrinciple(account-transfer, t8, t10b).

Most of these requirements apply to all processes in the system; however, it is also possible to associate a process parameter with a rule in order to apply it to a specific process or subprocess.

Practical Experience with Control Requirements

As computing speeds increase and prices drop, data analytics becomes more affordable and more applications for it arise in auditing. The "Big Four" accounting firms (Deloitte, PricewaterhouseCoopers, Ernst and Young, and KPMG) are all venturing into this space and embedding such principles into their auditing approach. Deloitte Netherlands used the approach described above for the validation of several business requirements on large log files from real information systems. Their experience with various scenarios that fall into the categories listed above is described below.

Ordering-based requirements. A utility company introduced the requirement that invoices could only be paid if there was a valid purchase order present in the system. This requirement was applicable for three months and was configured in their system as an automated control. However, in the process an invoice was registered in the system just before it was paid and the essence of the requirement was that the company wanted

Table 8.2 A task role matrix

Task	Customer representative	Banking specialist	Senior financial manager	Financial manager	Financial accountant	Financial clerk
Task t1	✓					
Task t2	✓					
Task t3						✓
Task t4					✓	
Task t5						✓
Task t6		✓				
Task t7					✓	
Task t8a				✓		
Task t8b				✓		
Task t9						✓
Task t10a					✓	
Task t10b						
Task t11						
Task t15						✓
Task t16			✓			
Task t17						
Task t18	✓					

to prevent placing orders that were not approved through the formal process. Therefore, they decided to run the task precedence business rule O1 above ("Task t1 always precedes task t2"), with t1="PO approval" and t2="Invoice registration," against the complete population of invoices of these six months. They found that in the first three months, a significant number of invoices were paid without a PO approval being present at all. However, in the last three months they noted that for all invoices paid a PO had been approved, but this approval in a significant number of cases had been "after the fact," i.e. it occurred *after* registration of the invoice.

Agent-based rule. At a large consumer products company, it was found that authorizations in their enterprise system allowed for booking and approval of purchase orders across business units. This was against company policy, and also posed a risk for the reliability of their financial statements. Using an extension of the business requirement, "Forbid agent to write," to distinguish between processes in business units, it was found that in the total population of 1,892 purchase orders there were 140 agents involved in 5 business units. The business rule held for all but one agent, who was involved in a process across two business units. Further inquiry about this exception with the agent confirmed that this assessment was correct, but that there was a plausible explanation for this fact.

Value-based rule. At a chemical company, it was found that the invoice verification option in SAP (which implements the three-way match) was set to optional. A quick sample drawn on the population showed that, indeed, the option had been disabled for certain purchase orders that were in the selected sample. Overruling this option posed the risk that invoice amounts, goods received, and goods ordered would not agree with one another, but the actual impact of this risk was hard to quantify. The "three-way match" business requirement was used to verify the full population of purchase orders based on the amount and monetary value. In this way, it was possible to assess the invoices that did not pass the three-way match criteria. These invoices were followed up, corrections were made in some cases, and credit notes were requested from suppliers.

RBAC – Role-Based Access Control

The Role-Based Access Control model (RBAC) is a well-accepted mechanism for implementing the security policy of an organization. It groups individual users into roles and assigns permissions to various roles according to their stature in the organization. A simple way to associate permissible roles for tasks is through a task-role matrix, as shown in Table 8.2. However, RBAC goes further than that. Roles are organized in a *hierarchy* or *lattice* (as shown in Figure 8.8 for the example discussed earlier). A higher role in a hierarchy normally subsumes the privileges of any subordinate role. In general, the *principle of least privilege* requires that a user be given no more privilege than necessary to perform a job. To ensure this requires us to identify what the user's job is, determine the minimum set of privileges required for the job, and to restrict the user to only those privileges and nothing more. It is also desirable that a task be performed by the lowest level role that is eligible to do it. Thus, in the context of Figure 8.8, if the financial manager is authorized to approve a transaction then it should not, in general, be done by the senior financial manager, since the latter is a more precious and expensive resource than the former. Nevertheless, on occasion, the senior financial manager may also perform the transaction to meet an urgent deadline when the financial manager is not available or otherwise preoccupied.

RBAC offers, therefore, an interesting and well understood paradigm that extends the simple use of roles employed in conventional workflow systems, yet shares the notion of employing roles as the semantic construct that lies at the heart of authorization. Formally, an RBAC model is described by:

(1)   **Entities**: users U, roles R, privileges P;
(2)   **Relationships** between these entities; and
(3)   **Constraints** over these relationships.

   In the model of Figure 8.9, user u ∈ U represents individual users and a privilege p ∈ P represents classes of rights. A right pertains to the ability of a user holding that right to

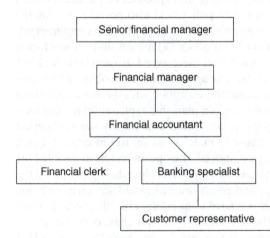

Figure 8.8 A role hierarchy

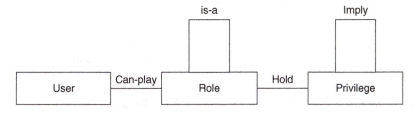

Figure 8.9 An RBAC model

perform various operations and tasks, read and write data, etc., possibly with explicit attributes. For example, `travel-approval(US$500)` represents the right to execute the task of approving travel expenses up to $500; a role $r \in R$ describes meaningful groupings of privileges or abilities that can be assigned to users, e.g. the roles of manager, auditor, and so on.

RBAC defines the following relationships between entities by means of relations:

`can-play(u; r)`, $u \in U$; $r \in R$, states that user u can play the role r. `can-play(mary, manager)` says that Mary can play the role of manager.

is-a(r1,r2), r1; r2 $\in R$, states that role r1 is a kind of (and thus inherits all privileges of) role r2. `is-a(javaprogrammer, programmer)` states that java programmers are a kind of programmer, and thus a "javaprogrammer" has all the rights that a "programmer" has, and possibly more.

If `is-a(r1, r2)` is true, we say that r1 is *larger* than (or a supertype of) r2, and conversely that r2 is *smaller* than (or a subtype of) r1. r1 is larger than r2 because it holds all the privileges that r2 does, and more:

`hold(r, p)`, $r \in R$; $p \in P$, states that role r holds the privilege p.

`imply(p1, p2)`; p1, p2 $\in P$, states that privilege p1 is stronger, or supersedes, or includes p2. For example, the right to approve travel expenses up to US$1000 *implies* (*is stronger than*) the right to approve travel expenses up to $500.

If `imply(p1, p2)` is true, we will say that p1 is stronger than p2.

There are some implicit inheritance structures in RBAC. The first one is defined by the `Is-a` relation among roles, that follows the RBAC model: if `is-a(r1, r2)` then for all p such that `hold(r2, p)`, it is also the case that `hold(r1, p)`.

The second inheritance structure is defined by the imply relation: if `imply(p1, p2)` then in every situation in which p2 is the appropriate right to accomplish something, p1 can also be used to accomplish that.

The RBAC model also includes the concept of constraints that can restrict the co-occurrence of different relations. For example, one may restrict the number of different roles that any user can play to, say, at most five. This constraint would not allow the co-occurrence of more than five instances of the can-play relation for any user.

The RBAC model contains another entity called *session*, which represents the (temporarily bounded) exercise of a role by a user. In the RBAC model, constraints that refer to session entities are called *dynamic constraints*, and constraints that do not refer to sessions are called *static constraints*. The RBAC framework has been widely implemented in database systems. Next, we shall develop the ideas of the RBAC framework further into the context of business processes.

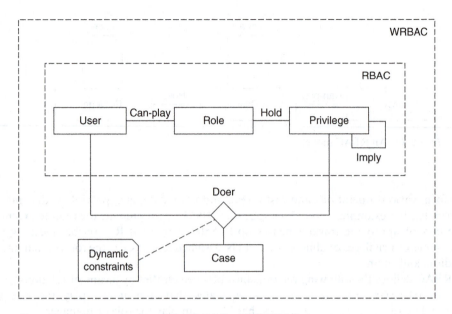

Figure 8.10 A conceptual model of RBAC and W-RBAC

W-RBAC

W-RBAC is a framework that extends RBAC in the context of workflow and business process management systems. A conceptual model for the RBAC and W-RBAC concepts is presented in Figure 8.10. W-RBAC extends RBAC with the notion of a case and a three-way relationship called doer between a user, privilege, and case. It also introduces dynamic constraints as a way of handling case-specific requirements, such as those involving binding and separation of duties.

The main components of W-RBAC are:

- the entity case which represents an instance of a workflow process;
- the relation **Doer**(U, T, C) states that user U executed the task T for a particular case C;
- dynamic constraints that limit who can execute a particular task for a particular case.

For example, a dynamic constraint would forbid the same person from performing the activities sign check and audit expenses for the same case, but not for different cases. Dynamic constraints are represented in W-RBAC as

$$\perp \leftarrow Cn$$

where Cn represents an invalid situation since the $\perp$ symbol represents null. Thus, to assert that no one can be the check signer and the auditor for the same process instance or case c, one would write

$$\perp \leftarrow doer(u, check\_signer, c), doer(a, auditor, c), u = a$$

Note that u, c and a are variables that represent a generic user, case and auditor respectively.

W-RBAC can be realized by adding a permission service to work in conjunction with a workflow engine, as shown in Figure 8.11. It employs a workflow component and an enhanced RBAC-based permission service. While the workflow component is responsible for process enactment, the permission service handles the selection of authorized and most appropriate users to execute each task, based on an organizational and authorization model that it manages. W-RBAC defines a protocol that regulates the interaction between these two modules, so that the workflow enactment and permission concerns are clearly separated, i.e. permissions are encapsulated in the permission service that is solely responsible for all authorization-related information.

The workflow system interacts with the permission system through a relatively simple interface such that, before a task is assigned to a user, the workflow module makes a call (who?) to the permission module to determine the users that can perform that task. The permission system will query the RBAC relations to verify which users have the right to perform the task and, for each user, it will verify if adding the corresponding doer relation will violate some of the dynamic constraints. The IDs of all users who do not violate the dynamic constraints will be returned to the workflow system as potential executors of the task. The workflow might then select among the potential candidates using various considerations and criteria.

Moreover, after each task is completed (done) the workflow system will notify the permission service of the user who actually performed the task (doer), so that the permission service can properly implement various dynamic constraints. The selection process is an important aspect of the workflow system. Many concerns may arise, such as optimization of some metrics like number of late jobs, quality of the work, etc. which are beyond the permission system and W-RBAC. W-RBAC will return the set of potential executors as an ordered list of sets of equally preferred users. The workflow may choose among

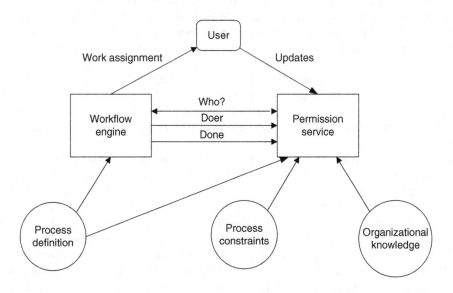

Figure 8.11 Interaction of a permission service with a workflow engine

Figure 8.12 Delegation

Source: www.businesswings.co.uk/articles/The-importance-of-delegating-authority.

the most preferred ones (regarding the ordering defined), or may choose another user who belongs to the list.

Delegation

In the security literature, the term delegation refers to the transfer or inheritance of rights from one user (delegator or transferor) to another user (transferee or delegate) who performs an action on behalf of the transferor. It may also describe the transfer of rights to a machine, that then acts as a surrogate for that user (as in an ATM transaction, for instance). The need for delegation arises when an individual to whom a task is assigned is not available. Say a director of finance, Sue, has been assigned the task of approving the travel expenses for a manager, Joe, who reports to her. However, Sue is on vacation. In such a situation, she may transfer some of her pending tasks such as this one to her colleague, Jane, who is the director of accounting. Now, Joe does not report directly to Jane; however, Jane has been given approval to serve as an alternate for Sue for certain kinds of matters. This is the main idea behind delegation. Figure 8.12 shows this idea symbolically.

Of course, Sue cannot choose any delegate for herself at will. Her delegates must be approved by company policy. Moreover, the permissions transferred to the delegate should in general not exceed the permissions of the delegator herself. In fact, if anything, the permissions of the delegate may be reduced. Thus, if Sue can approve expenses up to $5000 per trip, the approval limit of her delegate, Jane, may be kept the same as that of Sue or it may be restricted to $3000, since Jane does not know Sue's department so well.

Such a delegation may apply to a particular workflow case (say, Joe's travel to Rio for the BPM conference). This is called a specific delegation. Alternatively, Sue could confer on Jane a more generic form of delegation, in which she delegates just the right to execute a task, but does not specify the case. Now, Jane holds this right (until such time as it is revoked) to execute all instances where this right may need to be invoked and not just a specific case. There are two stages in a delegation:

(1)   First, Sue makes the delegation, which we call an assertion.
(2)   Second, the workflow engine determines that a next task has to be performed and asks the permission system for possible executors of that task.

The system will determine that Sue is the normal executor of the approval task. However, on checking availability of Sue, it might learn that Sue is not available and hence it will search for any delegates of Sue, thus leading to Jane. It is also possible that Jane is also not available, in which case the system will search for alternate delegates of Sue. If there is no alternate delegate for Sue other than Jane, then the system will look for delegates of Jane.

This second stage is called the execution of the delegation, although it may transpire that a delegation is asserted but never executed. In the above example, Jane may hold the right to approve travel expenses for Joe, but the need may never arise for her to exercise that right. In order for Sue to be able to delegate a right to Jane, she must possess the right to do so herself to start with. She may obtain the right by virtue of her position, or she may have received it through delegation. We say that Sue has *direct rights* to a privilege if the RBAC structure allows her to have that right, or, more formally, there is a role that Sue can play, and the role directly holds the specific privilege. On the other hand, Jane's right is an indirect one since she has received it through delegation. In general, Jane may further delegate her right to Bob provided she has the right to do so. Thus, the right to delegate a task is in itself a privilege that is separate from the right to perform the task. In this way, it is possible to have a chain of delegations though in actual practice such chains are not likely to be long.

Figure 8.13 shows the concepts of delegation in a model called DW-RBAC that is an extension of the W-RBAC model. As the figure shows, DW-RBAC further extends

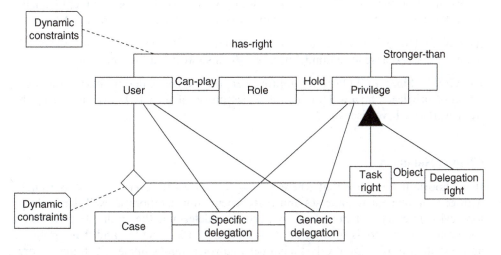

Figure 8.13 The DW-RBAC framework

W-RBAC by introducing two types of delegations: specific and generic. A specific delegation pertains to a user Delegate receiving the privilege P from another user Grantor as it relates to a specific case C. This can be expressed by a function or operation `delegate` `(Grantor, Delegate, P, C)`. In a similar way, a generic delegation is expressed without stating a case as: `delegate(Grantor, Delegate, P)`.

This figure also shows that "task right" and "delegation right" are two kinds of privileges. A delegation right pertains to a task such as "Approving travel expenses" or "Sanctioning leave request," etc. Hence, there is a link from delegation right to task right as well in the figure. Finally, the `stronger-than` (or imply) relation associates privileges with one another. For example, the privilege to "Approve travel expenses up to $5000" is stronger than (or implies) the privilege to "Approve travel expenses up to $3000." Since all privileges cannot be ordered relative to all other privileges, this relation is called a *partial order relation* (as opposed to a total order relation). However, some privileges can be compared with one another by using this relation.

A delegation can also be revoked by using the `revoke` function instead of the delegate function with the same arguments. Further extensions of delegation may restrict the time period for which the delegation privilege is extended and impose other conditions on it. If delegation is not used carefully, it can lead to some individuals inheriting multiple privileges through a series of indirect delegations that they should not have. Hence, safeguards are required to ensure that delegation occurs in a secure way.

Exercise 4: Say Jane reports to Sue, and submits her travel expenses to Sue for approval. Now, Jane is also a delegate for Sue and Sue is away on vacation. Can Jane approve her own expenses as a delegate of Sue? If not, then how will you prevent it?

Exercise 5: In a chain of delegations, where successive delegations are made to the next lower level, e.g. a CEO to a VP, a VP to a director, a director to a manager, etc., how will you prevent a manager from assuming the permission for a very important decision that is usually made by a CEO?

Exercise 6: How will you prevent a circular chain of conflict of interest from arising in an organization such that A can approve some expense (or, in general, an entitlement) for B, B can approve for C, ... , X can approve for Y, and Y can approve for A?

Exercise 7: How will you prevent a conflict of interest situation where someone is able to approve an expense for a family member who also works in the company.?

Exercise 8: Since a CEO cannot approve her own expenses, despite having the highest set of privileges, how will you handle the approval of the CEO's expenses using the frameworks we have discussed?

Chapter Summary

It is important to realize that where security is concerned, every solution is fraught with certain inherent weaknesses and cost–benefit considerations as well. Risk, therefore, exists in every system and it is important to determine the "right" level of risk a company is willing to assume, or an organization's "risk appetite," and then apply the appropriate controls. Fraud will still happen and you cannot eliminate it entirely. Moreover, a business cannot apply a "checkbox" mentality of merely satisfying industry and government regulations to security, as this is likely to result in inadequate protection. The security landscape facing a company changes every day and calls for constant vigilance. In essence you have to keep running just to stay in the same place. In this chapter, we have reviewed some approaches to improve security with a focus on business processes. We did not cover system-level security, as that is a separate topic in itself and falls outside the scope of the current book. As part of our discussion on security, we examined topics like compliance, authorization, and delegation.

The healthcare fraud problem is widely known; see for instance [6]. A lot of work on security has been done in transactional contexts, e.g. in database systems. SQL has a GRANT statement for giving permission to a user for accessing an object. General frameworks for process security, like the ones described here, have only been tried in prototype systems for the most part, and have still not been implemented in real-world BPM systems. To a large extent, security is still hard coded in application systems. The COSO Framework is described in [5]. An approach called security validation as a service for business process compliance has been described by Compagna et al. [4]. It is based on creating a BPMN2-SEC schema that extends the BPMN2 standard to capture the security-related aspects of a business process. A validation as a service-enabled client connects to a server that performs the validation by applying model checking techniques. Proof of concept prototypes have been developed in the context of SAP Netweaver and Activiti BPM systems. Control objectives are discussed in [16]. Schultz [19] has described ways to add access control features into process aware information systems, e.g. SAP, by means of patterns like double invoice check, three-way pattern match, etc.

Our discussion on the security framework and separation of duties is based on several works. The RBAC model was originally proposed by Sandhu et al. [18] and by Ferraiolo, Cugini, and Kuhn [8, 9]. It is implemented in several database systems. Ferraiolo and Kuhn also introduced the notions of separation of duties [8] and a language was proposed by Ahn and Sandhu [1]. The separation of duty framework is from Ernst and Young [7]. Some early work on supporting RBAC in the context of workflow systems was done by Bertino, Ferrari, and Atluri [3].

There is a large body of work on business process compliance with semantic constraints (see for instance [14, 15, 17]). A lot of such work in the context of process aware information systems has the aim of ensuring compliance with business rules and policies, also broadly called semantic constraints. To be able to implement the security policies a BPM first has to model the resource perspective that provides elements referring to organizational units, group roles, and staff members. The approach proposed by Knuplesch et al. [10] uses extended Compliance Rule Graphs to model the time, data and resource perspectives. Then, they are able to create rules consisting of antecedent and consequent patterns to describe relationships between elements of the resource perspective (and time and data perspectives as well). A further development of this approach proposes a visual framework to express compliance rules [11]. Another method for visualization of compliance violations is presented in [2]. A conceptual model for online auditing of process logs for applying detective, preventive, and proactive controls is discussed in [20]. Our case study and practical experiences are based on that work. An approach for verifying compliance of a process log based on model checking is given in [13].

For research on delegation, we refer the reader to [21, 22]. A basic model for incorporating security into a workflow system called W-RBAC has been discussed in [21]. This model has been extended by adding features for specific and generic delegation into the DW-RBAC model [22]. A very thorough and systematic survey of security issues in process aware information systems that highlights challenges and future directions in the context of 12 security controls within five broad categories was conducted by Leitner and Rinderle-Ma [12].

References

1. G. J. Ahn and R. Sandhu. The RSL99 language for role-based separation of duty constraints. In: *ACM RBAC Workshop*. Vol. 99, pp. 43–54, 1999.
2. A. Awad and M. Weske. Visualization of Compliance Violation in Business Process Models. In: Proceedings of the Business Process Management Workshops. *Lecture Notes in Business Information Processing*, Vol. 43, Springer, pp. 182–193, 2009.
3. E. Bertino, E. Ferrari and V. Atluri. The specification and enforcement of authorization constraints in workflow management systems. *ACM Transactions on Information and System Security*, Vol. 2, No. 1, 65–104, 1999.
4. L. Compagna, P. Guilleminot and A. D. Brucker. Business Process Compliance via Security Validation as a Service. In: M. Oriol and J. Penix (eds) *Testing Tools Track of ICST*. IEEE Computer Society, Washington, DC, USA, 2013.
5. COSO. Committee of Sponsoring Organizations of the Treadway Commission. www.coso.org/Pages/default.aspx.
6. *The Economist*. The $272 billion swindle. May 31, 2014.
7. Ernst and Young. A risk-based approach to segregation of duties, May 2010.
8. D. F. Ferraiolo and D. R. Kuhn. Role-based Access Controls. *Proceedings of the 15th NIST-NSA National Computer Security Conference*, Baltimore, Maryland, October 13–16, 1992.
9. D. Ferraiolo, J. Cugini and R. Kuhn. Role-based Access Control (RBAC): Features and Motivations. In: *Proceedings of 11th Annual Computer Security Application Conference*, New Orleans, LA, pp. 241–248, December 1995.
10. D. Knuplesch, L. T. Ly, S. Rinderle-Ma, H. Pfeifer and P. Dadam. On Enabling Data-aware Compliance Checking of Business Process Models. In: J. Parsons, M. Saeki, P. Shoval, C. Woo and Y. Wand (eds) ER 2010. *LNCS*, Vol. 6412. Springer, Heidelberg, pp. 332–346, 2010.
11. D. Knuplesch, M. Reichert and A. Kumar. A framework for visually monitoring business process compliance. *Information Systems*, Vol. 64, pp. 381–409, 2017.
12. M. Leitner and S. Rinderle-Ma. A systematic review on security in Process-Aware Information Systems – Constitution, challenges, and future directions. *Information and Software Technology*, Vol. 56, No. 3, pp. 273–293, 2014.
13. I. A. Letia and A. Goron. Verifying Compliance for Business Process Logs with a Hybrid Logic Model Checker. In: I. Hatzilygeroudis, V. Palade, J. Prentzas (eds) Combinations of Intelligent Methods and Applications. *Smart Innovation, Systems and Technologies*, Vol. 46. Springer, Cham, pp. 61–78, 2016.
14. L. T. Ly, S. Rinderle-Ma, K. Göser and P. Dadam. On enabling integrated process compliance with semantic constraints in process management systems. *Information Systems Frontiers*, Vol. 14, No. 2, pp. 195–219, 2012.
15. L. T. Ly, S. Rinderle and P. Dadam. Integration and verification of semantic constraints in adaptive process management systems. *Data and Knowledge Engineering*, Vol. 64, No. 1, pp. 3–23, 2008.
16. S. Sadiq, G. Governatori, K. Namiri. Modeling Control Objectives for Business Process Compliance. In: Proceedings of the 5th International Conference on Business Process Management (BPM), *Lecture Notes in Computer Science*, Vol. 4714. Springer, Berlin, Heidelberg, pp. 149–164, 2007.
17. S. W. Sadiq, M. E. Orlowska and W. Sadiq. Specification and validation of process constraints for flexible workflows. *Information Systems*, Vol. 30, No. 5, pp. 349–378, 2005.

18. R. Sandhu, E. Coyne, H. Feinstein and C. Youman. Role-based access control models. *IEEE Computers*, Vol. 29, No. 2, pp. 38–47, 1996.
19. M. Schultz. Enriching Process Models for Business Process Compliance Checking in ERP Environments. In: J. Brocke, R. Hekkala, S. Ram and M. Rossi (eds) *Proceedings of the 8th International Conference on Design Science at the Intersection of Physical and Virtual Design (DESRIST'13)*. Springer-Verlag, Berlin, Heidelberg, pp. 120–135, 2013.
20. W. van der Aalst, K. V. Hee, J. M. V. D. Werf, A. Kumar and M. Verdonk. Conceptual model for online auditing. *Decision Support Systems*, Vol. 50, No. 3 (February 2011) pp. 636–647, 2011.
21. J. Wainer, P. Barthelmess and A. Kumar. W-RBAC – A workflow security model incorporating controlled overriding of constraints. *International Journal of Cooperative Information Systems*, Vol. 12, No. 4, pp. 455–486, 2003.
22. J. Wainer, A. Kumar and P. Barthelmess. DW-RBAC: A formal security model of delegation and revocation in workflow systems. *Information Systems*, Vol. 32, No. 3, pp. 365–384, 2007.

9   Real-Time and Temporal Processes

Introduction

Thus far we have mentioned the notion of time only sparingly in this book. As you can well imagine, time plays an important role in a running process instance. In fact, it can even be of the essence if the process instance has a deadline by which it must finish. Sometimes there are written agreements between a customer and a service provider that require a process instance to finish in a pre-specified time duration. If the performance guarantees are not satisfied, then penalties are incurred by the provider. Hence, it is important to monitor a process from moment to moment, and make decisions based on its status. The most common types of time related considerations in a process pertain to durations of activities and elapsed times between activities. In general, processes that are sensitive to timing are called *temporal processes*.

In this chapter, we shall motivate the need for real-time and time sensitive business processes and then discuss techniques for modeling and executing such processes. We shall start with motivating temporal processes, intervals, and constraints. Then we introduce a running example, build a temporal model for it, and show how to analyze it using heuristic methods. A formal approach and ways to analyze it for managing violations are discussed next. Finally, we present ideas for applying optimization in real-time processes and monitoring them.

Motivation

Figure 9.1 shows a simple example of a real-time process involving dispatch of an emergency vehicle. When a person living in the US calls 911 for an emergency service, a dispatcher answers the call and records the address along with other important information about the caller, and then dispatches an ambulance to that address. However, some important information is missing from this simple process model.

The missing information relates to time. Clearly, time is an essential consideration in such a process because the activities must occur within prescribed time limits. Check out the modified process model in Figure 9.2 with the additional temporal information superimposed on the process model. The revised figure shows that the dispatcher must answer the call within 30 seconds and record the address within 1 minute of receiving the call. Further, she must locate an available emergency vehicle within the next 2 minutes. Finally, the vehicle should be at such a location from where it can reach the calling address within 5 minutes.

This is an example of a temporal process where each activity has a prescribed duration and it must be completed within that duration.

Consider another example of a customer stock purchase from an online broker. Online brokers usually offer execution guarantees to customers that they will execute a customer order within, say, 10 or 15 seconds after it is placed. If they fail to do so, then they charge a lower commission on the trade, or even waive the commission altogether. The process model for this stock purchase order fulfilment process is shown in Figure 9.3.

In this process, we employ a new structure called the **temporal-XOR gateway**. This gateway checks if the elapsed time since the start of the process (when the order is received) is more than 10 seconds. If so, the reduced fee is applied to this transaction, and then it is recorded and the customer is notified.

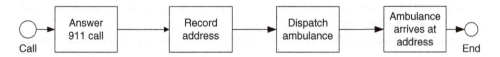

Figure 9.1 A 911 call dispatch process

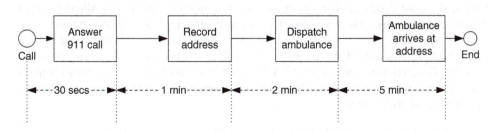

Figure 9.2 A 911 call dispatch process with temporal duration of tasks

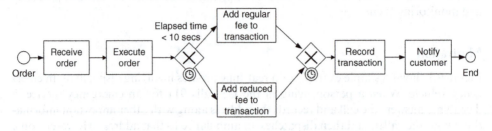

Figure 9.3 Fulfilment of a buy stock order process at an online brokerage

Exercise 1: How is the process of Figure 9.2 different from that of Figure 9.3?

If you compare the two processes, the emergency response process can take up to 8.5 minutes to finish. On the other hand, the stock buy order process takes just about 10 to 15 seconds. The second process is called a **real-time process** because the customer will receive an immediate response on her screen that the trade has been executed while she is waiting.

Exercise 2: Is the emergency response process a real-time process or not? Explain briefly.

There is another difference between the two process models that should be noted. In the process of Figure 9.2 we show the elapsed time between successive activities and this is equal to the duration of each activity. However, in Figure 9.3 we only show the elapsed time from the start of the process instance until the Temporal-XOR gateway (for split) that occurs immediately after the trade is executed. This means that all the activities until then should be completed in less than 10 seconds. As we shall see, there are different ways of representing temporal constraints in a process model.

It should also be noted that a large number of real-world business processes have deadlines. An application for a credit card can be processed in real-time, and a response is sent to the customer within a few seconds. A company may have a policy that all expense approval request must be processed within 7 days. Banks also have policies on how soon they can process mortgage loan applications, funds transfers, letters of credit applications, etc. In practice, actual instances are monitored and violations are reported to management on a regular basis.

Next, we'll provide some background on temporal intervals and temporal constraints.

Temporal Interval Patterns

One of the most significant early contributions to temporal modeling is Allen's Interval Algebra. In his work, Allen has described 13 possible temporal relations between two tasks, each of which has a specific start time, duration, and an end time. Figure 9.4 is a pictorial representation of Allen's 13 temporal relations between two events/processes: A and B. These relations can be described formally in terms of constraints using the maximum (max) and minimum (min) functions to represent the corresponding time points of the intervals as follows:

Interval A is before Interval B iff max(A) < min(B)
Interval A meets Interval B iff max(A) = min(B)

Interval A overlaps Interval B iff max(A) > min(B) and max(B) > max(A)
Interval A occurs during Interval B iff min(A) > min(B) and max(A) < max(B)
Interval A finishes Interval B iff min(A) > min(B) and max(A) = max(B)
Interval A is co-temporal with Interval B iff min(A) = min(B) and max(A) = max(B).

Another important idea described by Allen is the concept that a particular time interval (over which a property holds) can be divided into sub-intervals such that the property holds over each sub-interval as well. So, a statement such as, "I played soccer every day this week" implicitly implies that the person played soccer on Monday of the week that she is referring to. Thus,

"I played soccer every day this week" → "I played soccer on Monday"
"I played soccer every day this week" → "I played soccer on Tuesday"
"I played soccer every day this week" → "I played soccer on Monday and Tuesday" etc.

Exercise 3: Using two temporal intervals $[TS_i, TF_i]$ and $[TS_j, TF_j]$, write a constraint to express the idea that the maximum overlap between them should not exceed δ.

Exercise 4: Using three intervals $[TS_i, TF_i]$, $[TS_j, TF_j]$ and $[TS_k, TF_k]$, write a constraint to express the idea that the total elapsed time from the start of the first interval to the end of the last one should not exceed δ.

Types of Constraints

There are different types of constraints that are relevant in the context of a temporal process. We can think of constraints in terms of events. An event is assumed to occur

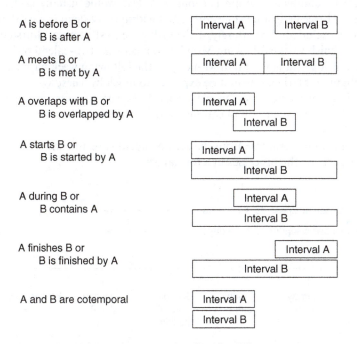

A is before B or B is after A	
A meets B or B is met by A	
A overlaps with B or B is overlapped by A	
A starts B or B is started by A	
A during B or B contains A	
A finishes B or B is finished by A	
A and B are cotemporal	

Figure 9.4 13 interval patterns described by Allen

at the start or end of an activity. Thus, TS_i and TF_i are time points at which the start and end events, respectively, occur for activity i. As noted above, we have task duration constraints and inter-task duration constraints. They can be specified in a common framework in terms of events.

Lower bound constraints. The duration between occurrences of events A and B is constrained by a lower bound. Thus, $TF_i - TS_i \geq \ell$ is a lower bound constraint that requires task i to consume at least ℓ amount of time. When you sit for a massage therapy the therapist may be required to perform, say, head massage on you for at least 5 minutes.

Upper bound constraints. The duration between occurrences of events A and B is constrained by an upper bound. Thus, $TF_i - TS_i \leq \upsilon$ is an upper bound constraint that requires task i to take no more than υ amount of time. In a massage therapy session, the therapist may be directed to not exceed 10 minutes of massage to prevent any harm to the patient.

Fixed date constraints. These constraints require that an event may occur only on certain dates. A date could refer to a specific calendar date and a time. It could refer to a calendar date and a range of hours on that date, say 9 a.m. to 5 p.m. It is also possible to specify that a task be performed during working hours. Working hours may correspond to the hours of operation of a business or a government agency.

Inter-task constraints. These constraints span two different tasks and specify a lower or upper bound (or even both) between the start (finish) of one task and the start (finish) of another task. The start (finish) time of a task i is denoted as TS_i (TF_i). Thus, $TF_i - TS_j \leq \upsilon$ denotes that the elapsed time from the start of task j to the end of task i must not exceed υ.

It is also important to note that while calculating elapsed time, the gap is not always determined as the exact time difference between two specific points in time. A requirement that a task must be completed within two business days would usually exclude weekends and holidays. However, if it must be completed within two calendar days then these days would not be excluded. Accordingly, if the task were to start on a Thursday, it would be expected to finish by the following Monday to meet the "two-calendar day" requirement. However, if it so transpired that Monday of the following week happened to be a holiday (see Figure 9.5), then it would be expected to finish by Tuesday.

Therefore, calculations involving time can get tricky. However, for our discussion in this chapter we will ignore such complications, and just assume that time flows continuously in calendar days.

Next, we shall give a running example from the area of healthcare and show how to model the temporal aspects of the processes in a formal way.

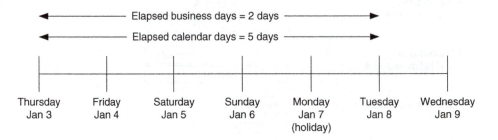

Figure 9.5 Measuring time intervals based on calendar days vs. business days

A Healthcare Example

In medical processes, it is especially important that strict temporal guidelines be observed for the success of various treatments and procedures. Some examples of such guidelines that arise in a medical process (say, for the treatment of a fracture) are:

- A patient may be prescribed two medicines together, but they should not overlap for more than three days.
- A radiologist's report must be submitted within 24 hours of a CT scan.
- If surgery is needed, it must take place within a week of the radiologist's report.
- Antibiotics must be administered for 3 days before surgery
- A blood thinner like Warfarin must be stopped 48 hours before surgery.
- The patient must recover in the hospital for two days before being discharged.
- The total time from patient admission to discharge should not exceed ten days.
- Adequate blood supply must be procured at least one day before surgery.

In modeling such time-aware processes, the duration of each activity (or task) is provided as a range with a lower and an upper bound. For example, in a medical process the duration of the patient admission activity is, say, between 10 and 20 minutes. By associating such durations with each activity, one can determine expected minimum and maximum times for each execution path of the workflow from start to end. Moreover, deviations from the expected times can be monitored, and appropriate messages and alerts can be generated to draw attention. In some cases, only one bound, either upper or lower, may apply.

Another aspect of temporal workflows relates to inter-activity constraints that impose restrictions on the elapsed time between one activity and another. Further, they may be specified with reference to the start or finish time of the respective activities. A variety of temporal constraints may be imposed on a workflow. While other types of constraints have been studied in literature, there has been less work on temporal constraints.

A Simple Temporal Model

A temporal model of a process is made by combining two types of constraints: (1) structural constraints, and (2) temporal constraints. The structural constraints capture the control flow of the process to coordinate the proper sequence in which the tasks occur. The temporal constraints specify the permitted durations of each activity and the minimum or maximum gaps between them.

Definition 1: A general temporal process model TP can be represented as:

$$TP = (T, A, X, E, TD, TI)$$

Where

T: set of task nodes, $T_1, T_2, \ldots$
A: set of AND control nodes, $A_1, A_2, \ldots$
X: set of XOR control nodes, $X_1, X_2, \ldots$
E: set of edges among the nodes in {T, A, X}
TD: set of task duration ranges: $\{(T_i, D_{i\_min}, D_{i\_max}), \ldots\}$, where $D_{i\_min}, D_{i\_max} \in R^+$

TI: set of additional inter-task constraints: $\{(T_i, T_j, S|F, S|F, TI_{i\_min}, TI_{i\_max}), \ldots\}$, $TI_{i\_min}, TI_{i\_max} \in R^+$

Figure 9.6 is an example of a simple temporal model. It shows the control flow, along with [min, max] durations of each task and inter-task constraints. It is expressed as:

T: $\{T_1, T_2, \ldots, T_6\}$
A: $\{A_1, A_2\}$
X: $\{X_1, X_2, X_3, X_4\}$
E: $\{(start, X_1), (X_1, T_1), (X_1, T_2), (T_1, A_1), (A_1, T_3), (A_1, T_4), (T_3, A_2), (T_4, A_2), \ldots\}$
TD: $\{(T_1, D_{1\_min}, D_{1\_max}), (T_2, D_{2\_min}, D_{2\_max}), (T_3, D_{3\_min}, D_{3\_max}), \ldots\}$
TI: $\{(T_1, T_5, S, S, TI_{1\_min}, TI_{1\_max}), (T_4, T_5, S, F, TI_{2\_min}, TI_{2\_max})\}$.

In addition to the time intervals of each task, an inter-task constraint (TI) can also be represented by a dashed line connecting the start(s) or end/finish (F) point of a task to the start or end point of another task. For example, in Figure 9.6, the inter-task constraint TI_2 between T_4 and T_5 requires that the elapsed time from the start of T_4 until the end of T_5 must lie in the $[TI_{2\_min}, TI_{2\_max}]$ interval. Also note that while we only consider task and inter-task durations, fixed time activities can also be modeled by setting their relative time with respect to the start time of a process instance and converting them into delays with respect to the start activity.

To illustrate our modeling approach, the treatment process of a patient suspected of having a proximal femoral fracture shown in Figure 9.7 will be used as a running example. This figure shows a simplified clinical pathway in BPMN notation. This process model consists of 14 tasks coordinated by sequential flows along with choice and parallel structures in BPMN notation. Briefly, after a patient is admitted (T_1), she undergoes anamnesis and examination (T_2). Following the initial examination, if there is any suspicion that the patient may have sustained a proximal femoral fracture, she is advised to

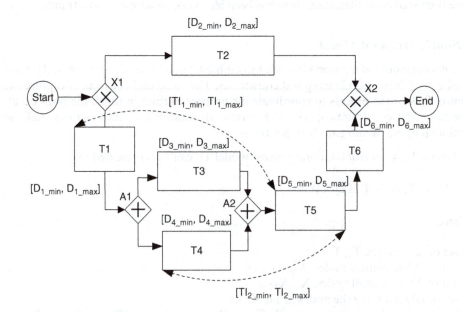

Figure 9.6 A basic temporal model with XOR and AND connectors

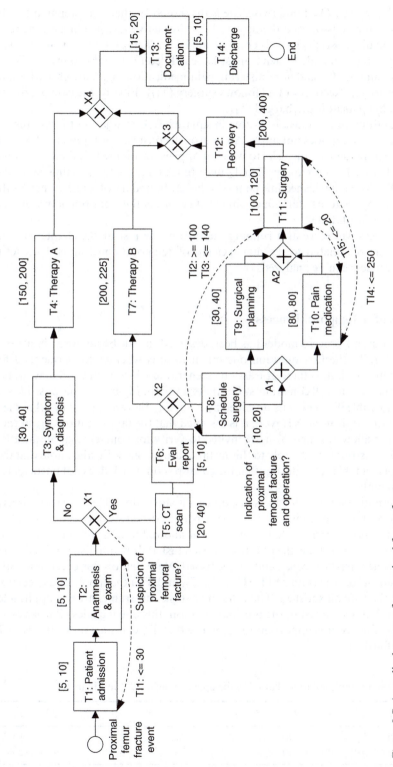

Figure 9.7 A medical process for proximal femur fracture

take a CT scan test (T_5); otherwise, she is diagnosed further and prepared for therapy (T_3), followed by customized therapy A (T_4). Alternatively, depending on the results of her imaging diagnosis (T_6), she is either treated with therapy B (T_7) or by surgery (T_{11}). If surgery is recommended, then it must be scheduled (T_8), and two prerequisite tasks: surgical planning (T_9) and administering pain medication (T_{10}), are carried out in parallel prior to T_{11}. Recovery (T_{12}) follows surgery (T_{11}). Finally, the case is documented (T_{13}) and the patient is discharged (T_{14}).

The duration for each task is written in square brackets adjacent to it (in time units). If a value is blank it does not apply. An inter-task constraint is represented by a dashed line connecting the pair of tasks to which it applies. In Figure 9.7, there is a constraint between T_1 and T_2 that requires that T_2 must finish no more than 30 time units after the start of T_1. When the dashed line connects the left boundary of a task, it means that the constraint applies to its start time, while if it connects the right boundary of a task, it applies to its finish time.

This process will serve as a running example in the rest of the chapter to illustrate various concepts related to the management of temporal constraints. Now let us see how this process can be analyzed.

Analysis of a Temporal Process

After a temporal process model has been designed, it can be analyzed in a variety of ways. Naturally, the first question one might raise is whether the model is a feasible one. This means that, is there at least one scenario in which the model may give a valid solution that satisfies all constraints? For the example in Figure 9.7, one possible solution is shown in Table 9.1. This was obtained by assuming that the workflow takes the upper branch at the XOR node X1. Also, it is assumed that the task durations are at the lower end of their allowed range. You are invited to verify for yourself that all duration and inter-task constraints that apply to this instance are satisfied. Further, note that the dash (-) symbol in a table cell indicates that the corresponding task does not participate in the execution path.

An alternative solution for the same process is shown in Table 9.2. Here it is assumed that the workflow execution takes the lower path at the XOR nodes X1 and X2. Again, the task durations are at the lower end of their allowed ranges. You may verify that this solution is also correct, i.e. the duration of each task falls within its permitted range and all applicable inter-task constraints are satisfied. Note that on this execution path there are five inter-task constraints (TI_1, TI_2, TI_3, TI_4 and TI_5) that apply and check to make sure that they are all satisfied. The other inter-task constraints are not applicable here. Also note that in contrast to the previous solution, this one includes all tasks except T_3, T_4 and T_7. Finally, it is important to recognize that T_{11} can start only after *both* T_9 and T_{10} have finished.

Table 9.1 An example solution that takes the upper branch at X1 in Figure 9.7

	1	2	3	4	5	6	7	8	9	10	11	12	13	14
Start	0	5	10	40	-	-	-	-	-	-	-	-	190	205
End	5	10	40	190	-	-	-	-	-	-	-	-	205	210

Table 9.2 Another example solution that takes the lower branches at X1 and X2 in Figure 9.7

	1	2	3	4	5	6	7	8	9	10	11	12	13	14
Start	0	5	-	-	10	30	-	35	45	45	145	245	445	460
End	5	10	-	-	30	35	-	45	75	125	245	445	460	465

Table 9.3 A solution that takes the lower branches at X1, X2 with maximum durations of tasks

	1	2	3	4	5	6	7	8	9	10	11	12	13	14
Start	0	10	-	-	20	60	-	70	90	90	190	310	710	730
End	10	20	-	-	60	70	-	90	130	170	310	710	730	740

Exercise 5: There is a third possible execution scenario for the process of Table 9.3. Can you identify this scenario and make a table to show its execution schedule assuming that each task takes its *longest permitted duration*? Check if this solution satisfies all constraints. If not, what are the violations?

In the healthcare example process of Figure 9.7, there are three possible execution paths as follows:

Path 1: T_1, T_2, T_3, T_4, T_{13}, T_{14}. (by taking the upper branch at XOR node X1)

Path 2: T_1, T_2, T_5, T_6, T_8, T_9, T_{10}, T_{11}, T_{12}, T_{13}, T_{14}. (by taking the lower branch at X1, X2)

Path 3: T_1, T_2, T_5, T_6, T_7, T_{13}, T_{14}. (by taking the lower branch at X1, and upper branch at X2).

In general, at an XOR split node, only one outgoing branch can be taken. Thus, each XOR branch in turn leads to a different execution path. The total number of execution paths is determined by selecting all valid combinations of outgoing branches at all XOR split nodes. However, as you can well appreciate by now, all outgoing branches are taken at an AND split node so this does not lead to multiple different execution paths.

Table 9.2 assumed that each task took its minimum duration to finish, an optimistic scenario. It is natural to ask how execution would proceed if each task was tardy and took its maximum permitted duration. Under this assumption, we obtain an execution schedule shown in Table 9.3.

The new solution in Table 9.3 takes considerably longer to finish. Again, it is possible to verify that this solution does indeed satisfy all the constraints. It turns out that if solutions can be found at both extreme values of a task duration range, then a solution will always exist at every value for the duration range of the task.

Exercise 6: Show that if a solution can be found at both extreme values of the duration range of a task, then it can be found at every duration value within its permitted range.

Thus, we can see that it is possible to identify all execution paths and, for each path, check if a valid solution that satisfies all constraints exists for (1) a lower bound constraint (let's call it the Lower Bound or LB solution); and (2) for an upper bound constraint (let's call it the Upper Bound or UB solution) of the task duration range of each task. If so, it means that a valid solution does exist for each value within the permitted task duration range.

Managing Violations by a Heuristic Approach

So far, we have only considered task durations within their permitted range. Now, say, a task exceeds its permitted duration. The natural question to ask is: Will this lead to any further violations of other constraints? Thus, we would like to understand the effect of this violation on the remainder of the process.

Now consider that the duration of task T_8 in path 2 (i.e. the path with tasks T_1, T_2, T_5, T_6 and T_8–T_{14}) of Figure 9.7 exceeds its upper bound by 10 time units and takes 30 time units.

Exercise 7: Modify the schedule of Table 9.2 to check if all constraints can still be satisfied if the duration of T_8 increases to 30.

Exercise 8: What is the maximum possible duration of T_8 beyond which some constraint will be violated?

Table 9.4 shows another scenario where the duration of T_8 is 50. What maximum permissible value for the duration of T_8 did you find in Exercise 8? At this point, we can clearly see that constraint TI_3 that requires $TS_{11} - TS_8 \leq 140$ is violated because $TS_{11} - TS_8 = 150$. Further, we can also examine the constraints along the two paths from the start of T_8 to the start of T_{11}, as follows:

Upper path from T_8 to T_{11}: $(TF_8 - TS_8) + (TF_9 - TS_9) \leq 140$, and
Lower path from T_8 to T_{11}: $(TF_8 - TS_8) + (TF_{10} - TS_{10}) + (TS_{11} - TF_{10}) \leq 140$.

While the upper path constraint is valid, the lower path constraint is not. This means that the maximum permitted value of T_8 is 40. In this way, it is possible to examine various run time scenarios to check for any cascading effects of a constraint violation on the rest of the process.

Now we know that increasing the duration of T_8 beyond a cut-off value will lead to violation of inter-task constraint TI_3. Let us say that TI_3 is inviolable! We may then ask: Is there another solution that satisfies TI_3 at the expense of another constraint? So, let us examine again the expression that causes TI_3 to be violated along the lower path from T_8 to T_{11}:

Lower path constraint from T_8 to T_{11}: $(TF_8 - TS_8) + (TF_{10} - TS_{10})$
$$+ (TS_{11} - TF_{10}) \leq 140.$$

Given that the duration of T_8 is 50, we can rewrite it as:

$$50 + (TF_{10} - TS_{10}) + 20 \leq 140.$$

To satisfy this constraint, $TF_{10} - TS_{10} \leq 70$. This means that the duration of T_{10} should be no more than 70 to satisfy this constraint. However, the duration of T_{10} is exactly 80. Thus, *now we will have to violate the duration constraint of task T_{10} to satisfy the inter-task constraint TI_3.*

Table 9.4 A solution where the actual duration of task T_8 exceeds its upper bound by 30

	1	2	3	4	5	6	7	8	9	10	11	12	13	14
Start	0	10	-	-	20	60	-	70	120	120	220	340	740	760
End	10	20	-	-	60	70	-	120	160	200	340	740	760	770

Exercise 9: Can you see another way to satisfy constraint TI_3 without violating the duration constraint on T_{10} in the above scenario?

Well, let us revisit the lower path constraint again:

$$(TF_8 - TS_8) + (TF_{10} - TS_{10}) + (TS_{11} - TF_{10}) \leq 140.$$

This can be rewritten as:

$$(TF_8 - TS_8) + (TF_{10} - TS_{10}) + (TS_{11} - TF_{10}) \leq 140.$$

This implies that $TS_{11} - TF_{10} \leq 10$, i.e. the gap between the end of T_{10} and the start of T_{11} should not exceed 10. However, inter-task constraint TI_5 requires that this gap must be at least 20. Hence, we will have to violate TI_5 by 10 time units to satisfy both TI_3 and the T_{10} duration constraint. This shows that there are often alternatives that may be pursued in a running process. Hence, a physician faced with this scenario at the end of task T_8 will have these options:

Option 1: delay start of surgery by 10 time units beyond the guidelines
Option 2: reduce the duration of pain medicine by 10 time units from 80 to 70
Option 3: reduce the gap between the stopping of pain medicine and the start of surgery by 10 time units.

In a scenario like this where multiple options exist, a decision can be made by the physician based on her professional expertise.

Exercise 10: Write arithmetic expressions for the maximum, minimum, and overlap durations among three overlapping tasks using the TS and TF values of each task along with the min and max functions.

A General Approach for Managing Violations

What we described above was a heuristic approach for managing violations of temporal constraints at run time of a process. Next, we shall describe a more formal approach.

We first build a temporal model of the process by combining four types of constraints:

- structural constraints (SC)
- temporal flow constraints (TF)
- task duration constraints (TD)
- inter-task constraints (TI).

The structural constraints were described in Chapter 6, and they ensure the structural correctness of the process model. The flow constraints capture the temporal flow among successive activities. Thus, if activities T_1 and T_2 are in sequence we need to explicitly capture the idea that the start of activity T_2, denoted by TS_2 is no sooner than the finish time of activity T_1 denoted as TS_1. The temporal, and task and inter-task duration constraints have been described above.

By combining these four types of constraints we can obtain a complete formal model of the process. A (partial) formulation for the process model of Figure 9.7 is shown in Figure 9.8. This is called a model in the sense that it captures the exact requirements of the process in a formal way by a series of related equations. To create this formulation, we combine the SC, TF, TD, and TI constraints. Moreover, we have added an objective function at the top of the formulation in Figure 9.8. The objective function is meant to produce a solution with a specific goal. If we solved our system of equations without an objective function, then it would have an infinite number of solutions. However, by adding a specific objective it is possible to obtain a single solution. In the case of our example, the objective function is to minimize the time taken to finish the

---

Model MILP1
Minimize TF14   //Minimize end time of process
s.t.
//Structural constraints (SC)
Start. Start = 1;
End. End = 1;
SF0. T_1 = Start;
SF1. $T_2 = T_1$;
SF2. X1 = T_2;
SF3. $T_3 + T_5$ = X1;
SF4. $T_4 = T_3$; $T_6 = T_5$; X2 = T_6;
...

//Temporal flow constraints (TF)
TF$_1$. $TF_1 \geq TS_1$;
TF$_2$. $TS_2 \geq TF_1$;
TF$_3$. $XS_1 \geq TF_2$;
...

//Temporal duration constraints (TD)
TD$_1$. $T_1 == 1 \rightarrow TF_1 - TS_1 \geq 5$;
TD$_2$. $T_1 == 1 \rightarrow TF_1 - TS_1 \leq 10$;
...

//Temporal inter-task constraints (TI)
TI$_1$. $T_1 == 1$ && $T_2 == 1 \rightarrow TF_2 - TS_1 \leq 30$;
TI$_2$. $T_{11} == 1$ && $T_8 == 1 \rightarrow TS_{11} - TS_8 \geq 100$;
TI$_3$. $T_{11} == 1$ && $T_8 == 1 \rightarrow TS_{11} - TS_8 \leq 140$;
TI$_4$. $T_{11} == 1$ && $T_{10} == 1 \rightarrow TF_{11} - TS_{10} \leq 250$;
TI$_5$. $T_{11} == 1$ && $T_{10} == 1 \rightarrow TS_{11} - TF_{10} \geq 20$;

Figure 9.8 A (partial) formulation of a design-time temporal workflow for the example problem

process. This is denoted simply as the finish time of the last activity in the process. In this case, since T_{14} is the last activity for our example, we write the objective as **Minimize TF$_{14}$**.

One other observation about the model in Figure 9.8 is in order. Notice that the TD and TI constraints are written in the **if-then** ($\rightarrow$) style. This is done to ensure that these constraints apply only if the associated tasks are present in a solution. If the associated tasks are not selected in a solution, then these constraints naturally become invalid, e.g. if task T_i is not present in the solution then TS_i and TF_i do not have any meaning and are undefined, so they may be ignored.

A model such as this is called a mixed integer linear programming (MILP) model. There are many software programs for solving such models. A solution will give the values of the variables in the model such as $T_1, T_2, \ldots$; $TS_1, TS_2, \ldots$; and $TF_1, TF_2, \ldots$. We used the software tool CPLEX from IBM for solving the model. The CPLEX solution produced an objective function value of 210. In fact, it is the same solution as the heuristic solution we had obtained in Table 9.1. This is called a *design-time solution* because it was produced before we actually started running the model. It shows that the model is valid, since it has a feasible solution. The full solution consists of tasks $T_1, T_2, T_3, T_4, T_{13},$ and T_{14}. This corresponds to the path in Figure 9.7, where the upper outgoing branch is taken at node X1. The solution also shows the start and finish times of each activity.

Clearly, other outgoing branches could have been taken at X1 and then at X2. To find a design time solution that shows whether a path with X1 and X2 is feasible, we can force the lower outgoing path at X1 by adding a constraint $T_5 = 1$. This produced a solution with an objective function value of 465 and included tasks $T_1, T_2, T_5, T_6,$ and tasks T_8 through T_{14}. This is the same solution that was obtained by the heuristic approach in Table 9.2. Finally, we tried forcing a solution with the upper outgoing branch at X2 by adding $T_7 = 1$. In this case, the objective function value is 255, and it includes tasks T_1–T_2, T_5–T_7, and T_{13}–T_{14}.

Exercise 11: Make a full formulation of the optimization problem shown in Figure 9.7, and solve it in CPlex or another optimization tool.

Run Time Analysis

Above, we developed an "ideal," design-time solution that can be planned even before the process starts running. At run time, changes have to be made to the formulation in a running process based on its actual progress. So, say we have just completed task T_8 (schedule surgery) and while its planned completion time was 45, the actual completion time was 65 because of scheduling problems that necessitated manual intervention. We wish to determine what constraints, if any, will be violated on account of this delay, and how the process will run from here on. Hence, we perform the steps shown in Figure 9.9. These steps are carried out in the various run time scenarios that follow.

Run time scenario 1. Consider the situation where task T_8 is delayed. Its normal duration is [10, 20], but in this case, it has taken 30 time units as shown in Table 9.5.

To analyze the subsequent run time behavior of this process, we add the constraints that specify the exact TS and TF times of the completed tasks to our formulation and remove the duration constraints for these tasks (i.e. T_1, T_2, T_5, T_6) since they are already completed. We can also add the start time for T_8 and remove the upper bound constraint

Model variables: T[i], task start and finish times TS$_i$, TF$_i$

1. IP_run = IP_design

2. L = {T$_i$ s.t. task T$_i$ is completed}

3. Delete from IP_run any duration constraints ∀T$_i$ ∈ L, e.g.

    $D_{i\_max} \geq TF_i - TS_i \geq D_{i\_min}$

4. Add to IP_run the *actual* TS and TF of each completed task, i.e.

    $TS_i = TS_{i\_actual}$; $TF_i = TF_{i\_actual}$

5. Solve the modified IP_run formulation

Output: Tasks T$_i$ values as 0-1; and

TS$_i$, TF$_i$, i.e. start and finish times for each task where T$_i$=1.

Figure 9.9 Procedure for performing run time analysis

Table 9.5 Partial run time schedule where T$_8$ is delayed beyond its maximum duration

	1	*2*	*3*	*4*	*5*	*6*	*7*	*8*	*9*	*10*	*11*	*12*	*13*	*14*
Start	0	5	-	-	10	30	-	35						
End	5	10	-	-	30	35	-	?						

on the duration of T$_8$ because we know that it is already late. Next, we modify the objective function as follows:

Maximize TF$_8$ − TS$_8$

The purpose of doing so is to find the maximum possible duration of T$_8$ without violating any other task duration or inter-task constraints. Upon solving the new formulation, an optimal value of 40 is found. This means that we can increase the duration of T$_8$ to 40, even though it was normally supposed to take no more than 20 time units without violating any other constraint. Thus, the advantage of a formal approach is that it can help us to calculate the "optimal" value of such upper and lower bounds directly without having to test various values of, say, the duration of T$_8$ and then heuristically finding the optimal.

In general, if a design-time solution exists but a run time solution is not found, then it means that the problem has become infeasible on account of either duration or inter-task constraints. In this situation, it is helpful to know the reason for the violation and its extent. For instance, we would like to know that a certain constraint C1 is violated by X1 time units. To deal with such situations we will introduce the notion of constraint violations in the next section.

Process changes. Our approach can also deal with process changes. If the process changes through insertions and deletions of activities, or if the activity durations are revised, the corresponding information in the formulation of Figure 9.8 is modified. Moreover, it is very easy to force certain branches to be taken in the process path, say, at an X-split connector. Thus, if there are two outgoing branches from an X-split connector Xi that have tasks T_{iA} and T_{iB} in their paths, then one of these branches can be forced by setting either $T_{iA} = 1$ or $T_{iB} = 1$.

"What-if" analysis. As a further benefit, various kinds of what-if analyses can also be performed with this approach. To find the maximum or minimum possible duration of a task (say, T_5) without violating any constraints, we modify the objective function to: **Maximize ($TF_5 - TS_5$) or Minimize ($TF_5 - TS_5$)**, and solve the new MILP. Finally, we can also assign specific duration values to a combination of tasks and check if these values still lead to a feasible solution.

Exercise 12: Modify your formulation to find the maximum duration of task T_9 without violating any other constraint. What solution did you get?

Modeling Temporal Constraint Violations with Constraint Relaxation

Constraint Relaxation Variables

The main idea for dealing with violations is to introduce relaxation variables for each constraint in such a way that if a constraint is violated then the variable takes on a positive non-zero value, and otherwise it is 0. Thus, a duration constraint such as, say, "schedule surgery" (T_8) with a duration of [10, 20] is expressed as:

$$TF_8 - TS_8 \geq 10$$

By introducing a constraint relaxation variable CD_8, we may rewrite this constraint as:

$$TF_8 - TS_8 + CD_8 \geq 10$$

Now, CD_8 is a relaxation variable that assumes a non-negative value. If the actual duration of T_8 is less than 10, say, the duration is 5, then $CD_8 = 5$. Thus, the constraint is satisfied and CPLEX can find a solution for the formulation. CD_8 is an example of a *lower bound relaxation variable*. The upper bound constraint in our example on the duration of T_8 is 20. In this case, a similar *upper bound relaxation variable*, say CD'_8 is introduced as follows:

$$TF_8 - TS_8 - CD'_8 \leq 20$$

Notice that the negative sign before CD'_8 means that the relaxation allows us to satisfy the upper bound constraint by again assuming a positive value. If the duration lies between 10 and 20, then CD'_8 is 0.

Relaxation for *inter-task constraints* is modeled in the same way. Constraint TI_2 of Figure 9.8, for instance, is:

$$TS_{11} - TS_8 \geq 100$$

Again, by adding a new relaxation variable, say, $C\dot{I}_2$ we can rewrite this constraint as:

$$TS_{11} - TS_8 + CI_2 \geq 100$$

The corresponding upper bound constraint TI_3 in the formulation of Figure 9.8 is relaxed by another relaxation variable CI_3 as follows:

$$TS_{11} - TS_8 - CI_3 \leq 140$$

Run time Scenario 2. When we revised these constraints by adding the relaxation variables in the MILP formulation, and solved it for the case where $TF_8 = 85$, we found a solution with an objective function value of 505 for TF_{14}. Moreover, the value for CI_3 was 10, indicating that constraint TI_3 was violated by 10 time units due to the delay in completion of T_8.

Controlled Violation with Penalties

The notion of controlling a temporal process means that after detecting a violation, it is also necessary to further explore the effects of the violation and suggest possible corrective actions. In the above example for run time scenario 2, we noticed that the delay in the surgery scheduling activity leads to the violation of constraint TI_3 by 10 and also an overall delay of 50 in the completion of the process. Hence, it is necessary to dig deeper to see if any corrective action is possible to: (1) rectify the violation in constraint TI_3 by making changes to the succeeding tasks; or (2) reduce the delay in completion time of the process. It is also useful here to distinguish between *strict* and *violable* constraints.

Run time Scenario 3. If, say, constraint TI_3 is strict, then we would like to see whether there is an alternative solution that would restore TI_3 but force changes in another constraint. In order to check for this, we might remove the relaxation variable CI_3 for the constraint TI_3 to make it a strict constraint and add relaxation variables to the remaining constraints TI_1, TI_2, TI_4, TI_5. In addition, we should also add the corresponding relaxation variables CI_1, CI_2, CI_4 and CI_5 to the objective function because we wish to minimize the extent of the violation. Now, we are able to find a solution in which $CD_{10} = 10$ and $TF_{14} = 495$. This means that by reducing the duration of pain medication (T_{10}) by 10 time units, we are able to satisfy constraint TI_3 and obtain a solution.

Associating Penalties with Slack Variables

In run time scenario 3, we assumed that the general form of the objective function was given by the sum of the finish times of the last task in the process and the values of all relaxation variables as follows:

$$\textbf{Minimize } TF_{\text{'Last'}} + \sum CD_i + \sum CD'_i + \sum CI_i$$

This means we added the violations due to each relaxation variable taking a non-zero value to the finish time of the process. However, this objective function treats each violation equally. In real practice, it is likely that the various constraint violations might have different degrees of impact on the outcome. Hence, in general, a different penalty may be assessed for the violation of each constraint. Such penalties would be determined by the domain experts. Therefore, the revised objective function should be:

$$\textbf{Minimize } TF_{\text{'Last'}} + \sum PD_i * CD_i + \sum PD_i' * CD_i' + \sum PI_i * CI_i$$

In this objective function, PD_i, PD_i' and PI_i are penalty weights associated with a one-unit violation of CD_i and CI_i, respectively.

Run time Scenario 4. In our running example, a doctor may feel that violation of constraint CI_5 is less important than a violation of the other constraints. Based on this information, we could assign, say, a penalty of just 0.5 to CI_5 and of 1 to the other constraints. When we rerun the MILP with this change, we get a solution in which $CI_5 = 20$. Now the process completion time TF_{14} drops to 485. Clearly, since the penalty for CI_5 is smaller, the optimal solution is one which relaxes this constraint as much as possible to minimize the objective function value.

In general, each constraint may have a different penalty assigned to it, and the appropriate determination of the penalty amount is left to the domain experts who understand the application area. In this way, it is possible to evaluate the tradeoffs between different constraints and find multiple alternate solutions at run time from which one may be selected.

Controlling the Extent of Violation

In addition to associating weights with penalties, it should also be possible to limit the extent of the violation in a duration or inter-task constraint through constraint relaxation. While some relaxation is reasonable, beyond a certain point it may become unacceptable. To restrict the amount of relaxation of a constraint, we could add a constraint like $CI_5 \leq 10$ to specify that the maximum relaxation (or violation) allowed in constraint TI_5 is 10, i.e. the gap between stopping pain medication (T_{10}) and the start of surgery must be at least 15 time units.

Run time Scenario 5. To illustrate this new condition, we modify the formulation of our running example by adding constraint $CI_5 \leq 5$ to the formulation in run time scenario 4. This means that now the constraint TI_5 can only be relaxed up to 5 time units. Thus, the gap between T_{10} and T_{11} that should normally be at least 20 can just be reduced to 15, but not anymore. On solving the formulation now, we get a solution with $CI_5 = 5$ and $CD_{10} = 5$. This means that in addition to reducing the gap between T_{10} and T_{11} by 5, we must also reduce the duration of the pain medication from 80 to 75 time units. The new process completion time TF_{14} is now 495.

Optimized Interactive Processes

To further appreciate the value of the optimization approaches described above, let us return to the 911 call dispatch process introduced at the start of this chapter. This process is an example of an emergency response system where real-time response is critical. Moreover, there is a need to coordinate physical, digital, and human systems. Such a process has been called an **optimized interactive process (or OIP)**. In general, it should interact with a variety of service systems, communication systems and collaboration systems in real-time. It also needs to receive data from a large number of sensors, make decisions, and respond in real-time.

Say, in the context of the 911 dispatch service, no emergency vehicle is available within a 5-minute radius of the incident site. Then a decision has to be taken in real-time on whether to accept a delay or arrange for a vehicle through a sub-contractor. Similarly, a situation could arise where there are two simultaneous incidents and only one vehicle is available that is within a 5-minute radius of both incident sites. In such scenarios, the process flow must be modified accordingly, based on real-time decisions. Yet certain constraints cannot be violated at all, or violated only in a controlled manner. Moreover, the assignment of activities to resources has to be optimized in real-time given that there are competing demands for the resources from multiple simultaneous process instances. Since traditional workflow systems are not designed for this sort of real-time interaction, there are several issues that need to be explored here; we explain these next.

Table 9.6 contrasts OIPs with conventional BPM systems. In an OIP it is possible to communicate using multiple channels. For instance, a message may be sent to an agent or worker by email first. If a response is not received within 5 minutes, then a text message would be sent. Finally, if a response is still not received in the next 3 minutes, then a phone call is placed to reach the person, first to their primary number and then to their alternative number. A BPM system has limited human interaction channels. Further, in an OIP it is possible for participants to collaborate during execution of the process freely. In BPM, support for collaboration is still rather limited. Moreover, an OIP can be dynamically optimized based on the exact location of resources (both human and physical) in real-time. Such capabilities are not present in BPM systems. Hence, there is much room for the kind of optimization methods discussed earlier in this chapter to be applied there.

New architectures are also needed to design OIP systems. These architectures should be flexible and extendable, so new types of services can be introduced. They should also be safe, secure, and reliable. A proposed architecture is shown in Figure 9.10. The BPM system has a communication layer on top of it, and it interacts with an optimization module that manages the resource and constraints modules in real-time. The resource module manages assignments of specific resources to agents (or workers) based on their skills, availability, and current location. The constraint module manages additional constraints related to the sequencing of the tasks, their timing as well as their resource needs. Finally, the communications layer manages interactions with agents by multiple means. Thus, if an emergency worker is not reachable by email within a certain duration, then she is texted and if no response is received for the text within a short time window, then an attempt is made to reach her by phone.

Table 9.6 Comparison of BPM and optimized interactive processes (OIPs) (adapted from Yellin et al. [23])

Feature	BPM	OIPs
Communication media	Communication through limited human interaction channels	Common devices like cell phones and other communication media, such as social networks, are used
Participant collaboration	Usually not supported	Sharing of resources is possible
Optimization of human-centric tasks	Assignment of human tasks takes place based on static attributes	Assignment of human tasks based on dynamic attributes (for example GPS coordinates of participants, etc.)

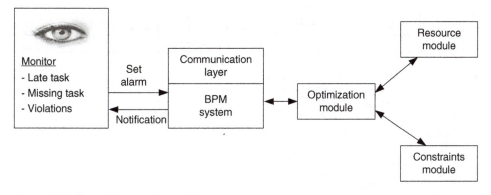

Figure 9.10 An architecture for an OIP

Conventional process management systems are not able to operate in this manner. Another aspect of Figure 9.10 is the monitoring system that looks for violations of various types of constraints related to timing, resources, activities, etc. More details of monitoring are discussed in the next section.

Support for Monitoring Temporal Processes

Business process monitoring enables an organization to measure and analyze process performance to identify critical process problems proactively, using data to make decisions that will improve the speed, quality, and efficiency of business processes. At process design time, most designers do not consider how a workflow they are designing will be monitored at run time. Ideally, *a process designer should be able to specify what kind of metrics of a process are to be monitored*, e.g. the throughput time of a task, a subprocess, or the entire process, etc. In addition, the resources that are actually deployed in the process execution can also be monitored in terms of the time they spent on a task. In a temporal process, the actual duration (versus the planned duration) of a task is an important KPI, as we have seen in some of the examples earlier in this chapter. If the actual duration exceeds a limit, then some alerts and notifications should be generated for the process owner and other parties.

More complex kinds of monitoring are also needed. Consider the well-known example of a travel booking process. Typically, a traveler will perform three main steps in sequence: book a flight; book a hotel; and book a taxi for local transportation from the airport to the hotel (see Figure 9.11(a)). After this process completes, a travel reservation has been successfully made and a traveler itinerary is created. However, it is also important to monitor this process. In order to do so, a monitoring dependency diagram such as the one in Figure 9.11(b) is developed. This diagram describes the monitoring steps that must be performed and the dependencies between them. Thus, this diagram shows that the flight schedule must be monitored by applying rule R1. This rule is defined as follows:

Rule R1: If new_flight_dep_time $\neq$ Itinerary.sched_flight_dep_time
then alert(Itinerary.traveler, "Your flight departure time has changed.")

The diagram also shows that if rule R1 is triggered (i.e. its left-hand side is satisfied), then rules R2 and R3 should also be checked to see if they are triggered. However, if rule

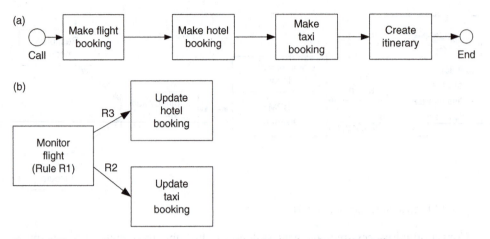

Figure 9.11 A travel arrangements process and its monitoring dependency diagram

R1 is not triggered, then it is not necessary to check rules R2 and R3. Rules R2 and R3 are stated as follows.

Rule R2: If new_flight_arr_time – Itinerary.sched_flight_arr_time > 1 hour
　　then alert(Itinerary.traveler, "Please reschedule your taxi reservation.")
Rule R3: If new_flight_arr_time > 12 am
　　then alert(Itinerary.traveler, "You might need to change your hotel reservation.")

　　Rule R2 reminds the traveler to change her taxi reservation if the flight will arrive more than one hour after its scheduled time, while rule R3 advises the traveler to modify the hotel booking if the flight will arrive after midnight. By associating a monitoring process with a related process, it is possible to track the status of a running process. Further, one can also create an itinerary monitoring app that can display the latest itinerary of a traveler in real-time when launched as shown in Figure 9.12. In addition, it may also show additional information such as the weather at the destination, current activities, and so on. In the absence of such an app, a traveler has to check the status of the flight, taxi, and hotel information separately.

　　Timers can also be associated with the process and invoked at required times. Other features of this app could include information for the traveler about the weather forecast at the destination, say, one day before travel date, etc. It could also automatically notify the hotel and the taxi service that the flight is late. In addition to an itinerary process, the same monitoring approach would apply to other kinds of service processes, healthcare processes, even manufacturing processes, etc. We still do not have an ability to design and run such processes.

Exercise 13. Make a dependency diagram for the healthcare process in Figure 9.5 and write the corresponding rules for it.

Chapter Summary

Our approach in this chapter was based on making optimization models for temporal workflows and solving them using the CPLEX tool [6]. This tool is available from

```
┌─────────────────────────────────────────────────────┐
│                                                       │
│                    Itinerary monitor                  │
│                                                       │
│  Flight:                                              │
│  Dep. New York (EWR) 5.30 PM (Scheduled 4.30 PM)      │
│  Arr. Tampa (TPA) 7.30 PM  (Scheduled 6.30 PM)        │
│                                                       │
│  Car rental:                                          │
│  Pick up at TPA 8 PM (Scheduled 7 PM)                 │
│                                                       │
│  Hotel:                                               │
│  Marriott, Late arrival until midnight                │
│                                                       │
│  Destination weather: 75°                             │
│                                                       │
└─────────────────────────────────────────────────────┘
```

Figure 9.12 An itinerary monitoring app

IBM and the user interface is quite straightforward. The early efforts towards formally describing temporal patterns are due to Allen [1] who developed a general theory of action and time for reasoning about actions based on temporal logic, and introduced relations between time intervals, and ways of reasoning about them. However, Allen's work was not done in the context of workflows. Temporal reasoning in the context of workflows is discussed in [4]. By far, the early efforts on introducing time into workflow systems were due to Marjanovic and Orlowska [18], Sadiq et al. [19] and Eder et al. [8, 9]. The approach of Eder et al. [8, 9] relies on ideas from project planning and critical path methods to determine various metrics like earliest start date, latest finish date, etc. for various activities.

Zhao and Stohr [24] also developed a framework and algorithms for temporal work-flow management in the context of a claims handling system based on turnaround time prediction, time allocation and task prioritization. They used reward functions to guide workers' behavior. The approach for analyzing temporal workflows and dealing with violations presented in this chapter is based on the work of Kumar and Barton [14]. These techniques are yet to be implemented in process modeling and management tools.

Lanz et al. presented several time patterns (TP) that represent temporal constraints of time-aware processes [16, 17] in the context of the ATAPIS project [3] at the University of Ulm. These patterns are in four groups: durations and time lags; restricting execution times; variability; and recurrent process elements. These patterns can also be represented using our approach. Time-BPMN is a proposal for incorporating temporal features and constraints into BPMN [10].

The approaches of Lanz et al. [15] towards dealing with time-aware processes have relied on the conditional simple temporal networks (CSTN) as a representational technique [20]. These networks were originally developed in the context of planning problems and allow a mapping from points in time at which observations are taken to propositional statements (that are true or false) attached to nodes. These statements are checked for their truth values at the observation times and the corresponding actions at the nodes are performed if the statements are true. Later, Combi et al. [5] extended CSTNs to the more general CSTNUs (CSTNs with uncertainty) and developed techniques for checking their correctness.

Dynamic controllability [12, 15, 20] is also a related concept in the context of temporal workflows. In this view, a temporal workflow consists of contingent links whose actual duration is determined by nature within a given range, and agent-controlled links whose actual value is under the control of and determined by an agent at execution time. The actual values of the durations of the contingent links are known only at run time. It is not possible to compare our approach directly with dynamic controllability because in our formulation there are no contingent links. All our task duration and inter-task duration ranges are determined based on, say, medical (or some other kind of) guidelines.

Healthcare is a particularly important application for management of temporal constraints. Workflows in a healthcare enterprise must respond and adapt in real-time [2] making temporal constraint management particularly important. A lot of effort in the ADEPT project [7] was devoted to the context of change and flexibility in healthcare. An approach for scheduling clinical pathways is described in [22]. The work in [11] shows how to translate a time-annotated clinical pathway model into a temporal hierarchical task network (HTN). Temporal constraints on this network can be checked and managed using techniques from the HTN planning domain.

A rather different perspective for controlling violations is to proactively undertake certain measures or escalation steps when it is anticipated that the deadline for the completion of a process instance will be missed. In this line of research (e.g. [21]), escalation may imply performing a task in a different way, allowing less qualified people to do certain tasks, or making decisions based on incomplete data. Such measures can help reduce the number of missed deadlines. Optimized interactive processes are discussed in [23] in the context of service-oriented architectures and unified communications and collaboration. Lastly, another optimization approach based on mixed-integer programming for dealing with violations is described in [13].

References

1. F. J. Allen. Towards a general theory of action and time. *Artificial intelligence*, Vol. 23, No. 2, pp. 123–154, 1984.
2. K. Anyanwu, A. Sheth, J. Cardoso, John A. Miller and K. Kochut. Healthcare enterprise process development and integration. *Journal of Research and Practice in Information Technology*, Vol. 35, No. 2, pp. 83–98, 2003.
3. ATAPIS: Adaptive Time- and Process-aware Information Systems. University of Ulm. www.uni-ulm.de/en/in/dbis/research/projects/atapis.html.
4. C. Bettini, X. S. Wang and S. Jajodia. Temporal reasoning in workflow systems. *Distributed and Parallel Databases*, Vol. 11, No. 3, pp. 269–306, 2002.
5. C. Combi, M. Gozzi, R. Posenato and G. Pozzi. Conceptual modeling of flexible temporal workflows. *TAAS*, Vol. 7, No. 2, pp. 19:1–19:29, 2012.
6. CPLEX. Reference Manual. IBM Corporation, 2009.
7. P. Dadam and M. Reichert. The ADEPT project: a decade of research and development for robust and flexible process support. *Computer Science R&D*, Vol. 23, No. 2, pp. 81–97, 2009.
8. J. Eder, P. Euthimios, H. Pozewaunig and M. Rabinovich. *Time Management in Workflow Systems*. Proceedings of BIS 1999, pp. 265–280, 1999.
9. J. Eder, W. Gruber and E. Panagos. Temporal Modeling of Workflows with Conditional Execution Paths. In: M. Ibrahim, J. Küng, N. Revell (eds) DEXA 2000. *LNCS*, Vol. 1873. Springer, Heidelberg, pp. 243–253, 2000.
10. D. Gagne and A. Trudel. Time-BPMN. In: B. Hofreiter, H. Werthner (eds) *Proceedings of the Conference on Commerce and Enterprise Computing (CEC)*. IEEE Computer Society, Vienna, pp. 361–367, 2009.

11. A. González-Ferrer, A. Ten Teije, J. F. Olivares and K. Milian. Automated generation of patient-tailored electronic care pathways by translating computer-interpretable guidelines into hierarchical task networks. *Artificial Intelligence in Medicine*, Vol. 57, No. 2, pp. 91–109, 2013.

12. L. Hunsberger, R. Posenato and C. Combi. *The Dynamic Controllability of Conditional STNs with Uncertainty*. Proceedings of PlanEx 2012, 2012.

13. A. Kumar, W. Yao and C. Chu. Flexible business process compliance with semantic constraints using mixed-integer programming. *INFORMS Journal on Computing*, Vol. 25, No. 3, pp. 543–559, 2013.

14. A. Kumar and R. R. Barton. Controlled violation of temporal process constraints—models, algorithms and results. *Information Systems*, Vol. 64, pp. 410–424, 2017.

15. A. Lanz, R. Posenato, C. Combi and M. Reichert. *Controllability of Time-Aware Processes at Run Time*. Proceedings of CoopIS, pp. 39–56, 2013.

16. A. Lanz, B. Weber and M. Reichert. Time patterns for process-aware information systems. *Requirements Engineering*, Vol. 19, No. 2, pp. 113–141, 2014.

17. A. Lanz and M. Reichert. Dealing with Changes of Time-Aware Processes. In: *BPM*, Vol. 8659, pp. 217–233, 2014.

18. O. Marjanovic and M. E. Orlowska. On modeling and verification of temporal constraints in production workflows. *Knowledge and Information Systems*, Vol. 1, No. 2, pp. 157–192, 1999.

19. S. W. Sadiq, O. Marjanovic and M. E. Orlowska. Managing change and time in dynamic workflow processes. *International Journal of Cooperative Information Systems*, Vol. 9, Nos. 1–2, pp. 93–116, 2000.

20. I. Tsamardinos, T. Vidal and M. Pollack. CTP: A new constraint-based formalism for conditional, temporal planning. *Constraints*, Vol. 8, No. 4, pp. 365–388, 2003.

21. W. M. P. van der Aalst, M. Rosemann and M. Dumas. Deadline-based escalation in process-aware information systems. *Decision Support Systems*, Vol. 43, No. 2, pp. 492–511, 2007.

22. A. Wolf. Constraint-Based Modeling and Scheduling of Clinical Pathways. In: *CSCLP*, Vol. 6384, pp. 122–138, 2009.

23. D. Yellin, Y. Yulevich, A. Pyasic and A. Houri. Optimized interactive processes. *Computer*, Vol. 45, No. 4, pp. 74–81, 2012.

24. J. Zhao and E. Stohr. *Temporal Workflow Management in a Claim Handling System*. Proceedings of Work Activities Coordination and Collaboration (WACC'99), San Francisco, California, pp. 187–195, 1999.

10 Social BPM

Introduction

Business processes are integral to the operations of an organization. Since processes are enacted within organizations and are performed by humans, it is natural to expect that they will have a social element. In fact, at their very heart, processes involve people or stakeholders such as customers, employees, third-party contractors, etc. At the core of a process lie the interactions among these individuals, and such interactions are crucial, if not critical, for the successful completion of the process. In fact, some tasks are even performed by teams of individuals, e.g. two engineers may work together to produce the design of an electronic circuit, or two executives may collaborate to prepare the draft of a sales forecast for their sales director. A departmental meeting held to select a new sales representative from a list of candidates is another example of a team task.

> "We found that patients whose surgical teams exhibited less teamwork behaviors were at a higher risk for death or complications" (Mazzocco et al. [14]).

This quote above from an academic article written by medical practitioners emphasizes the importance of teamwork in no uncertain terms. A surgical procedure is a complicated process consisting of pre-surgery, surgery and post-surgery subprocesses, each of which in turn is comprised of other tasks that must be planned, coordinated and executed very carefully by a team of professionals from whom a different subset may participate in each task. It is essential that this group of individuals cooperate and communicate with each other effectively for a successful outcome.

Social BPM is an emerging area within BPM. The main focus lies in understanding how agents or actors in an organization collaborate in the successful execution of processes. The emphasis here is on understanding collaboration within and across tasks of a process. In this chapter, we will motivate some basic ideas of social interaction in a process, and then introduce a social process lifecycle and social modeling concepts. Next, we shall discuss some approaches for extracting and building a socially enhanced organizational resource model, and finally present techniques for assigning actors to a process instance in an optimal way.

Background

Most business processes in an organization inhabit a social context. An understanding of this context can help improve collaboration among actors with the support of appropriate tools. This leads to improved communication and coordination, and thus better results, in knowledge-intensive tasks. Some tasks in a process are performed individually and others by teams. Understanding the social context of an end-to-end process can help in two ways:

(1) by forming teams in which the members work well with each other to perform a task; and
(2) by assigning related tasks of a process instance to users who cooperate well with each other.

Social technologies provide a range of collaboration and communication tools such as blogs, wikis, forums, chat platforms, etc. that support user interaction through social computing features. These features enable users to easily capture and share the knowledge and expertise that is needed to do their work. This sharing of information encourages collaboration, improves innovation, and targets relevant content to the people who have to see it. More broadly, social software supports the interaction of humans for the production of artifacts by combining ideas and inputs from independent contributors without predetermining the way to do this. Currently, these types of social technologies are not embedded in a process context.

Conway's law, proposed in 1967, states that *organizations have a tendency to design systems that mirror their communication structures*. Thus, it assumes a strong association between a system's architecture and the communication structure of the organization that designs it. This means that if the structure of the organization is decentralized and modular, it is more likely to lead to a modular software design, while if it the organization has a more centralized structure then the software design will reflect that. This "law" recognizes that software development (among other things) happens in a socio-technical context, i.e. the social considerations affect the technical work, and it is difficult to divorce the social aspect of work from the purely technical aspect.

> **Conway's Law**
>
> Any organization that designs a system (defined broadly) will produce a design whose structure is a copy of the organization's communication structure.

Consequently, a *socio-technical system* recognizes the complex set of interactions among people, processes, and technology. Hence, approaches to organizational work design in such systems should be developed accordingly for success. Many have suggested that software creation should be conceived of as a sociotechnical concept by arguing that design, execution, and productivity of software process models can be improved by mapping the social network among developers who contribute to components of a software application onto the network of connections among the software components. It was also shown in studies that the failure-proneness of a software component can be predicted more accurately by considering the combined socio-technical network of a software application. In a socio-technical setting, interactions among actors take place through handoffs.

Soft and Hard Handoffs

A *handoff* occurs when one task of a process instance is completed and the next one begins. In a typical insurance claim process (e.g. see Figure 10.1), several tasks, such as receive, validate, settle, approve, and pay a claim, must be carried out by different employees or actors performing possibly different roles in a certain order. After an actor completes her task, she hands over the process instance to the next actor. In a *hard handoff*, no further interaction between the two actors is necessary. But in a *soft handoff*, the two actors may still need to interact later for queries and clarifications even though the process definition may not reflect it. Thus, in practice, there is a series of overlapping and nested roles and responsibilities, where the transitions between tasks are somewhat fuzzy.

In general, an actor doing a later task in a workflow may need to refer back and consult with an actor who did a previous task for the same case. By the dotted lines between pairs of activities in Figure 10.1, we are trying to capture the fuzziness in the process model to show that the reviewer may contact the customer service representative occasionally if there is some information on the application that is not clear or incomplete. Similarly, the manager may contact the assessor if, for a certain case, she does not agree with his estimate for the settlement amount. These interactions do not happen for every instance, rather only for certain special cases and, hence, we cannot include them in the

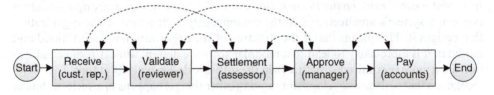

Figure 10.1 A simplified insurance claim process with several tasks and roles (dashed lines show the need for cooperation among actors of pairs of tasks)

formal process model. Yet it is important to realize that cooperation is necessary between various actors of successive tasks so that the workflow can proceed smoothly. We shall develop this example later on in this chapter.

In the context of a medical process for a patient at a hospital, a day nurse must "hand-off" to a night nurse at the end of her shift. In doing so, she must make sure to inform the night nurse (see Figure 10.2) about any particular symptoms or abnormal conditions that may have arisen during the day and that need particular attention. At any rate, a systematic and smooth handoff is critical to this patient care process.

The execution of a process instance is, in reality, a team effort involving multiple hand-offs, and ideally the handoffs should be as smooth as possible. To facilitate teamwork the actors of related tasks must be compatible with one another. The Free Dictionary

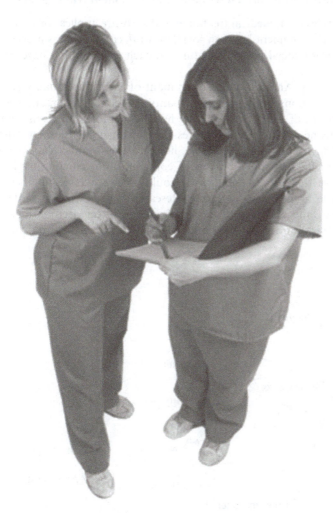

Figure 10.2 A handoff from the day shift nurse to the night shift nurse

Source: https://blog.nurserecruiter.com/wp-content/uploads/2012/10/Norman-Pogson-Fotolia1.jpg.

(www.thefreedictionary.com) defines *compatible* as: "capable of existing or performing in harmonious, agreeable, or congenial combination with another." Thus, *compatibility is a measure of the degree to which actors cooperate with one another in a workflow*. Hence, compatibility between actors should be a key consideration, in addition to qualifications of course, while assigning tasks to actors.

In this chapter, we shall use the term *synergy* to capture the degree of compatibility or the level of cooperation that exists between two actors (or more broadly resource). Synergy has a value between 0 and 1, where 0 reflects complete lack of synergy and 1 the highest level of synergy.

Examples from Healthcare, Software Development and Incident Management

Next, we introduce examples from medical treatment and software application areas to illustrate the importance of alignment between social networks and business processes, and discuss a few significant social network features in each example that have been explored in literature.

Medical Treatment Process. An important determinant of healthcare quality is the effectiveness of social interactions among the participants of the provider organization. Figure 10.3 shows a network of interactions among healthcare professionals in a hospital environment. In this network, there are professionals like surgeons, anesthetists, nurses, operating department practitioners (ODPs), home care assistants (HCAs), and administrators. The directed edges show the flow of communications among the individuals involved. Observe that Nurse manager 1 would receive a large number of communications by virtue of her large in-degree. Research has shown that patterns of communication among the operating team members can affect decision-making patterns, lead to communication breakdowns and drastically affect patient outcomes.

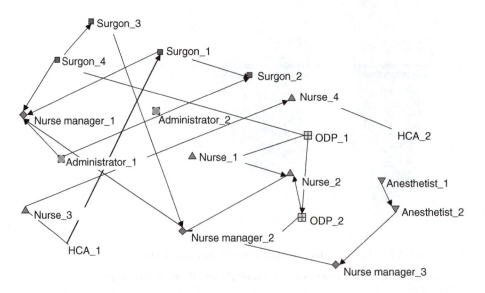

Figure 10.3 A healthcare professional social network

In particular, social network metrics like density and clustering have an impact on performance. Many resources from this network participate in a patient's process instance and the closeness among them has an impact on the patient outcome.

Software Development Process. Software development is a process that includes many activities like design, coding, testing, quality assurance, and documentation. The social networks among resources in such a process can have a large impact on the quality of the final software they produce. In most cases, resource social networks are an important factor to be considered during task assignment. Figure 10.4 shows development tasks in a software development project. These tasks are associated with each other due to shared artifacts (e.g. data tables, code, user interface, etc.). To reduce dependencies and also improve efficiency, a common practice is to group tasks into clusters and try to assign a cluster of tasks to one resource (or resources) with strong ties. For the example in Figure 10.4(a), these tasks may be grouped into three clusters, as highlighted in different shades of grey. Moreover, some tasks, e.g. T_6 and T_7, may be identified as critical ones, as they have stronger associations with others as indicated by their higher degree.

We can leverage social network features to optimize resource allocation. A *community* is a group of resources that is densely interconnected. Usually, resources within a community share common interests, e.g. database, BPM communities, etc. Figure 10.4(b) shows the corresponding social network of resources in a software development project. These resources can be clustered into three communities as highlighted in different shades. For example, tasks T1, T2, T5, and T6, all related to data model development, can be assigned to resources in a database community consisting of resource nodes 1–5.

In addition, some studies have shown that resource *closeness*, *betweenness*, and *degree* metrics (discussed in Chapter 7) are significantly correlated with the proneness to software failures. These metrics need to be considered during task assignment. Further, a critical task can be assigned to a resource that is well-connected and centrally placed in the community, so they can take advantage of their social position to improve process performance. Thus, task T6 may be assigned to node 4 (or node 8), as this resource is the center of the community and also bridges communication among them. A formal method for resource allocation by utilizing social networks is discussed later in the chapter.

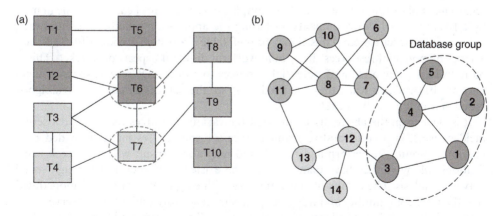

Figure 10.4 Software development tasks and resource community

IT Incident Management Process. Many enterprises outsource the management of their IT systems to professional IT service providers. In the case of overseas providers, outsourcing is called offshoring. When faced with systems issues, business users of the IT systems submit incidents to a service provider. Appropriate resources from the service provider are then assigned to work on the incidents and resolve the issues within timelines as defined in a service level agreement (SLA). An SLA may require that a certain type of problem be resolved in no more than 24 hours, failing which the vendor would have to pay a penalty to the client. Typically, resources are organized into different support teams by their specialty, e.g. database, operation system, etc.

Figure 10.5 illustrates an IT incident management process from a technology company. A problem or issue faced by a business user is reported to a help desk of the company. The help desk agent creates a new incident (see task "Open Incident" in Figure 10.5) in a ticketing tool and records the description of the issue faced by the user. Then the incident is assigned to a specific support team based on the nature of the problem (see the "Validate and Assign Incident" task in Figure 10.5). The incident, once assigned to a support team, is picked up by an available resource within the team. The resource acknowledges the receipt of the incident by claiming the ownership of the incident (task "Update Incident Ownership") and then diagnoses it (task "Analyze Incident"). If needed, the resource may communicate with the customer for additional information.

It may also transpire that, during the course of the incident analysis, the incident is transferred to another resource in the same support team or to another support team (task "Transfer Incident") for a number of reasons: (1) the assigned resource may have been diverted to a higher priority incident and thus become unavailable; (2) another resource may be better qualified than the current one; and/or (3) the complexity of the issues involved in the incident may call for multiple resources with different specialties to diagnose and resolve it. A transfer is made in two ways: (1) a resource directly transfers the incident to an alternate resource to work on it; or (2) a resource simply returns the incident to a dispatcher to determine the next appropriate resource. An incident is usually assigned to one resource at a time. After an incident is resolved, the functionality of the system as required by the business user (task "Restore Service") is restored. The business user validates and confirms the service provided by the resource (task "Confirm Service"). Once confirmed by the user, the incident is closed (task "Close Incident").

In general, for the resolution of complex issues multiple resources with different specialties may be required in diagnosis and resolution. Incidents, particularly ones regarding application outages, are often complicated as their root causes may lie in multiple layers in the IT environments, including the application, middleware, hardware, network infrastructure, etc. Thus, it may be preferable if a system can identify in advance a series of potential resources that would work on different aspects of a ticket. This is more like assigning a team of potential resources to a ticket. Of course, some of them may not be available when they are needed. If so, the team is dynamically reassigned based on the state of the ticket.

It is clear from the above discussion that the various resources that resolve a severe incident work in a collaborative manner since a resource uses inputs provided by a previous resource in performing its task and may also consult with it to seek clarifications. Many studies have demonstrated the existence of such ties through social network analysis. The results of these analyses with empirical data have demonstrated that there are communities and workgroups in such a network and resources serve social roles such as *contributor, influencer, coordinator*, etc. These roles are identified based on

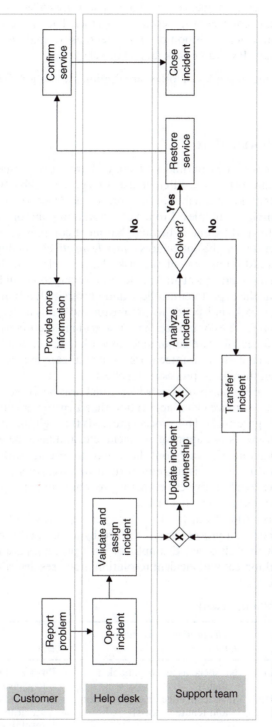

Figure 10.5 A process model for incident resolution

Source: CollaborateCom'14.

social analytics metrics like degree of connectedness (e.g. in-degree and out-degree) and betweenness. Roles such as influencer and coordinator are called *authorities* and *hubs* that provide advice and connect other resources together. They serve as a "glue" in facilitating smoother and faster resolution of an incident, as we shall see later. But first we will introduce a social BPM framework and a lifecycle.

Exercise 1: Give some examples of other applications where a social BPM would be useful.

A Framework for Social BPM

In the context of a process we can think of teamwork from two perspectives: teamwork within a task; and teamwork across different tasks of a process. Table 10.1 shows a simple framework for understanding collaboration in processes. Processes consist of tasks and each task may be simple or complex. From a collaboration point of view, low complexity tasks can be performed by one individual, but more complex ones require multiple individuals to cooperate and this introduces a *task team effect* that might determine the completion and successful outcome of the task. An example of such a task would be the promotion and tenure process at an American university. A candidate is reviewed by several committees at the department, college and university levels in that order. However, each committee works independently as a team and sends its recommendations to the next level committee. The committees have minimal interaction with each other and there is never really a need for two committees to work together as a larger team. Thus, here it is important that each committee works well as a team in a way that we call task team effect. However, there is no process team effect.

In contrast, there are other processes where collaboration is required across tasks. Take for instance an insurance claim application that a customer submits to the insurance company (see Figure 10.1). This process proceeds through various steps within the company such as review, assess, approve, payment, etc. and here there is much need for various (individual) actors who carry out these steps to interact with each other as we shall see shortly. In this case, it is more important to have synergy across tasks than within tasks, and the collaborative effect that is predominant is the *process team effect* because it relates to interaction across tasks.

Finally, the last scenario of our framework requires synergy both within and across tasks. Here many tasks in a process are performed by teams, and some of these teams need to cooperate with each other. Examples of such processes are the medical treatment, software development and incident resolution processes described above.

Table 10.1 A social BPM framework

		Collaboration across tasks	
		Low	High
Task complexity	Low	No social aspect (e.g. book a flight)	Process team effect (e.g. insurance claim process)
	High	Task team effect (e.g. promotion and tenure process)	Process + task team effect (e.g. application software incident resolution, heart surgery)

Most BPM systems thus far have been designed for the situation where the social aspect is neglected, i.e. the scenario of low task complexity and low collaboration across tasks in Table 10.1. However, there is a need to provide support for the other three categories in this table as well. In subsequent sections of this chapter we shall study some ways of adding such support.

A Social BPM Lifecycle

We saw earlier on in Chapter 1 that traditional BPM processes are developed according to a lifecycle. The key phases in the lifecycle of such a process are design, modeling, execution, process monitoring and optimization. The Gartner consulting firm defines *social BPM as the effort of designing and executing business processes collaboratively*. With regard to a lifecycle, social BPM embraces the notion of "design by doing," while traditional BPM is usually described as "doing by design." A social BPM lifecycle would still contain similar phases to a traditional BPM process but each phase would be enriched with social engagement (see Figure 10.6). Moreover, the boundaries between phases may also be somewhat blurred.

Process design could be performed in a collaborative manner by setting up a discussion group where multiple stakeholders may offer their inputs to create an initial design. This phase is followed by the *process modeling* phase in which a formal design is created from the collaborative inputs of the users. In this phase, there is less social involvement and it is primarily performed by one or two technical experts who understand the modeling

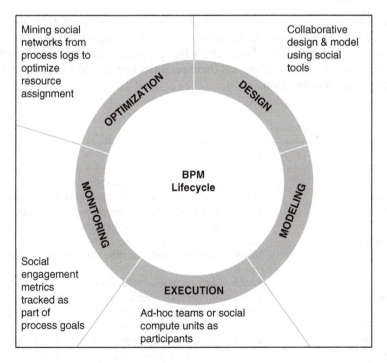

Figure 10.6 A social BPM lifecycle

language and tools. Building a social process model would require knowledge of various kinds of social tools and platforms that may be integrated into the process. Current modeling tools would need to be enhanced with a vocabulary of primitive types to support such modeling.

The next phase of *process execution* will likely involve collaboration for many of the activities of the process. This may be accomplished through ad hoc teams or social compute units working collaboratively with the help of social tools. For instance, if a task requires an online discussion or participation in a Doodle poll then each user will follow a link to a website and participate in the discussion. In the *process monitoring* phase, social engagement metrics, such as the level of interaction among participants, comments offered, participation in voting, etc., are also tracked as part of the process goals. These metrics measure how well participants in the process interact with each other and contribute to it.

Based on the results of the monitoring phase, changes may be required in the process and thus the *process optimization* phase would also be a social activity in which several users would participate and provide their inputs on how the process may be improved. Another important task in optimization of a social BPM is to understand the structure of participant social networks and leverage this structure in resource assignment since the social network plays a key role in the task and the overall process performance. Thus, most activities in the lifecycle would have a social aspect to them. In the next section we shall describe social BPM modeling along with some examples.

Social BPM Modeling

To allow a tighter integration of social tasks into a business process model, languages like BPMN can provide a new type of tasks called social tasks. The creation of primitive modeling constructs can simplify the design of social processes. Table 10.2 shows some primitives of social activities. As you can see, these primitives pertain to common social activities related to group interactions.

Table 10.2 Primitives for social process modeling

Primitive	Description
Create group	Set up an ad hoc group for collaboration
Invite to join group	Give a list of addresses of invitees and contact them
Invite to comment	Invite selected individuals to comment on your group
Add post/comment	Add a new post or comment on an existing post
Reply to a post/comment	Send a reply to another group/user
Start/close poll for meeting	Invite people to provide the time slots when they can meet
Open/close comments	Enable/disable a post so others can(not) comment on it
Collect responses	Compile all the responses to a post together
Tally votes	For a voting activity, summarize the votes
Set up conference call	Arrange for a call with a selected set of users
Send meeting reminders	Remind participants of a previously scheduled meeting
Accept/reject invite	Accept or reject an invitation to a group or meeting

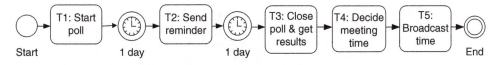

Figure 10.7 A social process to conduct a vote and arrange a meeting

Figure 10.7 shows how these primitives can be used in a process to set up a meeting time by polling the likely participants and deciding the time that is convenient to the largest number. This can simplify many aspects of this process such as starting and closing the poll, sending reminders, vote collection and tallying the results. Having predefined social primitives makes it easier to design such processes. Thus, the "start poll" primitive would allow the organizer to identify a list of invitees quickly from the address book and select possible meeting times. After, say, one day has elapsed (modeled with a timer), a reminder would be sent to the invitees. Then, after another day the poll is closed and the results made available to the organizer. Finally, a meeting time is selected by the organizer and communicated to all the invitees. Of course, a similar process could also be used to conduct a poll on some policy issue.

Exercise 2: Redraw the process of Figure 10.7 in BPMN assuming that you did not have any access to social BPM primitives.

Exercise 3: Make a process model for a conference review system that consists of inviting people to serve as reviewers and senior reviewers, receiving and acknowledging their replies, receiving paper submissions from authors, assigning papers to reviewers and senior reviewers, receiving reviews, having senior reviewers prepare reports, and sending out notifications to authors.

Another idea for social process modeling is the *Social Compute Unit* (SCU), a collaborative resource unit formed dynamically during task execution. Often, complex activities of a process require ad hoc teams or Social Compute Units to work collaboratively with the help of social tools. A Social Compute Unit is an ad hoc collaborative resource unit formed dynamically for the execution of a process instance to work on problems related to a group of components. SCUs are formed only for tasks of a complex nature requiring collaborative effort as opposed to the normal "business as usual" tasks. Figure 10.8 shows a model for implementing the SCU approach in the context of the incident management example described earlier. An SCU is an abstraction of a team consisting of human resources that bring together expertise to solve a problem. The SCU is a dynamic unit or team in which resources join, contribute and leave such that each resource contributes to a different aspect of a problem.

A simulation study in the context of an incident resolution problem showed that the SCU approach is superior to a conventional "business as usual" approach under certain circumstances. As shown in Figure 10.8, SCUs may be dynamically reconfigured as resolved components are removed and new components are added. Moreover, they are dissolved when the problem is fixed. Next, we shall see how social roles (in contrast to formal, technical roles) can be assigned to various actors who collaborate on a process instance by introducing the idea of a socially enhanced resource model.

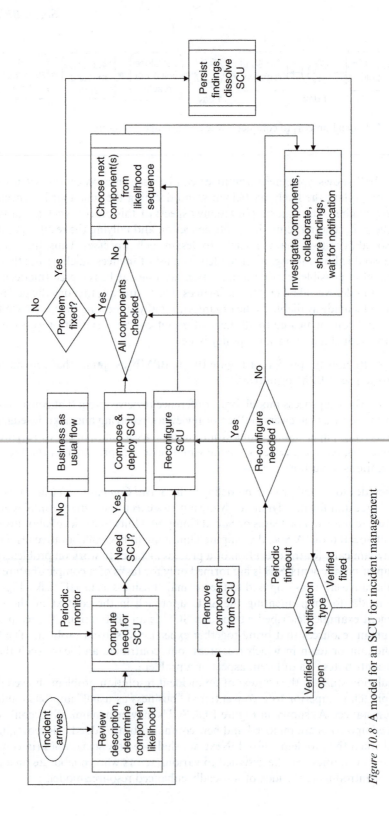

Figure 10.8 A model for an SCU for incident management

Building a Socially Enhanced Organizational Resource Model

A typical organizational model can be viewed as a hierarchical chart that shows the title or official organizational position of individuals in an organization from the CEO downwards. However, when multiple actors collaborate together on a task or a process instance with a specific goal (say, to perform a heart valve replacement operation on Liz Smith), they work as a team in which different actors also assume informal, social roles that are different from their formal, organizational positions. An organizational model that also captures the social positions of resources is called a **socially enhanced organizational resource model**. This is a kind of *organizational mining* in that we are trying to discover roles in an organizational setting from hidden patterns of interaction in historical logs.

In contrast to the *formal* model in Figure 10.9, such an *informal* model would capture the *social positions* of various resources. It cannot be shown as a hierarchical tree because the social positions do not fit into a top-down pattern. In fact, some individuals may have multiple social positions. Thus, such a model is shown in the form of a graph or a network diagram as will become clear shortly. Perhaps it deserves clarification that an *organizational position* is one that is assigned to an individual in her official capacity in an organization, while a *social position* is one that an individual assumes on the basis of her interactions with others in the organization. Informally, it represents the *social capital* of this person within an organization.

Typically, social positions can be identified by performing social network analysis on a network. *In a social network, resources are represented as nodes and edges are used to*

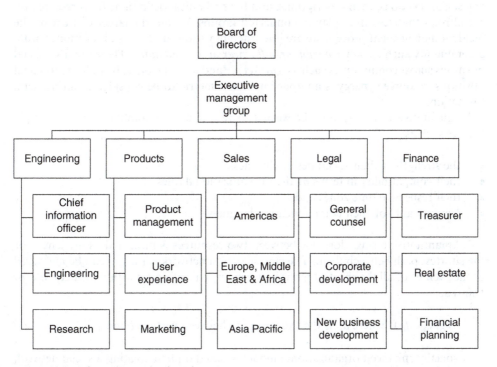

Figure 10.9 A formal organization chart

Table 10.3 Intra- and inter-community social positions and their descriptions

	Social position	Description	Technical definition using social network metrics
Intra-community	A key contributor	One who actively participates in completing a task in a community.	A node with high node degree.
	An influencer	Exercises influence by taking leadership roles in a community.	A node with high eigenvector centrality, i.e. a large influence in a network.
	A coordinator	Facilitates connections among others (a broker) in a community (e.g. IT architect, manager).	A node with high betweenness, i.e. it is on many shortest paths between other nodes.
Intra-community	A gatekeeper	Point of contact between two communities.	A node with many incoming edges from other communities.
	A representative	Represents a community to others, or acts as an interface.	Certain nodes with many outgoing edges to other communities.

denote resource connections that are established through joint participation in collaborative tasks. Thus, if actors A1 and A2 work together on an evaluation of a loan application, it creates a link between them by virtue of this joint activity. Table 10.3 shows some key social positions, their descriptions, and their technical definitions from research on social roles that resources play in connected groups. Within the larger context of the incident management process, we are interested in various useful social positions within a community such as: *key contributor, influencer* and *coordinator*. There are also social positions across communities such as: *gatekeeper* and *representative*. In addition to social positions, resource synergy is another important metric to be considered during team formation.

In qualitative terms, *synergy* between two resources is a combination of multiple factors such as:

- the strength of their social ties or closeness
- their compatibility in terms of their organizational roles
- their respective time zones and
- commonality of their communication languages.

In quantitative terms, closeness between two resources is measured as the length of the shortest path between them. The closeness of a network (or team) can be measured as the average of all the shortest paths between any pair of nodes within the network (or team) as:

$$Avg_{i,j \in V}(d_{ij}), \text{ where } d_{ij} \text{ is the shortest path between vertices } i \text{ and } j$$

A socially enhanced organizational model is based on first creating a social network among all the actors in an organization, like the one we saw in Chapter 7. Moreover, the social network must be analyzed to determine how many communities exist in it. A well-known technique for community detection is called the Girvan-Newman algorithm that we discuss next.

Girvan-Newman Algorithm

This algorithm is named after its two inventors. The main steps of this method are described next.

Girvan-Newman community (or workgroup) detection algorithm
(1)   Calculate the betweenness of all existing edges in the network.
(2)   Remove the edge with the highest betweenness > betweenness threshold.
(3)   Recalculate the betweenness of all edges affected by the removal.
(4)   Repeat Steps 2 and 3 until k components remain.

This algorithm works by repeatedly splitting a connected network into subgroups based on a metric called edge betweenness. This is somewhat similar to the *node betweenness* metric discussed in Chapter 7. Note that, analogously to node betweenness, *edge betweenness* of an edge is the number of shortest paths between pairs of nodes that pass through the edge. By applying this algorithm, we are able to find communities (or workgroups) that are tightly joined together within themselves but less so with the other communities. The edges with high betweenness serve as bridges between these communities. The parameter k in step 4 above determines when the algorithm will stop. The value of k is determined partly by judgment so as to obtain a logical grouping of communities where no community is too small and the total number of communities is also not very large. The betweenness threshold in step 2 above is also a parameter of the algorithm that is determined by the user. A higher value for it will create fewer communities, while a lower value will lead to more splits and hence more communities will be formed.

Example 1: For an illustration of this algorithm, let us see how we can make communities in the social network in Figure 10.10(a), assuming each edge has a distance of 1. We first find the edge betweenness of all edges. The highest betweenness value is 16 for edge 7–8. After removing this edge two communities remain. Next, we recalculate the betweenness values of all edges and find that the highest betweenness is 6.23 for 2 edges: 1–5 and 5–3. After removing these two edges, the edge betweenness is calculated

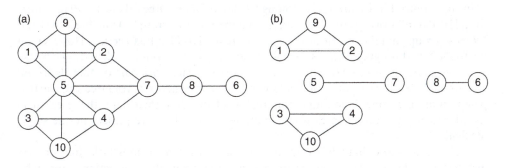

Figure 10.10 An example to illustrate the Girvan-Newman algorithm

again. Now, the highest value is 7.5 for 4 edges: 2–5, 5–4, 2–7 and 4–7. After removing these edges, we obtain four communities as shown in Figure 10(b). These calculations were made using RStudio using functions like graph and edge_betweenness in the igraph package.

In a similar way, this algorithm can be applied to a larger network to determine workgroups, and then relate these groups and individuals within them to the social roles described above. The next section will describe the results of an actual experiment on real data.

Exercise 4: Apply the steps of the Girvan-Newman algorithm to the graph shown in Figure 7.9 (in Chapter 7) using the actual distances shown on the edges and find the communities in it.

A Community Detection Experiment

Researchers from IBM analyzed a log of about 1500–1600 incidents from one of their clients in the travel and entertainment industry in the context of the incident management process. This process produced more than 23,000 task execution log entries reflecting the various tasks that were performed for these tickets by various individuals and the transfers that took place among them during the resolution process. A network based on these incident transfer log entries was constructed. In this network, each node is a resource and a directed link between a pair of nodes indicates that an incident is transferred from the source to the target node. They used the number of incidents along an edge as a weighting factor. In this setup they built a network of about 150 nodes and more than 200 edges as shown in Figure 10.11.

After creating this network, the researchers applied the Girvan-Newman algorithm to detect communities within it. The algorithm partitions the set of nodes into smaller subsets or groups, such that a pair of nodes within a group are much closer to each other than a pair of nodes across groups. By removing the edges across groups, each group becomes an island or a "community" On the bespoke dataset, the algorithm produced 21 communities of which only four are significant and interconnected (Communities 0, 1, 2 and 3) as shown in Figure 10.11. The other communities were relatively small and many were isolated from each other in terms of the closeness metric. Further, some communities were aligned with workgroup structures of the resources, while others were spread across multiple work groups, indicating the presence of strong collaborative activity across these groups.

In community 1 in Figure 10.11, among a total of 28 resources, there are 10 resources from HR Payroll work group, 7 resources from the Security group, 3 from the Travel and Expense group, and the rest from a few groups related to IT infrastructure. However, on the top left of this figure, there is a small community of 5 resources solely from a workgroup in charge of certain HR applications. Though the network partitioning algorithm assigns each resource to only one community, yet in practice a resource can participate in more than one. Upon analyzing real incidents from their data, the researchers found evidence of several cases where multiple social roles were present in one single incident.

Their results show that while creating a team to perform various tasks in a process instance, one should first try to satisfy resource requirements by selecting actors who meet the technical role requirements for the task. Next, among the qualified actors

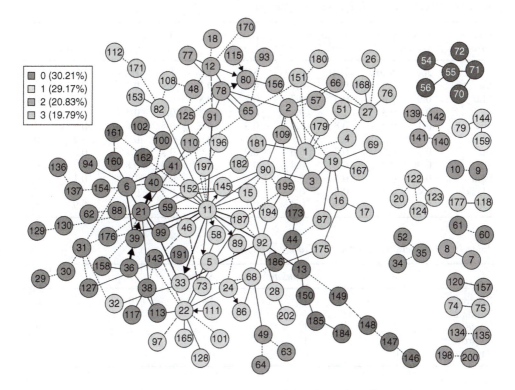

Figure 10.11 A resource social network of 4 communities (shown in different shades)

who are available, select ones who can also meet the social role requirement such as coordinator, gatekeeper, etc.

A Model for Resource Assignment across Tasks of a Process Instance

In this section, we shall discuss an approach that can take synergy among actors of various tasks in a process instance into consideration while assigning tasks to them in addition to their suitability in terms of their qualifications, experience, etc. Most approaches simply consider the suitability of actors for different tasks but disregard the synergy aspect. To see how an optimal assignment can be produced we shall first introduce some basic notation and vocabulary, and then use it to create an optimal resource assignment model.

To begin, we must specify synergies among actors in a synergy matrix such as Table 10.4 that shows the actors who perform various tasks and also their synergy with one another on a scale of 0 to 1. Thus a value of 0.9 between John and Jen indicates high synergy, while a 0.1 between Mike and Lin shows rather low or poor synergy. This information can be used in assigning tasks to resources in a more systematic way than making a random assignment. Such tables can be constructed from historical logs of complete process instances and from social networks derived from the logs.

In addition to pair-wise synergy between actors, we also need to know whether cooperation is required between a pairs of tasks or whether they are independent. To model

Table 10.4 Actor–actor synergy matrix (*synergy*)

Role > (*task*) >	*Cust. rep* (*receive*)		*Reviewer* (*validate*)		*Assessor* (*settle*)		*Manager* (*approve*)		*Accounts* (*pay*)	
	Joe	Mary	Beth	Sue	Mike	Jim	Jen	Pam	Mark	Lin
Joe	1.0	0.9	0.8	0.1	0.8	0.3	0.9	0.3	0.4	0.2
Mary	0.9	1.0	0.3	0.7	0.2	0.8	0.9	0.2	0.1	0.8
Beth	0.8	0.3	1.0	0.8	0.3	0.8	0.7	0.3	0.2	0.9
Sue	0.1	0.7	0.8	1.0	0.9	0.6	0.4	0.6	0.8	0.4
Mike	0.8	0.2	0.3	0.9	1.0	0.9	0.3	0.9	0.8	0.1
Jim	0.3	0.8	0.8	0.6	0.9	1.0	0.8	0.1	0.3	0.9
Jen	0.9	0.9	0.7	0.4	0.3	0.8	1.0	0.8	0.7	0.3
Pam	0.3	0.2	0.3	0.6	0.6	0.9	0.8	1.0	0.1	0.8
Mark	0.4	0.1	0.2	0.8	0.8	0.3	0.7	0.1	1.0	0.9
Lin	0.2	0.8	0.9	0.4	0.1	0.9	0.3	0.8	0.9	1.0

Table 10.5 Cooperation matrix (*task_task_coop$_{t1,t2}$*)

	Receive	Validate	Settle	Approve	Pay
Receive	–	1	1	0	0
Validate	1	–	1	1	0
Settle	1	1	–	1	0
Approve	0	1	1	–	1
Pay	0	0	0	1	–

this aspect, we introduce a task–task cooperation matrix as shown in Table 10.5. If cooperation is required between a pair of tasks (t1, t2) this is represented by a 1 in the corresponding entry in the matrix, else it is 0. Now we define an overall (and average) synergy for an assignment of resources to tasks in a process instance as follows:

$$Overall\ Synergy = \sum_{\forall(u1,u2,t1,t2)} actor\_task\_pair\_fit_{u1,u2,t1,t2} * task\_task\_coop_{t1,t2}$$
$$* synergy_{u1,u2}$$

$$Average\ Synergy = \frac{Total\ Synergy}{\sum_{t1,t2} coop_{t1,t2}}$$

Where

$synergy_{u1,u2}$: *synergy of actors* $u1$, $u2$ *on a continuous scale of* $0-1$

$$task\_task\_coop_{t1,t2}: \begin{cases} 1, & if\ cooperation\ is\ required\ between\ tasks\ t1\ and\ t2 \\ 0, & otherwise \end{cases}$$

$$actor\_task\_pair\_fit_{u1,u2,t1,t2}: \begin{cases} 1, & if\ actor\ pair\ (u1,u2)\ perform\ task\ pair \\ & (t1,t2)\ respectively \\ 0, & otherwise \end{cases}$$

The *overall synergy* is a measure of the total amount of synergy that is present in the process instance, while *average synergy* captures the synergy per every task pair for which interaction between actors is required. It is a measure of synergy between a typical pair of actors in the instance. Also, note that the binary variable $actor\_task\_pair\_fit_{u1,u2,t1,t2}$ is introduced here to show a work arrangement where actor u1 performs task t1, while actor u2 performs task t2. In such a case, this variable assumes a 1 value and otherwise it is 0. Let us see some examples to illustrate calculation of overall synergy.

Example 2: Partial cooperation case. Below we calculate average synergy using the values in Tables 10.4 and 10.5 There are five main tasks in this instance. Moreover, as per Table 10.5 there are only six interactions where cooperation is required; hence it is a case of *partial cooperation*. Clearly, several combinations of actor assignments are possible here. Let us look at two assignments, one random and another optimal.

Assignment 1 (random):
Customer rep: Joe; reviewer: Sue; assessor: Jim; Manager: Pam; accounts officer: Mark

Average synergy $= (0.1+0.3+0.6+0.6+0.1+0.1)/6 = 0.3$

Assignment 2 (optimal):
Customer rep: Mary; reviewer: Beth; assessor: Jim; manager: Jen; accounts officer: Mark

Average synergy $= (0.3+0.8+0.8+0.7+0.8+0.7)/6 = 0.683$

Notice how large a difference (of more than 100 percent) there is in average synergy between these two assignments. In the next example, we assume that all pairs of tasks require cooperation with each other.

Example 3: Full cooperation case. Next consider a variation of the above example. Instead of assuming that cooperation between some pairs of participants is necessary, let us assume that all participants who work on an instance of a process must cooperate with each other. The corresponding cooperation matrix is shown in Table 10.6. The solutions from the random assignment and the optimal assignment are as follows.

Assignment 3 (random):
Customer rep: Mary; reviewer: Sue; assessor: Jim; manager: Jen; accounts officer: Lin

Average synergy $=$
$(0.7+0.8+0.9+0.8+0.6+0.4+0.4+0.8+0.9+0.3)/10 = 0.66$

Table 10.6 Cooperation matrix (*full* cooperation required)

	Receive	Validate	Settle	Approve	Pay
Receive	–	1	1	1	1
Validate	1	–	1	1	1
Settle	1	1	–	1	1
Approve	1	1	1	–	1
Pay	1	1	1	1	–

Assignment 4 (optimal):
Customer rep: Mary; reviewer: Beth; assessor: Jim; manager: Jen; accounts officer: Lin

Average synergy $=$

$$(0.3+0.8+0.9+0.8+0.8+0.7+0.9+0.8+0.9+0.3)/10=0.72$$

In this example, the difference in average compatibility between the optimal and random assignments is much smaller than in Example 2. The improvement through an optimal reassignment of tasks in the full cooperation case is less because, in general, few actors cooperate well with all other actors in a process. In general, the cooperation matrix could vary, and the best assignment will also be different accordingly. Next we describe our model for finding an optimal solution so as to maximize cooperation within the team. Now, we shall apply these concepts to develop an optimization model called ORAM.

Exercise 5: Assume that all the entries for cooperation in Table 10.5 are 0, and recalculate the average synergy in Examples 2 and 3 for the random and optimal assignments.

Exercise 6: Write a simple greedy algorithm that looks just one step ahead at a time and makes resource assignment. Compare its results with those of the random and optimal algorithms.

An Optimal Resource Assignment Model (***)

Our model is shown in Figure 10.12. An optimal synergy model (ORAM) in general has an objective function and a set of constraints. Our objective is to maximize total synergy. However, in our model, for mathematical reasons, we express this objective function equivalently so as to *minimize total non-synergy*. To do so we replace $synergy_{u1,u2}$ by $(1 - synergy_{u1,u2})$. We shall use the notation described in the previous section.

There are three kinds of constraints in this model, as shown in Figure 10.12. Constraint 1 of the OSM model requires that every task must be assigned to exactly one actor. The second constraint forces the fit variable $actor\_task\_pair\_fit_{u1,u2,t1,t2}$ between an actor (or user) pair and a task pair to be 1 when the actors perform the corresponding tasks. Finally, the third constraint is needed to ensure that the actor u who is assigned to perform task t ($does_{u,t}$) must be qualified to do it ($cando_{u,t}$). We assume that $cando_{u,t}$ is a binary variable that is 1 if actor u is qualified to perform task t, and 0 otherwise.

The model in Figure 10.12 is called an integer programming (IP) formulation. Solving the ORAM model is an NP-complete problem (of exponential complexity); however, it can be solved quite efficiently with a tool like CPLEX. The solution of the model gives the optimal assignment by finding the values for the variable $does_{u,t}$ for all u, t pairs. Additional constraints can be added to this basic model to enforce minimum (maximum) limits on number of tasks assigned to any actor. Note that the objective function assumes that overall compatibility is linear in individual actor-pair compatibility.

Some experiments were conducted to compare the performance of this model versus the solution from a "greedy" algorithm that successively finds the best actor at each step in a greedy way by maximizing the synergy of the actor with the actors already assigned to previous tasks. These experiments were based on synthetic data with 10 tasks and

Model ORAM

$$Minimize \sum_{u1,u2,t1,t2} actor\_task\_pair\_fit_{u1,u2,t1,t2} * (1 - synergy_{u1,u2})$$

Subject to:

$$\sum_{u} does_{u,t} = 1, \forall t \tag{1}$$

$$does_{u1,t1} + does_{u2,t2} - actor\_task\_pair\_fit_{u1,u2,t1,t2} \leq 1,$$

$$\forall t1, t2 \ where \ coop(t1, t2) = 1 \tag{2}$$

$$does_{u,t} \leq cando_{u,t} \tag{3}$$

Where:

$$fit_{u1,u2,t1,t2} = \begin{cases} 1 & if \ actors \ u1, u2 \ perform \ tasks \ t1, t2 \ respectively \\ 0, & otherwise \end{cases}$$

$$does_{u,t} = \begin{cases} 1, & if \ actor \ u \ is \ assigned \ to \ perform \ task \ t \\ 0, & otherwise \end{cases}$$

$$cando_{u,t} = \begin{cases} 1, & if \ actor \ u \ is \ qualified \ to \ perform \ task \ t \\ 0, & otherwise \end{cases}$$

$$coop_{t1,t2} = \begin{cases} 1, & if \ cooperation \ is \ needed \ between \ t1 \ and \ t2 \\ 0, & otherwise \end{cases}$$

$$cweight_{u1,u2}: compatibilty \ between \ actors \ u1, u2$$

Figure 10.12 Model ORAM for optimal resource assignment

20 actors, assuming that each task could be done by either 2 or 3 actors, and there were 2 or 3 qualified actors for each task. It was assumed that each task i must cooperate with its successive task with probability 1.0, and with the tasks two and three steps removed with a probability of 0.5. The synergy matrix among actors was created by randomly assigning values between 0 and 1. Using these parameters, many scenarios were generated. The results showed that that the optimal algorithm outperformed the greedy one on average by about 20 percent, and in some cases by even as much as 40 percent. Clearly, there is value in finding optimal or near-optimal assignments.

Exercise 7: In the model above, we have a binary variable $coop_{t1,t2}$ that determines whether cooperation is required between two tasks t1 and t2. Now, let us say we have another variable $degree_{t1,t2}$ that takes a value between 0 and 1 to signify the extent of cooperation required between t1 and t2, assuming $coop_{t1,t2}$ is 1. If $coop_{t1,t2}$ is 0, then the $degree_{t1,t2}$ does not have any significance. Modify the ORAM model to incorporate this new feature.

Chapter Summary

Wikipedia, Facebook, WhatsApp, Twitter, WordPress, etc. are well-known examples of tools for collaboration. Users can adapt their own content, set policies to protect their privacy, and selectively share their content by controlling the permissions of others in their network to see it.

There are few tools that support the design of social processes fully and adequately. Hence, there is a need for BPM vendors to enhance or "socially enable" their products so that they can support social features. This would require modifications to the modeling language and also the execution engine. The modeling language must be extended to allow designers to use various social features in the processes they design. The execution engine will need "hooks" into the platforms of social software vendors so that they can invoke social activities and return the results to the users at run time.

SharePoint Server 2013 from Microsoft [15] implements features that make enterprise social computing and collaboration easier. These features are built upon a database that integrates information about people from many kinds of business applications and directory services. SharePoint includes several built-in workflows for common scenarios like approvals, feedback and signature collection, etc. It also enables users to add simple custom workflows of their own to lists which can be used for document/item review or approval cycles. This is ideally suited for a business team collaborating on document resources. However, SharePoint lacks an ability to design complex, cross-enterprise processes, with advanced business logic, systems integration and mobile support without extensive programming. It certainly does not provide full-fledged BPM support or integration. Advanced developers could consider programming custom workflows from scratch using InfoPath and Visual Studio, but this requires rather sophisticated coding ability. Besides, it is costly and time-consuming requiring local installation of development tools.

The importance of socio-technical networks is recognized in early works of Conway [5] and Trist and Labour [23]. The need for teamwork in healthcare is emphasized in [14]. Early proposals for assigning or distributing work to teams in a workflow are discussed in [9, 24]. The research of Balkundi and Harrison [1] showed how the network structure affects the success of teams. Evidence to show that social ties lead to higher-quality software appears in the work of Bird et al. [2]. Social processes and lifecycles are discussed in [3, 8, 13]. An introduction to SharePoint is found in [15].

The proposal on social compute units and their evaluation is due to Dustdar et al. [6, 20]. The Girvan-Newman algorithm for discovering communities in a social network is described in [7, 16]. Liu et al. [11] show how to apply the Girvan-Newman algorithm to derived social roles and enhanced organization structures. The experiment reported here is based on their work at IBM.

Work on resource and organizational mining to understand organizational structure and relationships from process logs appears in [12, 19, 22]. An approach for analyzing healthcare social networks is described in [17]. Other techniques for resource assignment are found in [4, 18, 21]. The resource assignment model and the optimization approach described in this chapter are based on the work of Kumar et al. [10]. Integration of resource assignment methods into BPM systems is still not mainstream or quite "technology ready," but we expect it will happen soon.

References

1. P. Balkundi and D. A. Harrison. Ties, leaders, and time in teams: strong inference about network structure's effects on team viability and performance. *The Academy of Management Journal*, Vol. 49, No. 1, pp. 49–68, 2006.

2. C. Bird, N. Nagappan, H. Gall, B. Murphy and P. Devanbu. Putting It All Together: Using Socio-technical Networks to Predict Failures. *Proceedings of the 2009 20th International Symposium on Software Reliability Engineering (ISSRE'09)*, 2009.

3. M. Brambilla, P. Fraternali and C. Ruiz. Combining Social Web and BPM for Improving Enterprise Performances: The BPM4People Approach to Social BPM. *Proceedings of the 21st International Conference Companion on World Wide Web*, pp. 223–226, 2012.

4. C. Cabanillas, M. Resinas and A. Ruiz-Cortés. Defining and Analysing Resource Assignments in Business Processes with RAL. In: G. Kappel, Z. Maamar, H. R. Motahari-Nezhad (eds) Service-Oriented Computing. ICSOC 2011. *Lecture Notes in Computer Science*, Vol. 7084. Springer, Berlin, Heidelberg.

5. M. Conway. How do committees invent? *Datamation*, Vol. 14, No. 4, pp. 28–31, 1968.

6. S. Dustdar and K. Bhattacharya. The social compute unit. *IEEE Internet Computing*, Vol. 15, No. 3, pp. 64–69, 2011.

7. M. Girvan and M. E. J. Newman. Community structure in social and biological networks. *PNAS*, Vol. 99, No. 12, pp. 7821–7826, 2002.

8. A. Koschmider, M. Song and H. A. Reijers. Social Software for Modeling Business Processes. In: First Workshop on BPM and Social Software, *LNBIP*, 2009.

9. A. Kumar, W.M.P. van der Aalst and H. M. W. Verbeek. Dynamic work distribution in workflow management systems: how to balance quality and performance. *Journal of MIS*, Vol. 18, No. 3, pp. 157–193, Winter 2001–2002.

10. A. Kumar, R. M. Dijkman and M. Song. Optimal resource assignment in workflows for maximizing cooperation. *BPM*, Vol. 8094, pp. 235–250, 2013.

11. R. Liu, S. Agarwal, R. R. Sindhgatta and J. Lee. Accelerating collaboration in task assignment using a socially enhanced resource model. *BPM*, Vol. 8094, pp. 251–258, 2013.

12. L. Linh Thao et al. Mining Staff Assignment Rules from Event-Based Data. In: *International Conference on Business Process Management*. Springer, Berlin Heidelberg, 2005.

13. P. Mathiesen, J. A. Watson, W. Bandara and M. Rosemann. Applying Social Technology to Business Process Lifecycle Management. In: *The 4th Workshop on Business Process Management and Social Software (BPMS'11)*, 2011.

14. K. Mazzocco, D. B. Petitti, K.T. Fong, D. Bonacum, J. Brookey, S. Graham, R. E. Lasky, J. B. Sexton and E. J. Thomas. Surgical team behaviors and patient outcomes. *American Journal of Surgery*, Vol. 197, No. 5, pp. 678–685, 2009.

15. Microsoft Cororation. Introduction to Sharepoint Workflow. https://support.office.com/en-us/article/Introduction-to-SharePoint-workflow-07982276-54e8-4e17-8699-5056eff4d9e3?ui=en-US&rs=en-US&ad=US&fromAR=1.

16. M. E. J. Newman. *Networks: An Introduction*. Oxford University Press, Oxford, UK, 2010.

17. M. Palazzolo et al. Measuring social network structure of clinical teams caring for patients with complex conditions. *Procedia-Social and Behavioral Sciences*, Vol. 26, pp. 17–29, 2011.

18. R.-M. Stefanie. *Life-Cycle Support for Staff Assignment Rules in Process-Aware Information Systems*, BETA working papers; Vol. 213. Eindhoven: Technische Universiteit Eindhoven. 2007.

19. S. Stefan et al. A framework for efficiently mining the organisational perspective of business processes. *Decision Support Systems*, Vol. 89, pp. 87–97, 2016.

20. B. Sengupta, A. Jain, K. Bhattacharya, H. L. Truong and S. S. Dustdar. Who Do You Call? Problem Resolution Through Social Compute Units. In: *Proceedings of the 10th international conference on Service-Oriented Computing (ICSOC'12)*, pp. 48–62, 2012.

21. R. Sindhgatta, A. Ghose, G. B. Dasgupta. Analyzing Resource Behavior to Aid Task Assignment in Service Systems. In: A. Barros, D. Grigori, N. Narendra, H. Dam (eds) Service-Oriented Computing. *Lecture Notes in Computer Science*, Vol. 9435. Springer, Berlin, Heidelberg, 2015.

22. M. Song and W. M. P. van der Aalst. Towards comprehensive support for organizational mining. *Decision Support Systems*, Vol. 46, No. 1, pp. 300–317, 2008.
23. E. Trist and O. M. O. Labour. *The Evolution of Socio-Technical Systems: A Conceptual Framework and an Action Research Program*. Ontario Ministry of Labour, Ontario Quality of Working Life Centre, 1981.
24. W. M. P. van der Aalst and A. Kumar. A reference model for team-enabled workflow management systems. *Data & Knowledge Engineering*, Vol. 38, No. 3, pp. 335–363, 2001.

11 Process Analytics

Introduction

Process analytics is a broad area of research with the goal of extracting as much information as possible about a process from a process execution log. Process mining or process discovery is a subfield of process analytics with the aim of extracting the control flow and related information about a process from historical execution logs. In this chapter, we will discuss process analytics in a broader sense but devote a large part of our discussion to process mining, since this is one sub-area of process analytics that has received a large amount of attention within the BPM area.

Process analytics can lead to the discovery of a variety of valuable information related to:

- **Process models.** The control flow of a process and resource information such as who carries out what tasks, task duration, etc.
- **Business rules.** Some rules can be inferred regarding patterns of resource assignments to tasks. For instance, the resources that perform the approval task might all have the status of manager or higher. The rules may lead to an understanding of the policies of the business.

- **Resource networks.** As we saw in Chapter 10, resource or social networks emerge among the actors who collaborate on certain process instances by performing different tasks of the same instance. These networks can help us understand how well two agents work with each other.
- **Delays and bottlenecks.** From process metrics like mean, standard deviation, minimum, and maximum durations, it is possible to distinguish high variability tasks from low variability ones and gain a deeper understanding of delays and bottlenecks. It is also important to determine whether delays are caused from resource shortages or are due to the inherent nature of the task.
- **Handoff patterns.** When a task in a process instance finishes, it is handed over from one agent to the next one. Some instances may return to the same agent who had done an earlier task after other agents worked on intervening tasks. This gives rise to handoff patterns. There is some evidence to show that handoff patterns can influence the throughput time of process instances.

Process analytics is an emerging research area that has opened new possibilities of knowledge discovery. It complements data mining with many practical applications. In healthcare, it is possible to extract the process for providing care to a patient and also to identify anomalies that may hurt proper treatment. Moreover, based on such analyses corrective action may be taken. It has also been applied in health-care fraud and abuse detection, and in compliance. Process mining also has applications in social mining. Thus, by analyzing a log it is possible to determine which co-workers are more compatible with each other when they are collaborating on an insurance claim or a loan application. Such analysis could show that, say, Bob and Mike when they work together on handling a loan application perform much better than Joe and Bill.

In this chapter, we shall study techniques and tools for extracting process models from logs, called process mining or discovery. We shall provide some background about process logs, describe a special kind of process model called the universal model, and introduce concepts related to fitness and specificity of a model. Next, we'll explain a process mining method based on relationships, followed by the Alpha and Heuristics Miner algorithms. Later, we shall discuss ways of dealing with noisy logs and give a real-world example of mining a model from a noisy log. Finally, we present an overview and an example of how to use the Disco tool for process analytics.

Understanding Process Logs

Figure 11.1 shows a log with 10 execution traces or process instances obtained from a process within a company. Each trace shows the sequence in which different tasks A through K occur. Notice how there are different ways of performing the same process, since all the traces belong to the same underlying process. In general, in addition to the task name, a log may have additional information like the start and end times of a task, the name or ID of the resource who performed the task, the input and output data of the task, etc. In general, a log record may have additional information like time stamp, resource, result, outcome, etc.

Exercise 1: What inferences about the underlying process from which this log is created can you draw by examining this log?

Number	Log instance
1	A B C E F G H J
2	A C B F E G H K
3	A B B C F E G H K
4	A B C F E G H K
5	A C F E H G J
6	A C B F E G H K
7	A B C E F G H K
8	A C B E F G H J
9	A C B B E F G H J
10	A C B F E H G J

Figure 11.1 An example log with 10 traces

Upon a closer inspection, you might notice that:

- Tasks, B, C, E, F, G, and J appear in **all** log instances at least once.
- Task B can appear more than once in a single trace, e.g. traces 3 and 9.
- All the log instances start with task A.
- J and K are alternative tasks, since they do not appear together.

We can think of these observations as rules of thumb that have been derived from the log.

Exercise 2: By heuristic reasoning, try to discover and draw the process this log might come from.

Now let us consider another log that is shown in Figure 11.2. This log is actually a variant of the first log in Figure 11.1. It only shows the first five traces from that log. However, in this log there is additional information in the form of the resource that performs a task, the duration of each task, and the total duration of the instance. The duration is not specified explicitly but it may be inferred from knowing the length of each cell. Thus, for log instance 1, the duration of task B is about twice the duration of tasks A and C.

Number	Log instance									Duration
1	A Joe	B Meg	C Liz	E Tom	F Sue	G Tom	H Liz	J Joe		150
2	A Joe	C Liz	B Meg	F Sue	E Tom	G Liz	H Meg	K Joe		170
3	A Meg	B Joe	B Meg	C Liz	F Sue	E Tom	G Tom	H Liz	K Joe	150
4	A Meg	B Joe	C Meg	F Sue	E Tom	G Liz	H Joe	K Liz		140
5	A Joe	C Liz	F Sue	E Joe	H Meg	G Tom	J Joe			110

Figure 11.2 The example log with additional information

Exercise 3: What kinds of information can you infer from the log of Figure 11.2 about tasks, resources, and durations?

There are several observations that one might draw such as:

- Tasks A and B are performed by Joe or Meg.
- Tasks J and K are always performed by Joe.
- Task C is performed by Liz or Meg.
- Tasks E and F are performed by Sue and Tom.
- Task G is performed by Liz or Tom.
- Task H is performed by Liz, Joe, or Meg.

We could also say that the variability in the duration of tasks B and E is high, while that of other tasks is small. The total duration of an instance varies from 110 to 170 time units.

Now let us see what additional observations one can make from a deeper analysis of the log in Figure 11.2. First, notice that *no two successive tasks are performed by the same individual.* This may result from the policy of a company and could be related to the issues of security and separation of duty that were discussed in Chapter 8. Perhaps there is a view in the company that letting the same individual perform the two tasks in sequence poses a security risk. Hence, this requirement is necessary. Second, you should note that there are five actors who work on this process and all five are involved in the execution of every instance of this process.

Next, we can turn to see how we can discover a process model for the log in Figure 11.1 by a heuristic approach. From observation, we notice that:

- A is the first task in the process.
- B and C are together in all traces (except for trace 5 where B is missing) but their order can change. This leads us to realize that they are in a parallel structure; however, since B can occur 0 or multiple times, it is likely in a *loop* structure.
- E and F are always together in all log traces. This leads us to believe that they are in a parallel structure. Further since E can appear one or more times within a trace, it is in a loop.
- Tasks G and H are also together in every trace though their exact order may change, and they each appear once in a trace. Hence, they are in a parallel structure.
- Finally, every trace ends with J or K. This implies that they are in a choice structure.

Now we can combine the A, B-C, F-E, G-H, and J-K structures in a sequence in that order and we obtain the process model shown in Figure 11.3. Notice that we have added a start and an end node (in circles) to this process to denote the start and end of the process. These are normally not tasks of the process but represent events or markers.

Exercise 4: Check for yourself that the process model shown in Figure 11.3 is consistent with all the log traces in Figure 11.1. Are there any traces that do not conform to this log and why?

Next, we will discuss some challenges that occur in process mining by introducing universal models.

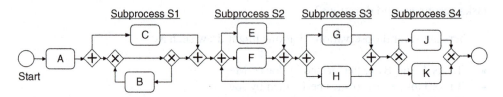

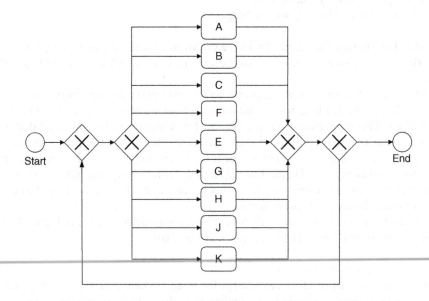

Figure 11.3 A process model that corresponds to the log of Figure 11.1

Figure 11.4 A universal process model that can explain the log of Figure 11.1

Universal Process Models

Let us turn now to examine the two models shown in Figures 11.4 and 11.5. The model in Figure 11.4 arranges the nine tasks of the example above: A, B, C, E, F, G, H, J, and K in a choice structure inside a loop. On the other hand, Figure 11.5 arranges this set of tasks in a sequence inside a loop. Also note that each task may be skipped because there is a self-loop around it.

A trace can be checked to see if it conforms to a process model simply by following each task in the trace and noting if it can logically be executed by the model. This is called *replaying* a trace.

Exercise 6: Check to see if the two models in Figures 11.4 and 11.5 can replay the log of Figure 11.1. If yes, how are these two process models different? Which one do you think is a "better" model?

As you can see, the *universal model* has an inner choice structure that allows you to choose any task at all and then there is an outer loop structure that allows you to return to the inner structure again. Thus, we can select the first task entry in a log trace from the inner choice structure, and then return to it to select the next entry in the trace, and so on.

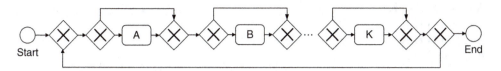

Figure 11.5 An alternative universal process model that can explain any log

At the end of the trace we can exit the model. It turns out that the universal models can explain any log at all! Problem solved, you might think. But not so soon! The drawback of the universal model is that it can explain literally *any* log because all sequences of tasks (even a random one) are explainable with the universal model. *This means that the universal model is a very general model.* It is like stating that all humans are less than 125 years old and shorter than 8 feet! While correct, such a broad, sweeping generalization is not at all informative. *Such models have an accuracy of 100 percent, but their precision is 0 percent.* These universal models are sometimes called flower models because they can also be drawn in the shape of a flower with a choice structure at the center and the tasks emerging radially from it.

Exercise 6: Draw a flower model with one choice control structure at the center and connect it to tasks A, B, C, ..., K, such that they loop back into the choice structure. Check if it is indeed a universal process model.

Desirable Properties of a Process Model – Fitness and Specificity

A major problem with the universal model is that its *quality* is "bad" since it can simulate every log. Thus, two logs with the same set of tasks can always be explained by the same model! Hence, this model lacks *specificity*. This has given rise to the issue of process model quality with a need for distinguishing good models from bad ones. Process models mined from logs are mainly evaluated in two aspects: *fidelity* (degree to which the model explains a log) and *specificity* (degree to which a model is specific to a given log). Fidelity is also referred to as *fitness* and specificity is also referred to as *appropriateness* or *precision*. These terms are defined more formally next.

$$\text{Fitness(PM)} = \text{fraction of log traces that can be correctly replayed by the process model}$$

$$\text{Precision(PM)} = \frac{\text{the amount of observed behavior as recorded in the log}}{\text{the amount of possible behavior as allowed by the model}}$$

The fitness of our example log in Figure 11.1 is 1, since every trace can be replayed by the model exactly. However, to calculate precision, we need to consider how many possible traces not shown in this log can be generated from the model.

Exercise 7: Make a list of all traces not present in the log of Figure 11.1 that can be generated from the model shown in Figure 11.3. Assume that the loop can occur only up to 2 times.

As it turns out, many additional traces can be generated such as:

A C B F E H G K
A C F E G H K
A C E F G H K
A C E F G H J
. . .

In fact, even if we limit ourselves to 0 or 1 occurrences of B there are 24 possible unique traces that can be generated in the process of Figure 11.3. Basically, this process consists of four structures or subprocesses S1–S4. Table 11.1 shows the possible trace subsequences that can be generated by each subprocess. When we combine these four sets of subsequences in all possible ways, we obtain 24 possible traces.

Exercise 8: Assume that B can occur up to a maximum of 2 times and calculate the total number of unique traces that can be generated by the process of Figure 11.3.

The fitness of the process model in Figure 11.3 with respect to the log in Figure 11.1 is 1, since it can replay all the log traces correctly. However, its theoretical precision is 0 because there is an infinite number of possible traces (and hence behaviors) that can be generated from this model due to the presence of the loop around B. Hence, we have to limit ourselves to a finite number of repetitions of B. If we assume that B occurs 0 or 1 times, then the precision is $10/24 = 0.42$. This means that the model is only about 42 percent precise or specific to the given log. It contains additional behavior that we do not see in the log.

Exercise 9: Can you redraw the process model of Figure 11.3 *without* the loop, but with the same behavior, if you know beforehand that B occurs only 0, 1 or 2 times?

Now let us consider the universal model of Figure 11.4.

Exercise 10: How many possible traces can be generated from the model of Figure 11.4? What is the precision of this model for the log of Figure 11.1? Assume that this model can have up to five tasks and that there are no loops.

These metrics relate to the quality of a model. Next, we shall describe algorithms for process mining.

Process Discovery Based on Relationships

This is a simple, intuitive approach based on making a relationship table that shows the relationships between all pairs of tasks. We assume a log L with n traces L_i,

Table 11.1 Possible valid subsequences that can be generated by each subprocess within the process of Figure 11.3 (assuming 0 or 1 occurrences of B)

S1	S2	S3	S4
C B	F E	G H	J
B C	E F	H G	K
C			
Count = 3	Count = 2	Count = 2	Count = 2

$i = 1, 2, \ldots n$, and the jth entry in trace L_i is L_{ij}. The rules for drawing this matrix are as follows:

Sequence (→): If log entry L_{ij} corresponds to an occurrence of task A, and entry L_{ik} corresponds to an occurrence of task B, then $k > j$ for all i implies that there is sequence relationship such that A always precedes B in the log. This is written as A → B. A reverse sequence is expressed as B ← A.

Parallel (‖): If log entry L_{ij} corresponds to an occurrence of task A, and entry L_{ik} corresponds to an occurrence of task B, and $k > j$ for some values of i, and $j > k$ for some other values of i, then there is a parallel relationship between A and B.

Choice (# or X): If log entry L_{ij} corresponds to an occurrence of task A, and there does not exist any entry L_{ik} corresponding to an occurrence of task B, and vice versa (i.e. A appears in some log traces and B in others but both *never* appear together), they are said to be in a choice relationship.

Table 11.2 shows a relationship matrix (similar to the ones we saw in Chapter 7) for the example log of Figure 11.1 derived by applying the above rules. The next step is to use this matrix to derive the process model itself. Note that when a task appears successively, e.g. BB in the log, it immediately indicates that there is a self-loop around B. We can note this information separately. All the diagonal entries are filled with a dash sign (-).

The next step is to scan the relationship matrix row-wise from the top and find a pair of tasks such that both tasks have the same relationships with all other tasks. *This means that these two tasks may be combined into a subprocess structure.* For our relationship matrix, we can notice that B and C have the same relationships with all other tasks, i.e. A, E, F, G, H, J, and K. In particular, A precedes both B and C, while F, G, H, J, and K all succeed B and C. This means we can combine B and C into a parallel subprocess structure (since they have a parallel relationship between themselves) and call this structure, say S1. Next, we can replace the relationships of B and C in the matrix by relationships of the structure S1 as shown in the revised matrix in Table 11.3 and Figure 11.6(a).

Notice how the size of the matrix shrinks from 9 × 9 to 8 × 8. We continue scanning the table and next observe that E and F also have the same relationship with all other tasks (or subprocesses) in the matrix. Thus, E and F are combined into a new parallel structure S2, as shown in Figure 11.6(b) and the size of the relationship matrix falls to 7 × 7. In the next step, G and H are combined into an S3 parallel subprocess as shown in Figure 11.6(c) and this reduces the matrix to a 6 × 6 size. Finally, J and K are joined

Table 11.2 A relationship matrix (Rel) between all pairs of tasks in the log

	A	B	C	E	F	G	H	J	K
A	-	→	→	→	→	→	→	→	→
B	←	-	‖	→	→	→	→	→	→
C	←	‖	-	→	→	→	→	→	→
E	←	←	←	-	‖	→	→	→	→
F	←	←	←	‖	-	→	→	→	→
G	←	←	←	←	←	-	‖	→	→
H	←	←	←	←	←	‖	-	→	→
J	←	←	←	←	←	←	←	-	#
K	←	←	←	←	←	←	←	#	-

Table 11.3 A relationship matrix after merging tasks B and C into a subprocess S1

	A	S1	E	F	G	H	J	K
A	-	→	→	→	→	→	→	→
S1	←	-	→	→	→	→	→	→
E	←	←	-	||	→	→	→	→
F	←	←	||	-	→	→	→	→
G	←	←	←	←	-	||	→	→
H	←	←	←	←	||	-	→	→
J	←	←	←	←	←	←	-	#
K	←	←	←	←	←	←	#	-

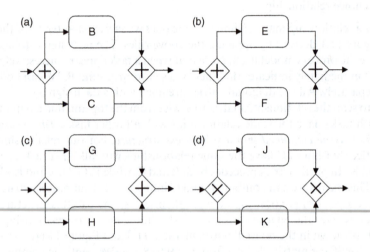

Figure 11.6 Four subprocesses S1–S4 that are generated based on relationships: (a) S1; (b) S2; (c) S3; (d) S4

Table 11.4 A relationship matrix after merging four pairs of tasks

	A	S1	S2	S3	S4
A	-	→	→	→	→
S1	←	-	→	→	→
S2	←	←	-	→	→
S3	←	←	←	-	→
S4	←	←	←	←	-

in a choice subprocess S4, as shown in Figure 11.6(d). At this stage we have a 5 × 5 relationship matrix, as shown in Table 11.4.

Now, we may repeat the same steps as before (you get the idea!) by combining the remaining tasks and/or subprocesses. Thus, A, S1, S2, S3, and S4 are combined in a sequence. Lastly, some post processing is required to put loops around tasks that repeat to get the final process resulting in the process shown in Figure 11.3. The formal algorithm REL can be described as follows.

Algorithm REL

1 Preprocess: Scan the log for any successive repeating task names and make a list of repeating tasks. The set P is initially empty, i.e. P = {}.
2 Create a relationship matrix (Rel).
3 Scan the matrix by rows to find the first pair of tasks T_i, T_j, that have the same relationship with all other tasks.
4 Combine this (T_i, T_j) into a structure $S_{i\cdot j}$ based on the Rel(T_i, T_j), i.e.

    a   Add an entry to process set P s.t. $P = P \cup \{S_{i\cdot j} = R(T_i, T_j)\}$
    b   Delete the row and column for T_j.
    c   Rename the row column for T_i to $S_{i\cdot j}$.

5 Repeat steps 3 and 4 until only 1 entry is left in the table
6 Scan set P from left to right, and build the process.
7 Make a self-loop around the tasks that are in the RPT list.

This algorithm assumes that: (1) the process from which the log is created is well structured; and (2) the log is complete, i.e. there are enough entries in the log to describe all the relationships among the tasks in an unambiguous way.

Exercise 11: Apply the REL algorithm to the log: {ABCD, ACBD, AED} and draw the discovered process.

This algorithm can handle self-loops but not general loops because in a loop multiple relationships can arise between pairs of tasks. This simple algorithm gives you the intuition behind process mining, but it only works when the log is from a fully structured model, for reasons we discussed in Chapter 7. Next, we shall describe the well-known Alpha algorithm that uses a different approach and is more advanced.

The Alpha Algorithm

The Alpha algorithm was the first major algorithm developed in the context of Petri nets. As we have discussed already in Chapter 2, most Petri nets can be converted into equivalent BPMN processes and vice versa. Thus, it is possible to feed a log as input into a process mining algorithm that discovers Petri nets and then convert the Petri net into a BPMN process. Most of the algorithms that are implemented for process mining and discovery in the **ProM** academic toolset have been devised for mining Petri nets.

The main idea of the Alpha algorithm is to scan a log and identify *causal, parallel,* and *choice* relations among tasks. A causal relation is different from the sequence relation described earlier in that a causal relationship arises when task A is *immediately* succeeded by task B (and the reverse is not true) in a trace. This means that if task A appears, say, in position j in trace i of log L denoted as L_{ij}, then task B would appear in position $j + 1$ of trace i or $L_{i(j+1)}$. This is denoted as $A \rightarrow_c B$. In such a case, we say that there is a causal relationship between t_i and t_j, i.e. t_i is the direct cause of t_j. The meaning of the choice and parallel relations is the same as before. By scanning the log, it is possible to identify the initial and final tasks in the log, and all such causal relationships among tasks (or transitions in the Petri net terminology).

So, let's consider a log with 2 traces: {ABCD, ABDC}. Upon examining the first trace ABCD alone in the log, one might infer that there are three possible causal relationships: $A \rightarrow_c B$; $B \rightarrow_c C$; and $C \rightarrow_c D$. However, on examining the second trace, it is evident that there is no causal relationship between C and D.

Once we have identified the pairs of tasks (or transitions) that have causal relationships, there is another important step. This requires combining such pairs to form sets by combining these causal pairs into *maximal* causal transition sets such that a set of transitions is caused by another set of transitions. Thus, in general, $\{t_{i1}, t_{i2}, \ldots\} \rightarrow_c \{t_{j1}, t_{j2}, \ldots\}$. *Moreover, the transitions in the causing set should all be in a choice relationship among each other, as also the transitions in the resulting set.* This causal relationship is mapped into a Petri net structure, as we shall show presently. Basically, there will be many such causal substructures resulting from the log, and each one is mapped into a substructure in a similar way.

By combining these sub-structures among themselves, and with the start and end places of the Petri net, it is possible to obtain a complete petri net solution for the log.

The full Alpha algorithm for mining a process model from a log W is given next.

Algorithm Alpha

1   $T_w = \{$set of all tasks in the log W (from all traces)$\}$
2   $T_I = \{$set of all initial tasks in the log, $T_{I1}, T_{I2}, \ldots\}$
3   $T_O = \{$set of all final (or output) tasks in the log, $T_{O1}, T_{O2}, \ldots\}$
4   $P = \{$start, end$\}$
5   $F = \{$(start, T_{I1}), (start, T_{I2}) $\ldots$, (T_{O1}, end), (T_{O2}, end) $\ldots\}$
6   Create set $C = \{$All causal relationship pairs, e.g. (t_{i1}, t_{j1}), (t_{i2}, t_{j2}), $\ldots$, (t_{ik}, t_{jk}), $\ldots\}$
7   Compute the **maximal** set $M = \{(LHS_i, RHS_i), i = 1, 2, \ldots\}$, such that the following conditions are satisified:

$\forall(l_{i1} \in LHS_i), \forall(r_{j1} \in RHS_i), (l_{i1}, r_{j1}) \in C$, and
$\forall(l_{i1}, l_{i2}) \in LHS_i, l_{i1} \# l_{i2}$, and
$\forall(r_{j1}, r_{j2}) \in RHS_i, r_{j1} \# r_{j2}$, and
$\forall(t_{ik}, t_{jk}) \in C, \exists(LHS_i, RHS_i)$, s.t., $t_{ik} \in LHS_i, t_{jk} \in RHS_i$, and
$\nexists(LHS'_i, RHS'_i)$ s.t. $LHS'_i \supset LHS_i$ OR $RHS'_i \supseteq RHS_i$

8   Then add one place $p_{ij\text{-}kl}$ to the set of places P corresponding to each subset in M. Moreover, we add a flow to the flow relation F for a directed edge from each t_{ik} to place $p_{ij\text{-}kl}$, and for a directed edge from place $p_{ij\text{-}kl}$ to each t_{ik}.
9   The final Petri net $PN = \{P, T_w, F\}$.

The idea of the *maximal* set in step 7 is that, if in step 6 we find two causal relationships, say, (A, C) and (B, C), then if we also determine that: (1) A and B have a choice relationship (i.e. A#B); (2) there is no other causal relationship (P, C) such that P#A#B; and (3) there is no other causal relationship (A, Q) where C#Q, then ({A, B}, C) is a maximal superset of (A, C) and (B, C). This algorithm was proposed by Wil van der Aalst and his colleagues. Our description above is slightly different from theirs.

The limitation of this algorithm is that it cannot deal with self-loops (i.e. a loop of length 1) and loops of length 2 as shown in Figure 11.7. Additional (minor) pre- and post-processing is required to handle those cases. Upon pre-processing a log, if we find that task B appears multiple times in succession it indicates a self-loop. Each occurrence of A can be replaced by three tasks, e.g. start A, execute A, and end A. In this way, the length of the A self-loop increases to 4. Similarly, if an A-B-A loop occurs, then B can

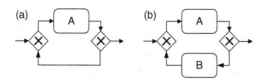

Figure 11.7 Special case loops of length 1 and 2: (a) loop of length 1; (b) loop of length 2

be replaced by start B, execute B to increase the loop length to 4. After the process model is discovered, the substitutions may be reversed to obtain the model showing only the activity names. We shall now illustrate the Alpha algorithm with an example borrowed from the paper of van der Aalst.

Example 1: Consider an example log, L = {ABCD, ACBD, AED}

T_w = {A, B, C, D, E}
T_I = {A}
T_O = {D}
Causal relationships = {(A, B), (A, C), (A, E), (B, D), (C, D), (E, D)}
Choice relationships = {(B, E), (C, E)}
Maximal causal relationship set = {(A, {B, E}), (A, {C, E}), ({B, E}, D), ({C, E}, D)}

Note that B and C do not have a causal relationship between them because both BC and CB subsequences appear in the traces. The maximal subset {(A, {B, E})} in M is created by combining (A, B) and (A, E) from C, since B#E. Similarly, the maximal subset ({B, E}, D) is created by combining (B, E) and (B, D), since B#D. To create the Petri net:

> Add a start place and connect it to A. Then add an end place and connect D to it. Next, each subset in the maximal causal relationship set is mapped to a Petri net substructure and they are connected together as shown in Figure 11.8.

The four places that correspond to the four maximal causal relationship sets are p1–p4. They have also been marked with their corresponding causal sets for clarity. An equivalent BPMN diagram for this Petri net is shown in Figure 11.9 for easier readability.

> Final Petri net PN
> = {{start, end, p1, p2, p3, p4}, {A, B, C, D, E}, {(start, A), (A, p1), (p1, B),
> (p1, E), (A, p2), (p2, C), (p2, E), (B, p3), (C, p4), (E, p3), (E, p4), (p3, D),
> (p4, D), (D, End)}}

Now, say, we added another trace "ACD" to the three traces in this example. We would still obtain the same process model by the Alpha algorithm since the causal relationships A $\rightarrow_c$ C, and C $\rightarrow_c$ D already exist in the other three traces. However, we cannot replay ACD in the discovered model. This is an instance of how the algorithm can remove noise, since ACD would be an example of it. Nevertheless, as noted earlier, the algorithm is not designed to handle noise.

Exercise 12: Apply the Alpha algorithm to the log of Figure 11.1 and draw a Petri net process diagram that you discover.

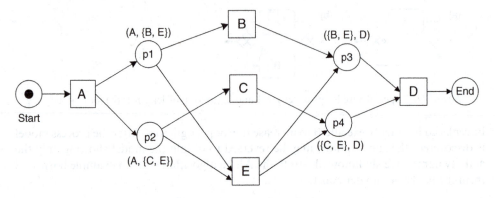

Figure 11.8 A Petri net derived from a log by applying the Alpha algorithm

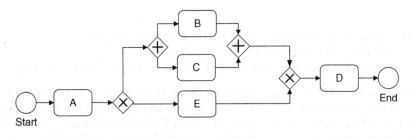

Figure 11.9 An equivalent BPMN diagram for the Petri net of Figure 11.8

The Heuristics Miner Algorithm

Next we describe the Heuristics Miner (or HM) algorithm. The greatest advantage of the HM algorithm over the Alpha algorithm is that by taking frequencies into account it can filter out noisy or infrequent behavior in a log.

The HM algorithm works by computing a number of metrics from the log for all task pairs such as frequency of each task, frequency of direct succession (i.e. an immediate sequence of two tasks), and frequency of indirect succession, and uses these metrics to compute dependency scores. The algorithm uses heuristic rules based on the dependency scores and frequency of direct succession to detect direct causal relationships between tasks, and form a dependency graph. The main steps of this algorithm are explained next in the context of a running example.

Step 1: The first step in HM is the construction of a *dependency graph*. A *frequency-based metric* is used to check the strength of the causality relationship between two tasks, t_i and t_j, or dependency. The calculated *dependency* (denoted as *Dep*) values between the tasks of a log L are used in a heuristic search to derive the relationships among tasks.

Thus, $\text{Dep}(t_i, t_j) = \left(\dfrac{\left| t_i \rightarrow_c t_j \right| - \left| t_j \rightarrow_c t_i \right|}{\left| t_i \rightarrow_c t_j \right| + \left| t_j \rightarrow_c t_i \right| + 1} \right)$

The terms $|t_i \rightarrow_c t_j|$ (and $|t_j \rightarrow_c t_i|$) represent the frequencies of the traces in the log where there is a causality from i to j (and vice versa). In this way, a dependency matrix showing dependencies between all pairs of tasks is constructed. The dependency values all lie between -1 and 1. A high positive dependency value indicates a strong causality from t_i to t_j, while a high negative value indicates a strong causality from t_j to t_i. A value of 0 indicates that there is no causality between two tasks. Consider a log such as:

$$\{ABCDEH^{(5)}, ACBDEH^{(5)}, ABDCFH, ACBDFH^{(5)}, ABCDHE, ABDFH\}$$

The same trace is often repeated multiple times in a log. The superscript of each trace represents the frequency of occurrence of the trace in the log. The dependency matrix is shown in Table 11.5.

Step 2: AND/XOR split/join and non-observable tasks

The next step is to infer causal relationships for AND/XOR control structures. Thus, in our example, it is clear that both B and C follow A, but how can we tell if they have an XOR or an AND relationship between themselves? Hence, we need to examine the dependency, Dep(A, B & C) further. The ratio is calculated as follows:

$$\text{Dep(A, B \& C)} = \left(\frac{|B \rightarrow_c C| + |C \rightarrow_c B|}{|A \rightarrow_c B| + |A \rightarrow_c C| + 1} \right)$$

When we perform the calculation on our example log, we get Dep(A, B & C) = 0.84. This large value suggests that this relationship is correct. A rule of thumb sets the threshold for this dependency at 0.1 and the calculated value is clearly much higher. Next, we also notice from the dependency matrix that there is a dependency from B to D (0.92) and from C to D (0.71). Hence, D should follow the B and C structure in the process model. From D there is a strong dependency to E (0.91) and to F (0.86). Based on this we can hypothesize that D is followed by either E AND F or (E XOR F) structures. If we calculate Dep(D, E AND F) using the above formula, we obtain a value of 0, since E and F never appear together in any trace of our example log. Hence, we rule out the structure E AND F, and determine that D is followed by E XOR F. Finally, there are strong dependencies from E to H (0.75) and from F to H (0.88). From this we can conclude that the E–F structure is followed by H. This process model can be represented as a Petri net as shown in Figure 11.10, and as a BPMN diagram as shown in Figure 11.11. This example relates to the procedure for obtaining an industrial engineer's license in Taiwan.

Table 11.5 A dependency matrix (Dep) for the example log

	A	B	C	D	E	F	H
A	0.0	0.89	0.91	0.0	0.0	0.0	0.0
B	−0.89	0.0	−0.24	0.92	0.0	0.0	0.0
C	−0.91	0.24	0.0	0.63	0.0	0.5	0.0
D	0.0	0.92	−0.63	0.0	0.91	0.86	0.5
E	0.0	0.0	0.0	−0.91	0.0	0.0	0.75
F	0.0	0.0	−0.5	−0.86	0.0	0.0	0.88
H	0.0	0.0	0.0	−0.5	−0.75	−0.88	0.0

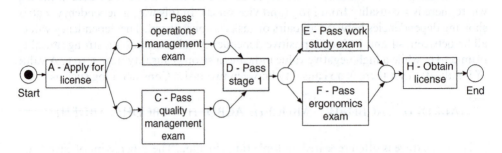

Figure 11.10 The mined Petri net model found by applying the Heuristic Miner algorithm on a log

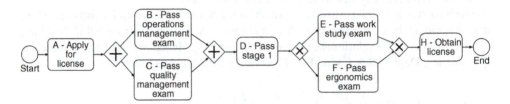

Figure 11.11 The mined BPMN model found by applying the Heuristic Miner algorithm on a log

Steps 1 and 2 are repeated on all dependency relationships until we obtain a full model. It is important to emphasize that the HM algorithm, as the name implies, is based on *heuristics*. It works by applying rules of thumb, as is evident from the running example we used above to illustrate it. In deriving the process model above, we used various values from the dependency matrix to determine the strength of a dependency. Thus, a user has to decide where the cut-off lies between a strong dependency and a weak one. This is a somewhat subjective assessment. Consequently, the algorithm defines three thresholds that are applied in deciding if a dependency value is a positive confirmation for a conjecture. These are:

Dependency threshold: a dependency relationship is accepted if the computed dependency value for it is above this threshold.

Positive observations threshold: a dependency relationship is accepted if its frequency of occurrence in the log is above this threshold.

Relative to best threshold: a dependency relationship is accepted if the ratio of the difference in the dependency measure relative to the best dependency measure is less than this threshold.

In practice, a user will need to vary these parameters and apply judgment based on how the model that is produced changes as the parameters are varied. Since this is a heuristic algorithm, it relies on some trial and error on the part of the user to achieve the best solution. Some typical values of these thresholds are:

Dependency threshold $= 0.45$
Positive observations threshold $= 1$
Relative to best threshold $= 0.4$.

However, in practice, a user must tune the settings based on the amount of noise present in the log. Some final observations about HM are in order here. Special processing is required for loops of length 2 and 3, as discussed above for the Alpha algorithm. Another special case that occurs sometimes relates to logs that are derived from *non-free choice Petri nets*. Practical examples of such scenarios occur when a transition is dependent on another transition that may be directly connected to it and also indirectly connected to it through another transition leading to a "long-distance dependency." Such process models are not very common, and we will give references to related work that discusses advanced techniques for dealing with such models at the end of this chapter.

Exercise 13: Add two more traces: {ABCEFGHJK, AEHGJ} to the ten traces of the log in Figure 11.1. Now apply the HM algorithm (with default thresholds above) to discover the underlying process model. Compare the model with the model in Figure 11.3.

Dealing with Noise in Process Logs

The heuristic miner represents a typical rule-based algorithm, which outputs a single model that is deemed to be *most probable* according to the observed log. As noted above, it could occur that by changing some threshold parameters the model will also change, and here users must assess, based on their understanding of the underlying process, which model is the best one. Such an approach relies heavily on how closely the observed execution patterns align with the heuristics used.

A major strength of the HM approach (and in contrast to the Alpha algorithm) is that it is forgiving of noise in the logs since it is based on frequencies and uses an adjustable threshold parameter to decide how much noise to tune out. If there are ten traces in a log and one or two patterns are in error, then this will not affect the ability of the algorithm to discover the correct model. This feature adds robustness to the algorithm. Let us reconsider the example log we used above to show how HM works:

$$\{ABCDEH^{(5)}, ACBDEH^{(5)}, ABDCFH, ACBDFH^{(5)}, ABCDHE, ABDFH\}$$

Exercise 14: Can you identify which of these log traces don't conform to the actual process model that we discovered in Figure 11.11 and why?

It turns out that the log trace ABDCFH (and two others) do not conform to the log because C and D are transposed. Yet, it is quite obvious that there is preponderance of correct traces, and, hence, we can still derive the correct process model despite 17 percent noisy traces in it. By adjusting the threshold values carefully, one can filter out a lot of this noise and find the correct model.

In fact, real-world logs are often noisy because some of their (sub-)traces are duplicated, incomplete, inconsistent, or reflect some other incorrect behavior. The noise can arise from data entry problems, faulty sensors, data transmission, or streaming problems and other technology limitations. Traces may be incomplete if some events are inadvertently missed due to our failure to capture them. Further, inconsistencies can arise from naming conventions. Events may also arrive in the wrong order. Sometimes infrequent correct behavior also gets confused with noise. Such behavior usually indicates the execution of exceptional paths in the process.

A Real-World Example

Case Example 1: To illustrate how process mining can be applied to a large, noisy real data set, we describe our experience with data from the United States patent application process (available at https://portal.uspto.gov/pair/PublicPair). This is a complex process with several hundred tasks. A patent application may have to go through multiple rounds of reviews before a decision is made. There is also an appeal mechanism whereby the applicant can file a response to a rejected patent and ask for reconsideration. An applicant may also ask for an extension to have more time to make a follow-up submission during the process. Thus a large number of execution scenarios are possible.

Data were collected for patents of the category 435 (Chemistry: molecular biology and microbiology) under the United States Patent Classification issued between 2000 and 2005. A total of 31,682 patent transaction instances contain 518 unique tasks. This dataset was analyzed with the Disco toolset to identify the most frequent tasks and the most frequent sequential relationships among them. From this analysis, a subset of 11 most frequent tasks was identified, as shown in Table 11.6. Moreover, based on the output from Disco about the sequential relationships among tasks and a basic understanding of the process, we developed a reference model as shown in Figure 11.12. All the 11 frequent tasks are included in this model and all the flow paths represent meaningful execution scenarios.

Then, for validation, a random subset of 1000 instances was selected from the log. All instances in a sub-subset of 100 instances were then manually marked as noisy or clean. Accordingly, ten instances were identified and marked as "noisy" and the rest as "clean." These 100 marked instances were used to generate rules using an algorithm called PRISM that can systematically induce rules by a separate-and-conquer kind of approach such that

Table 11.6 11 main tasks identified in the patents application process

Event ID	Description
A	Application captured on micro-film
B	Non-final rejection
C	Mail non-final rejection
D	Information disclosure statement filed
E	Request for extension of time granted
F	Response after non-final action
G	Notice of allowance data verification completed
H	Mail notice of allowance
I	Final rejection
J	Mail final rejection
K	Notice of appeal filed

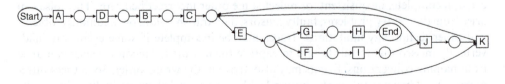

Figure 11.12 A reference model for the patent application process

the attributes in any pair of rules used for classification do not intersect. The rules were applied to the unmarked log and only the 827 instances marked as clean were retained. Subsequently, the HM algorithm in the **ProM** toolset was used to generate process models discovered from both the full (or "dirty") log and the "clean" log.

We found that the process model from the "clean" log was more compact and better. It had 30 places, 40 transitions, 122 arcs and 29 *silent transitions* (versus 31, 43, 130 and 32, respectively, in the "dirty" log). Further, we also calculated the *behavioral* and *structural precision* and *recall metrics* (see Chapter 7) for the two process models with respect to the reference model of Figure 11.12. Both behavioral metrics showed small improvements (precision by 2 percent and recall by 3 percent), while structural precision improved by 1 percent. Yet this suggests that any effort to clean the log before mining would help to produce a superior model.

Disco Tool

Considerable research on process mining has been done at Eindhoven University of Technology under the guidance of Professor Wil van der Aalst since 2002. As a part of this research, a large number of process mining algorithms and tools have been developed. These tools are prototypes and are not of industrial strength. The various algorithms for process mining have been included in the **ProM** toolset in the form of plug-ins (see the last section at the end of this chapter). There is also a video series that demonstrates use of the core **ProM** plug-ins such as the heuristics miner, the inductive visual miner, and various ways to filter event logs.

Disco is a commercial tool developed by Fluxicon that is owned by Anne Rozinat and Christian Gunther and based in Eindhoven. This company grew out of the research they both conducted at the University of Eindhoven. In this section we shall provide more details about Disco.

Disco allows automatic, high-speed discovery of process models based on imported data from logs. The input data can be in a variety of formats, and Disco can also deal with complex and heterogeneous process data. It has a very intuitive and powerful process visualization interface, and its interactive controls allow seamless blending in activities and paths. By using the slider control and your mouse wheel, you can zoom into the process to see just the more important core flow of the discovered process and then zoom out to see the entire process almost instantaneously.

The process mining algorithm used by Disco is called *Fuzzy Mining*. This algorithm applies concepts from roadmaps as a metaphor to show different degrees of detail about a process as the user moves the slider. The goal of the algorithm is to preserve significant behavior, and aggregate (into clusters) or abstract away from less significant behavior in the process. What is significant is determined by applying certain metrics. In this way, this algorithm helps to remove "spaghetti" from a model, and it caters to the needs of different users in the real world who would like to view the process model at different levels of detail.

Disco also generates a complete set of process metrics for activities and paths such as:

- absolute frequency
- case frequency
- maximum number of repetitions
- total duration

- mean duration
- maximum duration.

To support powerful process metric visualization and interactivity, Disco includes features like search in the process map, integrated process metric visualization, map metaphor with coloring of activities, and coloring and thickness of paths. There are also some very nifty bells and whistles like overlay popover, with all process metrics at a glance for a specific activity or path, and quick filter shortcuts to filter cases that contain a specific activity or path right from the map view.

Disco supports many import formats. The input files may be in formats like:

- CSV files
- MS Excel (XLS and XLSX) files
- MXML and MXML.GZ files (ProM 5)
- XES and XES.GZ files (ProM 6)
- FXL Disco log files
- DSC Disco project files.

Service ID,Operation,Start Date,End Date,Agent Position,Customer ID,Product,Service Type,Agent

Case 1,Inbound Call,9.3.10 8:05,9.3.10 8:10,FL,Customer 1,MacBook Pro,Referred to Servicer,Helen

Case 1,Handle Case,11.3.10 10:30,11.3.10 10:32,FL,Customer 1,MacBook Pro,Referred to Servicer,Helen

Case 1,Call Outbound,11.3.10 11:45,11.3.10 11:52,FL,Customer 1,MacBook Pro,Referred to Servicer,Henk

Case 2,Inbound Call,4.3.10 11:43,4.3.10 11:46,FL,Customer 2,MacBook Pro,Referred to Servicer,Susi

Case 3,Inbound Call,25.3.10 9:32,25.3.10 9:33,FL,Customer 3,MacBook Pro,Referred to Servicer,Mary

Case 4,Inbound Call,6.3.10 11:41,6.3.10 11:51,FL,Customer 4,iPhone,Referred to Servicer,Fred

Case 5,Inbound Call,18.3.10 10:54,18.3.10 11:01,FL,Customer 5,MacBook Pro,Product Assistance,Kenny

Case 6,Inbound Call,25.3.10 17:09,25.3.10 17:13,FL,Customer 6,MacBook Pro,Referred to Servicer,Harold

Case 6,Inbound Call,25.3.10 17:16,25.3.10 17:18,FL,Customer 6,MacBook Pro,Referred to Servicer,Nancy

Case 6,Inbound Call,26.3.10 8:36,26.3.10 8:40,FL,Customer 6,MacBook Pro,Referred to Servicer,Elena

Case 7,Inbound Call,18.3.10 11:49,18.3.10 11:50,FL,Customer 7,MacBook Pro,Product Assistance,Karen

Case 8,Inbound Call,11.3.10 9:20,11.3.10 9:23,FL,Customer 8,MacBook Pro,Referred to Servicer,Karen

Case 9,Inbound Email,19.3.10 19:47,21.3.10 8:17,FL,Customer 9,MacBook Pro,ProductAssistance,Samuil

Case 9,Call Outbound,21.3.10 8:32,21.3.10 8:33,FL,Customer 9,MacBook Pro,Product Assistance,Samuil

Case 9,Handle Email,21.3.10 8:33,21.3.10 8:33,FL,Customer 9,MacBook Pro,Product Assistance,Samuil

Case 10,Handle Email,27.3.10 11:29,27.3.10 11:30,FL,Customer 10,iPhone,Product Assistance,Jochem

---

Figure 11.13 Some sample log records from the log.csv input log file for the call center data

An Example to Illustrate Disco

Case Example 2: We shall use a call center data log to illustrate the use of Disco. This log has information about the activities of a call center. The log data is in a .csv file as shown in Figure 11.13. There are about 7500 log records.

The next step is to read this file into Disco. After reading the file, the screen shown in Figure 11.14 appears. On this screen, the user selects the first column of the spreadsheet and then clicks on the case icon in the top bar to indicate that this column corresponds to the case ID. Next the user selects the second column and clicks on the activity icon (shown as an email) to indicate that this is an activity. Further, the Start Date and End Date columns are similarly identified as time stamps by selecting these columns in turn and then clicking on the "clock" icon. The Agent column is identified as a resource by clicking on the "people" icon. Now we are ready to import the data into Disco.

After the user clicks the import button on the bottom of the data input screen, Disco analyzes the log and produces an initial process model as shown in Figure 11.15. In this process model, Disco shows the tasks or activities, the links connecting them, and

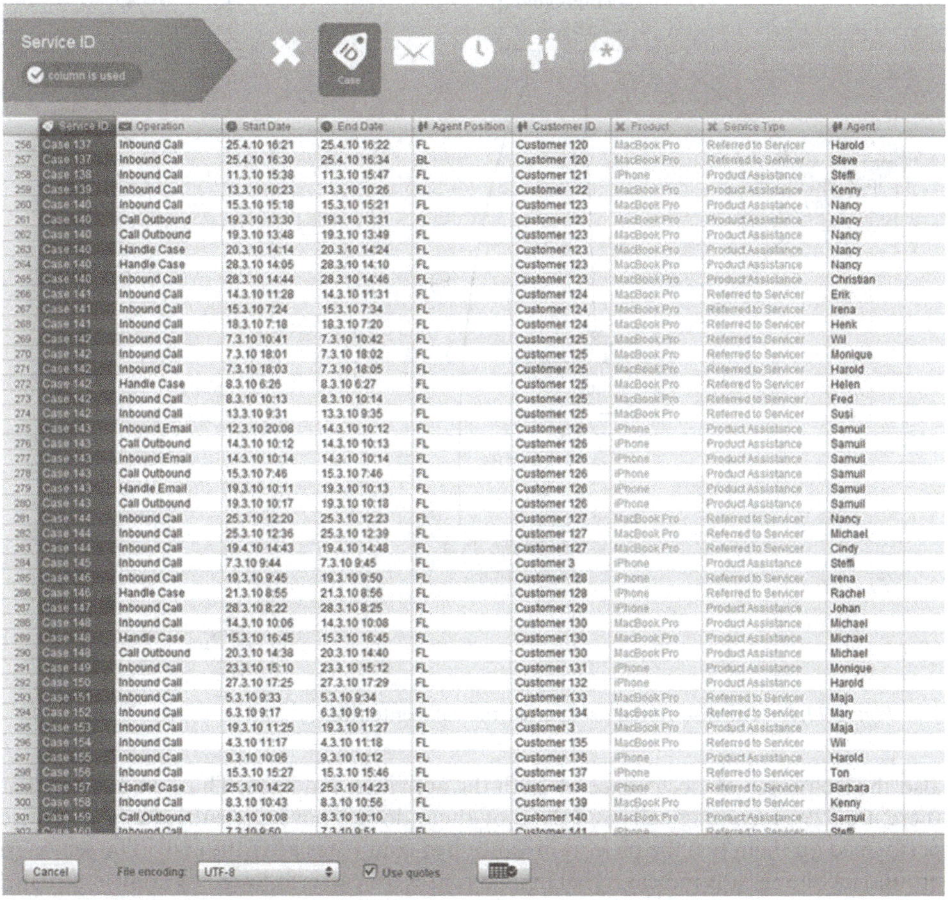

	Service ID	Operation	Start Date	End Date	Agent Position	Customer ID	Product	Service Type	Agent
256	Case 137	Inbound Call	25.4.10 16:21	25.4.10 16:22	FL	Customer 120	MacBook Pro	Referred to Servicer	Harold
257	Case 137	Inbound Call	25.4.10 16:30	25.4.10 16:34	BL	Customer 120	MacBook Pro	Referred to Servicer	Steve
258	Case 138	Inbound Call	11.3.10 15:38	11.3.10 15:47	FL	Customer 121	iPhone	Product Assistance	Steffi
259	Case 139	Inbound Call	13.3.10 10:23	13.3.10 10:26	FL	Customer 122	MacBook Pro	Product Assistance	Kenny
260	Case 140	Inbound Call	15.3.10 15:18	15.3.10 15:21	FL	Customer 123	MacBook Pro	Product Assistance	Nancy
261	Case 140	Call Outbound	19.3.10 13:30	19.3.10 13:31	FL	Customer 123	MacBook Pro	Product Assistance	Nancy
262	Case 140	Call Outbound	19.3.10 13:48	19.3.10 13:49	FL	Customer 123	MacBook Pro	Product Assistance	Nancy
263	Case 140	Handle Case	20.3.10 14:14	20.3.10 14:24	FL	Customer 123	MacBook Pro	Product Assistance	Nancy
264	Case 140	Handle Case	28.3.10 14:05	28.3.10 14:10	FL	Customer 123	MacBook Pro	Product Assistance	Nancy
265	Case 140	Inbound Call	28.3.10 14:44	28.3.10 14:46	FL	Customer 123	MacBook Pro	Product Assistance	Christian
266	Case 141	Inbound Call	14.3.10 11:28	14.3.10 11:31	FL	Customer 124	MacBook Pro	Referred to Servicer	Erik
267	Case 141	Inbound Call	15.3.10 7:24	15.3.10 7:34	FL	Customer 124	MacBook Pro	Referred to Servicer	Irena
268	Case 141	Inbound Call	18.3.10 7:18	18.3.10 7:20	FL	Customer 124	MacBook Pro	Referred to Servicer	Henk
269	Case 142	Inbound Call	7.3.10 10:41	7.3.10 10:42	FL	Customer 125	MacBook Pro	Referred to Servicer	Wil
270	Case 142	Inbound Call	7.3.10 18:01	7.3.10 18:02	FL	Customer 125	MacBook Pro	Referred to Servicer	Monique
271	Case 142	Inbound Call	7.3.10 18:03	7.3.10 18:05	FL	Customer 125	MacBook Pro	Referred to Servicer	Harold
272	Case 142	Handle Case	8.3.10 6:26	8.3.10 6:27	FL	Customer 125	MacBook Pro	Referred to Servicer	Helen
273	Case 142	Inbound Call	8.3.10 10:13	8.3.10 10:14	FL	Customer 125	MacBook Pro	Referred to Servicer	Fred
274	Case 142	Inbound Call	13.3.10 9:31	13.3.10 9:35	FL	Customer 125	MacBook Pro	Referred to Servicer	Susi
275	Case 143	Inbound Email	12.3.10 20:08	14.3.10 10:12	FL	Customer 126	iPhone	Product Assistance	Samuil
276	Case 143	Call Outbound	14.3.10 10:12	14.3.10 10:13	FL	Customer 126	iPhone	Product Assistance	Samuil
277	Case 143	Inbound Email	14.3.10 10:14	14.3.10 10:14	FL	Customer 126	iPhone	Product Assistance	Samuil
278	Case 143	Call Outbound	15.3.10 7:46	15.3.10 7:46	FL	Customer 126	iPhone	Product Assistance	Samuil
279	Case 143	Handle Email	19.3.10 10:11	19.3.10 10:13	FL	Customer 126	iPhone	Product Assistance	Samuil
280	Case 143	Call Outbound	19.3.10 10:17	19.3.10 10:18	FL	Customer 126	iPhone	Product Assistance	Samuil
281	Case 144	Inbound Call	25.3.10 12:20	25.3.10 12:23	FL	Customer 127	MacBook Pro	Referred to Servicer	Nancy
282	Case 144	Inbound Call	25.3.10 12:36	25.3.10 12:39	FL	Customer 127	MacBook Pro	Referred to Servicer	Michael
283	Case 144	Inbound Call	19.4.10 14:43	19.4.10 14:48	FL	Customer 127	MacBook Pro	Referred to Servicer	Cindy
284	Case 145	Inbound Call	7.3.10 9:44	7.3.10 9:45	FL	Customer 3	iPhone	Product Assistance	Steffi
285	Case 146	Inbound Call	19.3.10 9:45	19.3.10 9:50	FL	Customer 128	iPhone	Referred to Servicer	Irena
286	Case 146	Handle Case	21.3.10 8:55	21.3.10 8:56	FL	Customer 128	iPhone	Referred to Servicer	Rachel
287	Case 147	Inbound Call	28.3.10 8:22	28.3.10 8:25	FL	Customer 129	iPhone	Product Assistance	Johan
288	Case 148	Inbound Call	14.3.10 10:06	14.3.10 10:08	FL	Customer 130	MacBook Pro	Product Assistance	Michael
289	Case 148	Handle Case	15.3.10 16:45	15.3.10 16:45	FL	Customer 130	MacBook Pro	Product Assistance	Michael
290	Case 148	Call Outbound	20.3.10 14:38	20.3.10 14:40	FL	Customer 130	MacBook Pro	Product Assistance	Michael
291	Case 149	Inbound Call	23.3.10 15:10	23.3.10 15:12	FL	Customer 131	iPhone	Product Assistance	Monique
292	Case 150	Inbound Call	27.3.10 17:25	27.3.10 17:29	FL	Customer 132	iPhone	Product Assistance	Harold
293	Case 151	Inbound Call	5.3.10 9:33	5.3.10 9:34	FL	Customer 133	MacBook Pro	Referred to Servicer	Maja
294	Case 152	Inbound Call	6.3.10 9:17	6.3.10 9:19	FL	Customer 134	MacBook Pro	Referred to Servicer	Mary
295	Case 153	Inbound Call	19.3.10 11:25	19.3.10 11:27	FL	Customer 3	MacBook Pro	Product Assistance	Maja
296	Case 154	Inbound Call	4.3.10 11:17	4.3.10 11:18	FL	Customer 135	MacBook Pro	Referred to Servicer	Wil
297	Case 155	Inbound Call	9.3.10 10:06	9.3.10 10:12	FL	Customer 136	iPhone	Product Assistance	Harold
298	Case 156	Inbound Call	15.3.10 15:27	15.3.10 15:46	FL	Customer 137	iPhone	Referred to Servicer	Ton
299	Case 157	Handle Case	25.3.10 14:22	25.3.10 14:23	FL	Customer 138	iPhone	Referred to Servicer	Barbara
300	Case 158	Inbound Call	8.3.10 10:43	8.3.10 10:56	FL	Customer 139	MacBook Pro	Referred to Servicer	Kenny
301	Case 159	Call Outbound	8.3.10 10:08	8.3.10 10:10	FL	Customer 140	MacBook Pro	Product Assistance	Samuil
302	Case 160	Inbound Call	7.3.10 9:50	7.3.10 9:51	FL	Customer 141	iPhone	Referred to Servicer	Steffi

Figure 11.14 The Disco screen display after uploading data from a file

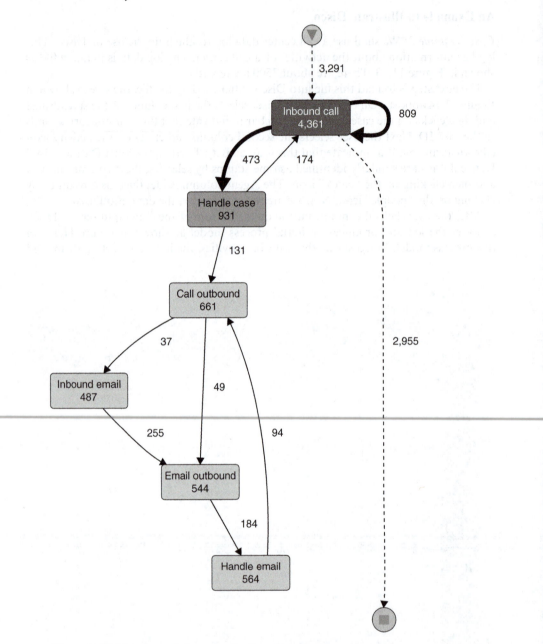

Figure 11.15 The discovered process for the call center log

also the frequency of occurrence of both the activities and links. Thus, we can see that there are 3291 incoming calls and 2955 of them do not have any subsequent activities performed on them (i.e. the process instance just completes after the call). The self-loop around incoming calls indicates that in many cases the call is followed by additional calls. For 473 cases, the inbound call is followed by the "handle case" activity. The numbers of the input and output flow for a node should normally add up for a task, but that does

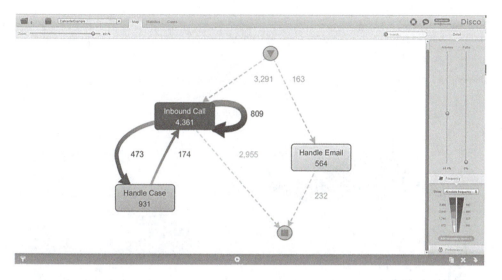

Figure 11.16 Zooming in on a process to see a core set of activities using the slider scale on the right

not occur for all the nodes because many cases may be unfinished, and at various stages of the process.

Next, notice the slider scales for activities and paths on the right of the screenshot. By adjusting the slider scale for activities on the right of the screen it is possible to zoom in on a subset of the core activities. This is shown in Figure 11.16. Upon clicking an activity, it is possible to see the frequency, repetition, and duration statistics for it as shown in Figure 11.17. Finally, there are color codes on the activities to indicate their relative frequencies.

It is also possible to use the animate feature of Disco to see actual running instances flowing through the process model. This feature is also very nice. For this feature, simply press the play button in the middle of the bottom bar of the screen in Figure 11.16. On the next screen, press the play/pause button the bar at the bottom to start/pause the animation. A screenshot obtained on pausing after running the animation for some time is shown in Figure 11.18. You can see the actual instances as circles at different stages of the process in this animation.

The purpose of this quick introduction is to show you how simple and easy to use Disco is! You should get a trial copy of the software and play around with it on your own logs or use the demo logs available on the website.

Chapter Summary

Process mining or discovery complements data mining [25] with many practical applications. There is such a large body of research on process mining that here we can only scratch the surface. A recent authoritative text book [28] by van der Aalst is an excellent resource for somebody who wants to study the area in depth. Some very early work was done by Cook and Wolf [6], and by Agrawal et al. [1] in the late 1990s. A lot of subsequent work on process mining was done by van der Aalst and his colleagues at the

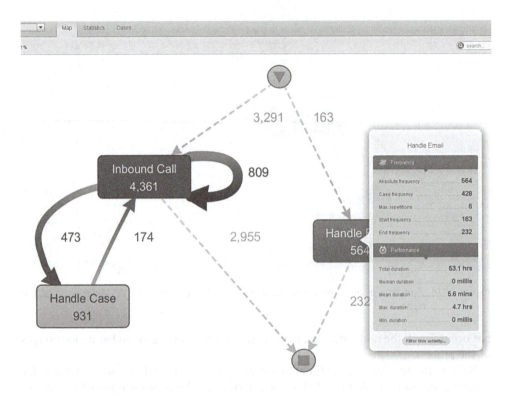

Map   Statistics   Cases

Figure 11.17 Frequency, repetition, and duration statistics

Eindhoven University of Technology. The Alpha algorithm was published in 2004 and is described in detail in [26]. The Heuristic Miner was described in [30]. A rule-based approach for process discovery appears in [17]. A genetic algorithm for process mining is proposed and evaluated in [7]. The Fuzzy Miner implemented in Disco creates hierarchical models at different levels of detail [10]. Another relatively newer algorithm called inductive miner [14] is based on recursively partitioning the log at logical points, and making process models for each partition. Later, the individual models can be joined together to obtain a complete model. The PRISM algorithm is described in [4], and more details of the patent application process are given in [5]. Some video tutorials on process mining developed by Eindhoven University of Technology are available through their website [8].

Process mining even has applications in social and organizational mining [23, 24, 27]. In this stream of work, the interest lies in the discovery of patterns related to resource assignments and relationships among various resource roles. Process mining from multiple perspectives such as data dependencies, resource assignments, and time constraints in addition to the control flow perspective is discussed in [15]. Work related to metrics like fitness, precision, etc. that relate to the quality of process models appears in [2, 12, 22]. Advanced process mining techniques related to refined ordering relations and non-free choice nets are discussed in [11, 13, 31]. There has also been work on mining of decisions [21], i.e. how a path is selected at an XOR-split connector based on

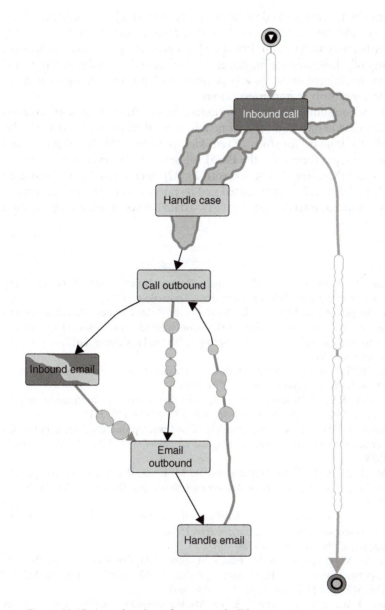

Figure 11.18 An animation of a process in Disco

the values of the data attributes of a process instance. Process mining in the context of healthcare processes has been discussed in [16]. This book presents a healthcare reference model and focuses on organizational healthcare processes rather than medical treatment processes.

The Disco tool from Fluxicon [9] was discussed at some length in this chapter. The company makes Disco software available for free to educational institutions. Rapid-Miner [20] is a data science platform with an easy to use GUI interface in the drag and drop style. Celonis PI [3] is another tool that is powered by AI and machine learning as per the company claims. It maps and visualizes processes as they actually occur, from beginning to end, in real-time, based on user data, thus ensuring maximum transparency and oversight over the user value chain. ProM [19] is a generic open-source framework from the University of Eindhoven for implementing process mining tools in a standard environment. It has implementations for a large number of process mining techniques, but note that these are prototype implementations.

There has been work on standards for storing execution logs from processes also called event logs since the start and/or end of each task is marked by an event. MXML [18] was an earlier de facto standard for storing event logs using an XML-based syntax and was used as the native input format for the **ProM** toolset [19]. However, it was recently superseded after XES (eXtensible Event Stream) [29, 32] emerged as the new standard for storing event logs. XES is also XML-based and its purpose is to provide a generally acknowledged format for the interchange of event log data between tools and application domains.

References

1. R. Agrawal and D. Gunopulos et al. *Mining Process Models from Workflow Logs.* 6th International Conference on Extending Database Technology, 1998.
2. J. Buijs, B. F. V. Dongen and W. M. P. van der Aalst. On the Role of Fitness, Precision, Generalization and Simplicity in Process Discovery. OTM Confederated International Conferences. *On the Move to Meaningful Internet Systems.* Springer, Berlin, Heidelberg, 2012.
3. Celonis. www.celonis.com/en/.
4. J. Cendrowska. PRISM: an algorithm for inducing modular rules. *International Journal of Man-Machine Studies*, Vol. 27, No. 4, pp. 349–370, 1987.
5. H.-J. Cheng and A. Kumar. Process mining on noisy logs—can log sanitization help to improve performance? *Decision Support Systems*, Vol. 79, pp. 138–149, 2015.
6. E. J. Cook and A. L. Wolf. Discovering models of software processes from event-based data. *ACM Transactions on Software Engineering and Methodology (TOSEM)*, Vol. 7, No. 3, pp. 215–249, 1998.
7. A. K. A. de Medeiros, A. J. M. M. Weijters and W. M. P. van der Aalst. Genetic process mining: an experimental evaluation. *Data Mining and Knowledge Discovery*, Vol. 14, No. 2, pp. 245–304, 2007.
8. Eindhoven University of Technology. *Introduction to Process Mining with ProM.* www.futurelearn.com/courses/process-mining/0/steps/15642.
9. Fluxicon. Disco. https://fluxicon.com/disco/.
10. C. W. Günther, W. M. P. van der Aalst. Fuzzy Mining—Adaptive Process Simplification Based on Multi-perspective Metrics. In: G. Alonso, P. Dadam, M. Rosemann (eds) BPM2007. *LNCS*, Vol. 4714. Springer, Heidelberg, pp. 328–343, 2007.
11. Q. Guo, L. Wen, J. Wang, Z. Yan and P. S. Yu. Mining invisible tasks in non-free-choice constructs. *BPM*, pp. 109–125, 2015.
12. Z. Huang and A. Kumar. A study of quality and accuracy trade-offs in process mining. *INFORMS Journal on Computing*, Vol. 24, No. 2, pp. 311–327, 2012.
13. T. Jin, J. Wang, L. Wen and G. Zou. Computing refined ordering relations with uncertainty for acyclic process models. *IEEE Transactions on Services Computing*, Vol. 7, No. 3, pp. 415–426, 2014.
14. S. J. J. Leemans, D. Fahland, W. M. P. van der Aalst. Discovering Blockstructured Process Models from Event Logs—A Constructive Approach. In: G. Ciardo, E. Kindler (eds) *Application and Theory of Petri Nets and Concurrency*, Vol. 8489. Springer, Cham, pp. 311–329, 2013.
15. F. Mannhardt et al. Balanced multi-perspective checking of process conformance. *Computing*, Vol. 98, No. 4, pp. 407–437, 2016.

16. R. S. Mans, W. M. P. van der Aalst and R. J. B. Vanwersch. *Process Mining in Healthcare: Evaluating and Exploiting Operational Healthcare Processes*. Springer, Heidelberg, 2015.
17. L. Măruşter, A. J. M. M. Weijters et al. A rule-based approach for process discovery: dealing with noise and imbalance in process logs. *Data Mining and Knowledge Discovery*, Vol. 13, No. 1, pp. 67–87, 2006.
18. MXML. Mining eXtensible Markup Language. www.processmining.org/logs/mxml.
19. ProM Toolset. www.processmining.org/prom/start.
20. Rapidminer. https://rapidminer.com/.
21. A. Rozinat and W. M. P. van der Aalst. Decision mining in ProM. *International Conference on Business Process Management*. Springer, Berlin, Heidelberg, 2006.
22. A. Rozinat and W. M. P. van der Aalst. Conformance checking of processes based on monitoring real behavior. *Information Systems*, Vol. 33, No. 1, pp. 64–95, 2008.
23. S. Schönig et al. A framework for efficiently mining the organisational perspective of business processes. *Decision Support Systems*, Vol. 89, pp. 87–97, 2016.
24. M. Song and W. M. P. van der Aalst. Towards comprehensive support for organizational mining. *Decision Support Systems*, Vol. 46, No. 1, pp. 300–317, 2008.
25. P.-N. Tan, M. Steinbach and V. Kumar. *Introduction to Data Mining*. Addison Wesley, Boston, MA, May, 2005.
26. W. M. P. van der Aalst, A. J. M. M. Weijters and L. Maruster. Workflow mining: discovering process models from event logs. *IEEE Transactions on Knowledge and Data Engineering*, Vol. 16, No. 9, pp. 1128–1142, 2004.
27. W. M. P. van der Aalst and H. A. Reijers et al. Discovering social networks from event logs. *Computer Supported Cooperative Work*, Vol. 14, No. 6, pp. 549–593, 2005.
28. W. M. P. van der Aalst. *Process Mining: Data Science in Action*. Springer, Berlin, Heidelberg, 2016.
29. B. F. V. Dongen, S. Shabani. Relational XES: Data Management for Process Mining. *Proceedings of the CAiSE 2015 Forum at the 27th International Conference on Advanced Information Systems Engineering*, Stockholm, Sweden.
30. A. J. M. M. Weijters, W. M. P. van der Aalst and A. K. A. de Medeiros. Process mining with heuristics miner algorithm. In BETA Working Paper Series, WP 166, Eindhoven University of Technology, Eindhoven, 2006.
31. L. Wen, W. M. P. van der Aalst, J. Wang and J. Sun. Mining process models with non-free-choice constructs. *Data Mining and Knowledge Discovery*, Vol. 15, No. 2, pp. 145–180, 2007.
32. XES. Extensible Event Stream. www.xes-standard.org/.

12 Future Directions

Introduction

This book is about how to induct process thinking into an organization to improve its performance. We have covered a broad range of topics, starting with various approaches for process modeling. We have shown that business process management encompasses a lot more than making boxes-and-arrows diagrams. Processes consist of related tasks that are performed by qualified resources. Further, they have input and output data requirements, deadlines, security, and compliance considerations, etc. Processes need to interact with other processes within the same or a different organization. Processes are dynamic, and may also be interrupted and resumed. Sometimes, they have to be cancelled or rolled back. Some processes run in real-time. We tried to stress the importance of socio-technical aspects and the role they play in process performance. Processes also need to be secure. Finally, process analytics has emerged as an important field of study itself.

This final chapter will give you brief insights into some new topics that are related to business process management, such as: decision model and notation; blockchain technology; and organizational routines.

Decision Model and Notation (DMN)

Decision Model and Notation (DMN) is a standard published by the Object Management Group. It is a step towards separating decision making from the control flow of a process. DMN makes this possible by allowing tasks to be linked to decision tables in such a way that the decision table can be invoked at run time with some input values of decision variables and the result (or output) of applying the decision table logic to the input values is fed back to the running workflow or process. This decision value is used to determine the correct path at the subsequent XOR node. Thus, decision making can be separated from the process flow. This makes process design easier, cleaner and less

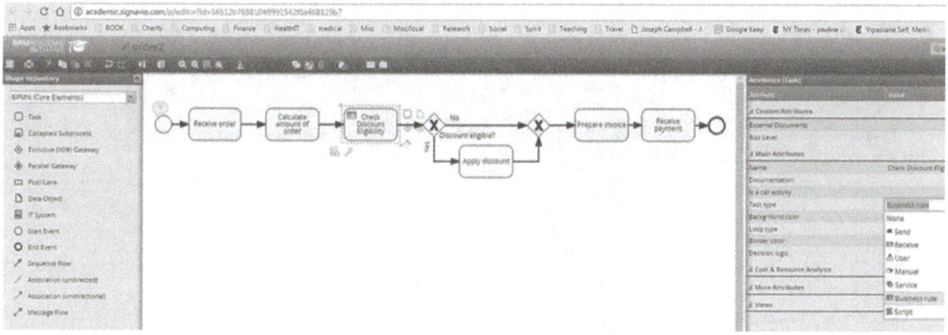

Figure 12.1 A process diagram in the BPMN 2.0 editor

error-prone. We shall illustrate how DMN can be integrated into BPMN by a simple example using Signavio.

We first create a process like the one shown in Figure 12.1 in the Signavio BPMN 2.0 editor. This process is designed to handle a customer order. After the order is received, we must check whether the customer is eligible for a discount and, if so, the discount is applied, an invoice is prepared, and the payment is received from the customer. As shown in the "check discount eligibility" task in this figure, the logic for checking if the customer is eligible for a discount is incorporated into a decision table using DMN (note the table symbol in the top left of the task box). To link a task to decision table, we set its task type attribute from the list of main attributes to Business Rule as shown in the attribute pane on the right side of this figure. Now if we click on the table icon it brings up a new pop up window as shown in Figure 12.2. This is called a DMN diagram and it shows how the two inputs, "Amount" and "Member?," are used to determine whether the customer is eligible for a discount.

The DMN diagram of Figure 12.2 was created in the DMN 1.1 editor and it was linked to a decision table shown in Figure 12.3. The DMN diagram shows that there are two input variables, Amount and Member?, that are required to decide if the customer is eligible for a discount. By clicking on the table icon in this diagram, we can open the decision table window shown in Figure 12.3. This table has the same two inputs, "Amount" and "Member?," in the first two columns, and an output ("New output") or result in the third column. Each row corresponds to a decision rule. The first row states that, if the amount of the order is $1000 or more, and the customer is a member, then she is eligible for the discount. The second row states that, if the order amount is $5000 or more, and even if the customer is not a member, then she is still eligible for the discount. Finally, the third row has blank values for the two inputs that match wildcards. Hence, this row applies if neither of the first two rows are satisfied with the actual input values for the two decision variables, and corresponds to the case where the customer is not eligible for a discount.

The set of rules should be *complete* so that at least one row of the table is applicable for all combinations of input values. The rules are selected accordingly to a *hit policy*. Here, the policy that is applied is called the *unique single rule policy* that is the default in the DMN standard. Only one rule is allowed to fire for any one combination of input values. Another alternative is the *first rule policy* where rules are evaluated from top to bottom

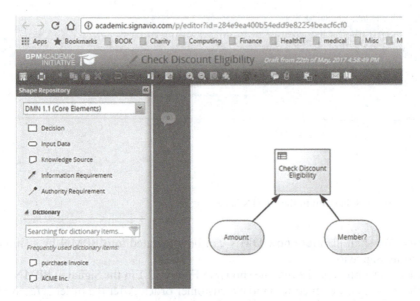

Figure 12.2   A DMN diagram can be edited in the DMN 1.1 editor

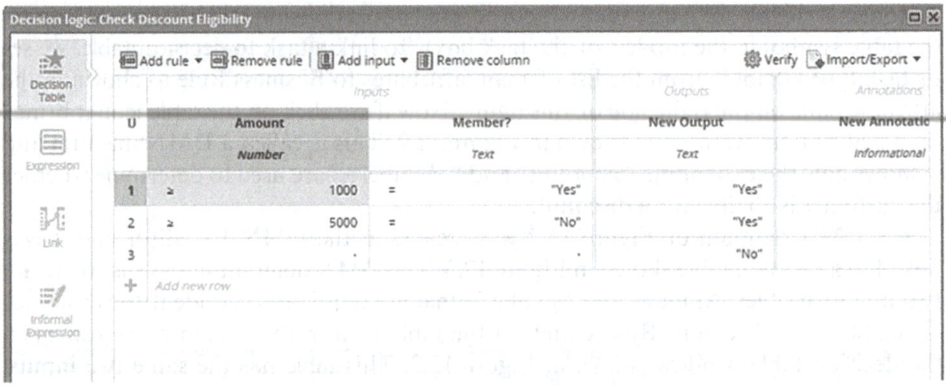

Figure 12.3   A Decision table related to the DMN diagram of Figure 12.2

and the first applicable rule fires. At execution time, the "check discount eligibility" task will invoke the decision table that will return a result or output value (yes or no) for whether the customer is eligible for a discount. Accordingly, one of the two paths is taken at the XOR split node in the process.

You can see how this approach allows the decision layer to be separated from the control flow layer. Business analysts can model the rules that lead to a decision in easy to read tables, and, after saving the model, the tables can be executed directly by a decision engine (like Camunda). This minimizes the risk of misunderstandings between business analysts and developers. Further, it makes it much easier to make changes to the decision logic. If the policy of the company for calculating discounts changes (say, they wish to make the discount available to non-members on order amounts higher than $3000 instead of $5000), they can simply change the decision table without making any changes to the underlying control flow of the process. As an exercise, you might like to create this example yourself.

Blockchain Technology

Blockchain is a new technology that became popular as a secure, safe, trusted and reliable mechanism for making digital payments. It gave rise to a digital and cyber currency called Bitcoin. Bitcoin is a peer-to-peer electronic cash payment system.

At the heart of blockchain technology is a *shared, serial, distributed ledger*. This ledger is shared among several participants or parties who interact with each other. Thus, everybody can be looking at the same copy of the ledger at the same time. As soon as a transaction is performed by one party it shortly afterwards appears on the ledger of all parties. Hence, it allows for secure record keeping in online ledgers. Another nice feature of blockchains is that the members share and confirm information with each other without the need for a central authority.

Figure 12.4 illustrates the idea underlying the operation of blockchain. The group of five interacting parties represented by the five boxes, A through E, in this network have a copy of the shared ledger or database. Each box in the figure shows a blockchain with five blocks, 1 through 5. Typically, a block contains about a few hundred transactions. These blocks are written sequentially. Say, A wishes to make a payment to B. A will create a chunk of data to represent this transaction. Then A will share the transaction with the rest of the group in a secure way. After a few hundred transactions have taken place, they constitute a block. Before being added to a sequential chain, a block has first to be confirmed by a decentralized group of participants or bitcoin miners to ensure that each transaction in it is legitimate and that no bitcoin has been reused. This is called reaching consensus. In this way, payments can be made securely and efficiently, and at low cost using this technology. Public key cryptography is used to encrypt the information stored on the blockchains to ensure its privacy.

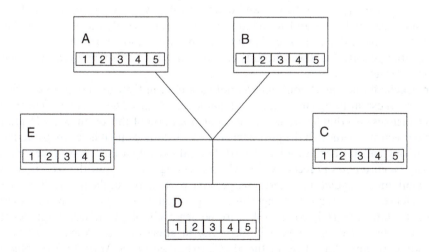

Figure 12.4 A Blockchain network with five parties

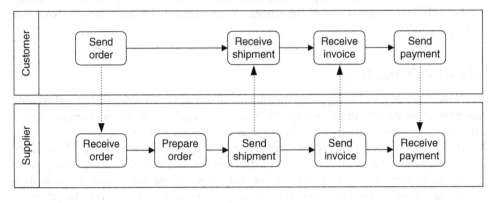

Figure 12.5 A supply chain example

The most popular application of blockchain technology so far is in bitcoins. However, in recent years, new applications for it are being found in supply chains, finance, healthcare, etc. as a secure method of performing transactions. We can think of a business process as a series of transactions (see Figure 12.5). A customer places an order. The supplier accepts the order. The supplier ships the order and the customer receives it. Finally, the customer pays the supplier. Each step in this process is a transaction. To apply the technology to this process (or an instance of this process) would require that each transaction be recorded on a blockchain. Since the blockchain is an immutable public ledger, it will be very easy for any of the parties (or a third party) to verify the legitimacy of each transaction performed. Moreover, the time stamp of a transaction would also appear in this ledger and can be verified.

This discussion is also related to the notion of a smart contract. *Smart contracts* are computer protocols that facilitate, verify, or enforce the negotiation or performance of a contract. Smart contracts can emulate the logic of various clauses in a contract. They can check whether contractual conditions (such as payment terms, liens, confidentiality, and even enforcement) were satisfied. and determine if any violations occurred. Thus, they can minimize malicious and accidental exceptions, and reduce the need for human intervention. In turn, this can lower fraud loss, arbitration and enforcement costs, etc. It also has the potential to speed up transactions, increase transparency, and prevent money laundering.

The blockchain and smart contract technologies have not yet been deployed widely for commercial use, although many large companies have started testing them. There are several challenges also that lie in the way of broad adoption of this technology. The first one is cybersecurity. Although the proponents of blockchain claim it is secure by design, the technology has not been seriously tested. Several hacking attacks have taken place against digital currencies in recent years, which is enough to warrant the security concern. Second, much regulatory uncertainty persists, particularly in the financial services industry. Hence, it may require changes in the legal frameworks globally before it can be adopted. Third, the likely costs to shift to the new technology are not insignificant. Finally, many technical challenges will also arise in integrating blockchain databases with existing systems. An article in the *Wall Street Journal* in April 2017 by Nikhil Lohade noted that Dubai is the first city to back the technology at a government level.

Table 12.1 Workflows vs. organizational routines

Dimension	Workflows	Routine
Purpose	Describe and enact work procedures in organization	Describe and enact work procedures in organization
Underlying premise about processes	Processes are standard with little variability	Processes change, decisions are dynamic
Description style	Process modeling languages to capture excruciating detail	Sequences of actions, networks of interdependencies
Underlying premise about actors	Actors are same, like interchangeable parts	Actors are different – their interpretations are different; they possess tacit knowledge
Topics of study	Process design, enactment, mining	Process variability, analysis of interdependencies
Focus	Focus on control flow, organizational, data and time perspectives	Focus on actions, people, technology
Performance analysis	Explained by model of tasks and control flows	Explained by deeper factors such as tacit knowledge, communication effectiveness, etc.

Organizational Routines

Organizational routines are "repetitive, recognizable patterns of interdependent actions." Such routines are followed in applying for approval for business or conference travel, getting reimbursement for travel, hiring of a faculty member in a department at a university, etc. Routines have an *ostensive aspect* (the ideal form of the routine) and a *performative aspect* (the routine in practice, with its actual place, time, context). Enacted actions are the "performative" aspect of a routine derived from the ostensive (or ideal) superset of routines defined by the organizational environment and standards. The ostensive aspect is akin to the standard operating procedure, while the performative aspect is subject to variation in part due to each participant's tacit and subjective understanding of the routine that in turn depends on her role and point of view. As actors recreate the ostensive aspect based on their own interpretations, the routine evolves from drifts in the ostensive aspect over time.

It is informative to draw some comparisons between workflows and routines based on our understanding of these terms as they are used in their respective research communities. Table 12.1 presents a summary of the comparison on various dimensions. In particular, scholars in the area of organizational routines accept a priori that variety exists in real-world processes and they develop approaches to quantify it, e.g. by posing questions like: Does the process in Department A have more variety than the one in Department B? Moreover, they attribute greater agency and tacit knowledge to actors of various tasks in terms of their interpretations of how the task should be done rather than treating actors as fully interchangeable agents.

It is evident from Table 12.1 that the underlying premises and approaches are quite different, yet the basic goal of the two communities is the same, i.e. to develop better ways to model and enact procedures to maximize organization efficiency.

Routines introduce a socio-technical aspect that takes into account the nature of social interactions and interdependencies among participants who collaborate on a routine.

Work is actually performed in an organization through handoffs among actors (or workers). A *handoff* is simply a transfer of work from one actor to another. The nature of these handoffs can affect the outcome and performance of a routine (or process instance) in terms of quality, failure rate, and other measures. In a nurse-to-nurse handoff at the end of a hospital shift, it is important that critical patient information must be exchanged. Similarly, in a transfer of software code between two developers, many issues related to status, bugs, unresolved issues, etc. should be addressed adequately. Failure to carry out such handoffs or transfers properly can lead to a breakdown in the process, with sometimes serious, even devastating, consequences. Some terminology from the area of organizational routines is introduced next.

Sequence analytics refers to the concept of analyzing the sequences of actions or elements to detect similarities and differences across the sequences. For example, in biology this concept is used to detect evolutionary patterns, rates of mutation, and any genetic modifications that occurred over time. This concept was later adopted by sociologists and more recently in information systems to gain a better understanding of the socio-technical aspects of work processes.

An *action pattern* (or a task sequence) is simply a series of possible orderings of related tasks to complete a routine or a workflow. Some examples are:

1   T1-T2-T3-T4
2   T1-T3-T4-T2
3   T2-T1-T4-T3

Variety in this context is a measure of variability in the possible action sequences of different processes. There are different ways of conceptualizing variety. One notion of variety called *string-match variety* is based on average edit-distance between all pairs of log sequences in a log. If we consider the first two task sequences above, we can see that to transform sequence 1 to sequence 2, we need to perform the two edit operations: delete(T2); insert(T2). Thus, the edit-distance between these two sequences would be two. By averaging the edit-distance across all pairs of, say, n possible sequences, where $d(i, j)$ is the distance between sequence i and sequence j, we can get a measure for string-match variety as follows:

$$\frac{2}{n(n-1)} \sum_{i=1}^{i=n} \sum_{\substack{j=2, \\ i<j}}^{j=n} d(i, j)$$

In a similar spirit, it is possible to also have actor sequences. An *actor sequence* would define a series of specific actors, such as A1-A2-A3-A4 or A3-A2-A4-A1, in the correct order in which the actors participate in the routine or workflow. Actor sequences can be further generalized into *actor patterns*. Thus, an actor pattern like 1-2-3-4 means that some (generic) actor 1, handed over the work to an actor 2 who in turn passed it along to 3, and so on. We call this a *straight pattern*. Another pattern may be 1-2-3-1. In this *loop pattern*, the work is returned at the end to the same actor who started it. Yet another pattern may be 1-2-1-2-1-3. This is a *pingpong pattern* since actors 1 and 2 alternate in it. It is important to note here that 1, 2, 3 are generic placeholders for actors, and not specific names of actors. See Figure 12.6 for examples of these patterns. It is possible that

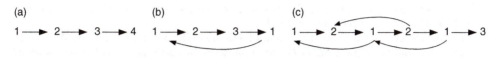

Figure 12.6 Different kinds of generic actor patterns

in the loop and pingpong patterns, perhaps generic actor 1 is acting like a coordinator and this may facilitate faster completion of work.

So the larger issue here is that task sequences, actor sequences, and actor patterns all have an impact on the performance of routines in an organization. By applying analysis techniques to actual logs, it is possible to gain a deeper understanding of the issues involved and improve work design in an organization.

Chapter Summary

The well-known Object Management Group issued the specifications of the DMN 1.1 standard in June 2016 [11]. The DMN standard is supported by several software products from companies like Camunda and Signavio. The conceptual issues related to separation of decision logic from control flow and integration of DMN with BPMN are discussed in [1, 5]. A nice tutorial introduction to DMN has also been developed by Signavio [15].

The original proposal for the bitcoin application based on the blockchain technology is described by its founder Nakamoto in [10]. Blockchain technology is discussed in further detail in [6, 16]. A recent position paper [9] lists challenges and opportunities in applying blockchains to business process management. Some key issues identified here relate to strategic alignment, governance, methods, information technology, people, and culture. Hull et al. [4] present ideas for how a business collaboration language that exploits the blockchain technology can be developed using an artifact-centric paradigm. This new technology has also sparked considerable interest in the popular press because of its potential impact on supply chains [8], and for maintaining medical records [14]. Some initiatives towards applying blockchain technology are called Hyperledger from Linux Foundation, Digital Asset, Ethereum and R3.

Organizational routines have been explored by Feldman and Pentland in several works; among them are [2, 12]. Some later work in this stream that relates interdependencies in networks appears in References [7, 13]. A recent special issue of *Organization Science* journal [3] has explored various issues related to routine dynamics such as routine interactions and networks, materiality, and embodiment.

References

1. K. Batoulis et al. Extracting Decision Logic from Process Models. *International Conference on Advanced Information Systems Engineering*. Springer International Publishing, Cham, 2015.
2. M. S. Feldman and B. T. Pentland. Reconceptualizing organizational routines as a source of flexibility and change. *Administrative Science Quarterly*, Vol. 48, No. 1, pp. 94–121, 2003.
3. M. S. Feldman, B. T. Pentland, L. D'Adderio and N. Lazaric. Beyond routines as things: introduction to the special issue on routine dynamics. *Organization Science*, Vol. 27, No. 3, pp. 505–513, 2016.

4. R. Hull et al. Towards a Shared Ledger Business Collaboration Language Based on Data-Aware Processes. *Proceedings of the International Conference on Service Oriented Computing (ICSOC)*, Springer, Cham, pp. 18–36, 2016.

5. L. Janssens et al. Consistent Integration of Decision (DMN) and Process (BPMN) Models. *Proceedings of the CAiSE'16 Forum, at the 28th International Conference on Advanced Information Systems Engineering (CAiSE)*. Springer, Cham, 2016.

6. A. Kosba et al. Hawk: The Blockchain Model of Cryptography and Privacy-Preserving Smart Contracts. *IEEE Symposium on Security and Privacy*, 2016.

7. A. Lindberg, N. Berente, J. Gaskin and K. Lyytinen. *Coordinating Interdependencies in Online Communities: A Study of an Open Source Software Project*. Information Systems Research, 2016.

8. N. Lohade. Dubai Aims to Be a City Built on Blockchain. *The Wall Street Journal*, 2017.

9. J. Mendling et al. *Blockchains for Business Process Management-Challenges and Opportunities*. arXiv preprint arXiv:1704.03610, 2017.

10. S. Nakamoto. Bitcoin: A Peer-to-Peer Electronic Cash System. http://bitcoin.org/bitcoin.pdf, 2008.

11. Object Management Group. Decision Model And Notation™ (DMN™). www.omg.org/spec/DMN/, 2016.

12. B. T. Pentland. Sequential variety in work processes. *Organization Science*, Vol. 14, No. 5. INFORMS, Catonsville, MD, USA, pp. 528–540, 2003.

13. B. T. Pentland, J. Recker and G. Wyner. A Thermometer for Interdependence: Exploring Patterns of Interdependence Using Networks of Affordances, Manuscript, 2015.

14. R. Plant. Can blockchain fix what ails electronic medical records? *The Wall Street Journal*, 2017.

15. Signavio. Quick Guide to Decision Modeling using DMN 1.0. www.signavio.com/wp-content/uploads/2015/04/Signavio-Whitepaper-Quick-Guide-DMN-en.pdf, 2017.

16. M. Swan. *Blockchain: Blueprint for a new economy*. O'Reilly Media, Inc., 2015.

Index

Note: Page references in bold refer to tables; those in italics refer to figures.